D0443817

HEROES & COWARDS

NBER Series on Long-term Factors in Economic Development
A National Bureau of Economic Research Series

Edited by Claudia Goldin

Also in the series

Claudia Goldin
Understanding the Gender Gap: An Economic History of American Women
(Oxford University Press, 1990)

Roderick Floud, Kenneth Wachter, and Annabel Gregory
Height, Health and History: Nutritional Status in the United Kingdom,
1750–1980 (Cambridge University Press, 1990)

Robert A. Margo
Race and Schooling in the South, 1880–1950: An Economic History (University of Chicago Press, 1990)

Samuel H. Preston and Michael R. Haines
Fatal Years: Child Mortality in Late Nineteenth-Century America (Princeton University Press, 1991)

Barry Eichengreen
Golden Fetters: The Gold Standard and the Great Depression, 1919–1939
(Oxford University Press, 1992)

Ronald N. Johnson and Gary D. Libecap
The Federal Civil Service System and the Problem of Bureaucracy: The Economics and Politics of Institutional Change (University of Chicago Press, 1994)

Naomi R. Lamoreaux
Insider Lending: Banks, Personal Connections, and Economic Development in Industrial New England, 1784–1912 (Cambridge University Press, 1994)

Lance E. Davis, Robert E. Gallman, and Karin Gleiter
In Pursuit of Leviathan: Technology, Institutions, Productivity, and Profits in American Whaling, 1816-1906 (University of Chicago Press, 1997)

Dora L. Costa
The Evolution of Retirement: An American Economic History, 1880–1990
(University of Chicago Press, 1998)

Joseph P. Ferrie
Yankeys Now: Immigrants in the Antebellum U.S., 1840–1860 (Oxford University Press, 1999)

Robert A. Margo
Wages and Labor Markets in the United States, 1820–1860 (University of Chicago Press, 2000)

Price V. Fishback and Shawn Everett Kantor
A Prelude to the Welfare State: The Origins of Workers' Compensation (University of Chicago Press, 2000)

Gerardo della Paolera and Alan M. Taylor
Straining at the Anchor: The Argentine Currency Board and the Search for Macroeconomic Stability, 1880–1935 (University of Chicago Press, 2001)

Werner Troesken
Water, Race, and Disease (MIT Press, 2004)

B. Zorina Khan
The Democratization of Invention: Patents and Copyrights in American Economic Development, 1790–1920 (Cambridge University Press, 2005)

HEROES & COWARDS

The Social Face of War

DORA L. COSTA & MATTHEW E. KAHN

PRINCETON UNIVERSITY PRESS
PRINCETON AND OXFORD

973.71
COS

Copyright © 2008 by Princeton University Press

Published by Princeton University Press, 41 William Street, Princeton, New Jersey 08540

In the United Kingdom: Princeton University Press, 3 Market Place, Woodstock, Oxfordshire OX20 1SY

All Rights Reserved

Library of Congress Cataloging-in-Publication Data

Costa, Dora L.

Heroes and cowards : the social face of war / Dora L. Costa and Matthew E. Kahn.

p. cm. — (NBER series on long-term factors in economic development)

Includes bibliographical references and index.

ISBN 978-0-691-13704-9 (hardcover : alk. paper)

1. United States—History—Civil War, 1861–1865—Social aspects.
2. United States—History—Civil War, 1861–1865—Psychological aspects. 3. Soldiers—United States—Biography. 4. African American soldiers—Biography. 5. United States. Army—Military life—History—19th century. 6. United States—Social conditions—To 1865. 7. Pluralism (Social sciences)—United States—Case studies. 8. Community life—United States—Case studies. 9. Social networks—United States—Case studies. I. Kahn, Matthew E., 1966– II. Title.

E468.9.C67 2008

973.7′1—dc22

2008016358

24.04

British Library Cataloging-in-Publication Data is available

This book has been composed in Janson Text

Printed on acid-free paper. ∞

press.princeton.edu

Printed in the United States of America

1 3 5 7 9 10 8 6 4 2

HELENA COLLEGE OF TECHNOLOGY LIBRARY
1115 NORTH ROBERTS
HELENA, MONTANA 59601

DISCARD

FOR ALEXANDER HARRY COSTA KAHN

NBER BOARD OF DIRECTORS BY AFFILIATION

OFFICERS

Elizabeth E. Bailey, *Chairman*
John S. Clarkeson, *Vice Chairman*
Martin Feldstein, *President and Chief Executive Officer*
Susan Colligan, *Vice President*

for *Administration and Budget and Corporate Secretary*
Robert Mednick, *Treasurer*
Kelly Horak, *Controller and Assistant Corporate Secretary*
Gerardine Johnson, *Assistant Corporate Secretary*

DIRECTORS AT LARGE

Peter C. Aldrich
Elizabeth E. Bailey
Richard B. Berner
John H. Biggs
John S. Clarkeson
Don R. Conlan
Kathleen B. Cooper
Charles H. Dallara
George C. Eads
Jessica P. Einhorn
Martin Feldstein
Roger W. Ferguson, Jr.

Jacob A. Frenkel
Judith M. Gueron
Robert S. Hamada
Karen N. Horn
John Lipsky
Laurence H. Meyer
Michael H. Moskow
Alicia H. Munnell
Rudolph A. Oswald
Robert T. Parry
Marina v. N. Whitman
Martin B. Zimmerman

DIRECTORS BY UNIVERSITY APPOINTMENT

George Akerlof, *California, Berkeley*
Jagdish Bhagwati, *Columbia*
Glen G. Cain, *Wisconsin*
Ray C. Fair, *Yale*
Franklin Fisher, *Massachusetts Institute of Technology*
Mark Grinblatt, *California, Los Angeles*
Saul H. Hymans, *Michigan*

Marjorie B. McElroy, *Duke*
Joel Mokyr, *Northwestern*
Andrew Postlewaite, *Pennsylvania*
Uwe E. Reinhardt, *Princeton*
Nathan Rosenberg, *Stanford*
Craig Swan, *Minnesota*
David B. Yoffie, *Harvard*
Arnold Zellner (Director Emeritus), *Chicago*

DIRECTORS BY APPOINTMENT
OF OTHER ORGANIZATIONS

Jean-Paul Chavas, *American Agricultural Economics Association*

Gail D. Fosler, *The Conference Board*

Martin Gruber, *American Finance Association*

Timothy W. Guinnane, *Economic History Association*

Arthur B. Kennickell, *American Statistical Association*

Thea Lee, *American Federation of Labor and Congress of Industrial Organizations*

William W. Lewis, *Committee for Economic Development*

Robert Mednick, *American Institute of Certified Public Accountants*

Angelo Melino, *Canadian Economics Association*

Harvey Rosenblum, *National Association For Business Economics*

John J. Siegfried, *American Economic Association*

DIRECTORS EMERITI

Andrew Brimmer
Carl F. Christ
George Hatsopoulos
Lawrence R. Klein
Franklin A. Lindsay
Paul W. McCracken
Peter G. Peterson
Richard N. Rosett
Eli Shapiro
Arnold Zellner

RELATION OF THE DIRECTORS TO THE WORK AND PUBLICATIONS OF THE NBER

1. The object of the NBER is to ascertain and present to the economics profession, and to the public more generally, important economic facts and their interpretation in a scientific manner without policy recommendations. The Board of Directors is charged with the responsibility of ensuring that the work of the NBER is carried on in strict conformity with this object.

2. The President shall establish an internal review process to ensure that book manuscripts proposed for publication DO NOT contain policy recommendations. This shall apply both to the proceedings of conferences and to manuscripts by a single author or by one or more co-authors but shall not apply to authors of comments at NBER conferences who are not NBER affiliates.

3. No book manuscript reporting research shall be published by the NBER until the President has sent to each member of the Board a notice that a manuscript is recommended for publication and that in the President's opinion it is suitable for publication in accordance with the above principles of the NBER. Such notification will include a table of contents and an abstract or summary of the manuscript's content, a list of contributors if applicable, and a response form for use by Directors who desire a copy of the manuscript for review. Each manuscript shall contain a summary drawing attention to the nature and treatment of the problem studied and the main conclusions reached.

4. No volume shall be published until forty-five days have elapsed from the above notification of intention to publish it. During this period a copy shall be sent to any Director requesting it, and if any Director objects to publication on the grounds that the manuscript contains policy recommendations, the objection will be presented to the author(s) or editor(s). In case of dispute, all members of the Board shall be notified, and the President shall appoint an ad hoc committee of the Board to decide the matter; thirty days additional shall be granted for this purpose.

5. The President shall present annually to the Board a report describing the internal manuscript review process, any objections made by Directors before publication or by anyone after publication, any disputes about such matters, and how they were handled.

6. Publications of the NBER issued for informational purposes concerning the work of the Bureau, or issued to inform the public of the activities at the Bureau, including but not limited to the NBER Digest and Reporter, shall be consistent with the object stated in paragraph 1. They shall contain a specific disclaimer noting that they have not passed through the review procedures required in this resolution. The Executive Committee of the Board is charged with the review of all such publications from time to time.

7. NBER working papers and manuscripts distributed on the Bureau's web site are not deemed to be publications for the purpose of this resolution, but they shall be consistent with the object stated in paragraph 1. Working papers shall contain a specific disclaimer noting that they have not passed through the review procedures required in this resolution. The NBER's web site shall contain a similar disclaimer. The President shall establish an internal review process to ensure that the working papers and the web site do not contain policy recommendations, and shall report annually to the Board on this process and any concerns raised in connection with it.

8. Unless otherwise determined by the Board or exempted by the terms of paragraphs 6 and 7, a copy of this resolution shall be printed in each NBER publication as described in paragraph 2 above.

CONTENTS

LIST OF PLATES

PREFACE

The stress of war tries men as no other test they have
encountered in civilized life. Like a crucial experiment it
exposes the underlying physiological and psychological
mechanisms of the human being.
— Grinker and Spiegel 1945

SHOULD MARRIED ACADEMICS WRITE PAPERS TOGETHER?
Our first collaborative project, written while one of us
was at MIT in Cambridge, Massachusetts, and the other
was at Columbia University in New York City, focused on
the rise of "power couples." Over the last 60 years, as
women have increased their labor force participation and
investment in their careers, they have often married men
with similar career ambitions. In our first paper, we documented a long-run trend: power couples are increasingly
clustering in big cities. Such cities attract both "power
singles," who then marry and remain in the city, and married "power couples," who recognize that big cities offer
a thick local labor market where both husband and wife can
pursue their careers without sacrificing for their spouse.

After we wrote this paper, we both read Robert Putnam's thought-provoking book *Bowling Alone* (2000). We
were fascinated by Putnam's account of the decline in
American civic engagement over time. Putnam emphasized the growing popularity of television as a pivotal

cause of the decline in community participation, but we wondered whether an unintended consequence of the rise of women working in the paid labor market was that PTAs and neighborhood associations lost their "volunteer army." We started to write a second paper testing whether the rise in women's labor force participation explained the decline in residential community participation. To our surprise, we found little evidence supporting this claim. Instead, our analysis of long-run trends in volunteering, joining groups, and trust suggested that, all else equal, people who live in cities with more income inequality were less likely to be civically engaged. These results contributed to a growing literature in economics documenting the disturbing fact that people are less likely to be "good citizens" when they live in more diverse communities.

Our early work on community participation attracted academic and popular media attention. Although we were flattered, we were aware that our measures of "civic engagement" bordered on "small potatoes." We were examining low stakes outcome measures such as entertaining in the household, joining neighborhood associations, and volunteering for local clubs.

In the summer of 2001, we realized that the American Civil War, 1861-1865, provided the ideal "laboratory." The setting was high stakes—roughly one out of every 6 Union Army soldiers died during the war. Unlike people in civilian life today, Union Army soldiers could not pick and choose their communities. Their "communities" were the roughly one hundred men in their units—men they lived with 24 hours a day.

This book is about the effect of peers on people's behavior. Using the life histories of 41,000 white and black

Union Army soldiers collected under the leadership of Robert Fogel, we study how social networks affected men's decisions to sacrifice their lives, help their fellow men, move away from home, and learn from their comrades. We study how comrades led men to risk their lives in the bloodiest war in our nation's history by sticking it out and not deserting. We demonstrate that comrades helped men survive POW camps. We examine how the large numbers of surviving veterans who had ever deserted were re-integrated into civilian life. We show how their comrades helped slaves forge a new, freeman's identity.

This book is targeted toward the broad social science research community. The study of peer effects has a long history in psychology and social science. In the 1920s and the 1930s, experiments examining the effect of changing work conditions and payment rules on productivity led researchers to study how workers interacted with each other. Since these first empirical studies, psychologists have studied social networks in the laboratory. Sociologists have used interviews and questionnaires to determine whether men fight for cause or comrade and to establish how social networks help people find jobs and helped women find an abortionist when abortion was illegal. Economists have used survey data to study how social networks determine where migrants go and how college roommates influence each other. Political scientists have used survey and voting data to determine who participates in a community. Legal scholars have used case studies of communities to examine how social sanctions, shame and ostracism, and other social incentives can create "order without law."

Even more has been written on the Civil War than on peer effects. Historians and political scientists have studied the causes of the war, the aims and war strategies of both sides, the impact of the war on the lives of ordinary people, and the war's economic, political and social legacy. Using official documents, newspaper accounts, memoirs, and private letters and diaries Civil War historians have analyzed men's reasons for enlisting and their combat motivations. They have documented prison experiences. They have examined how men remembered the Civil War and how the Civil War affected black soldiers. We examine many of the same issues, but by bringing the quantitative tools of the social sciences to the study of history, we base our evidence on men's deeds, not their words. And we can study "the short and simple annals of the Poor"–the men who left few traces of their lives.

There is a long-standing tension in how history should be written. Thucydides wrote in his *History*, "The absence of romance in my history will, I fear, detract somewhat from its interest; but I shall be content if it is judged useful by those inquirers who desire an exact knowledge of the past as an aid to the interpretation of the future, which in the course of human things must resemble if it does not reflect it. My history has been composed to be an everlasting possession, not the showpiece of an hour." History, as written by economists, will never be literature. Admittedly oversimplifying, economists are interested in numbers and historians in people. Economists and historians use different types of data and employ different types of methodologies. Economists seek the general patterns and historians treat each case as unique.

History has much to contribute to the social sciences. The past can provide better data. We have better measures of Civil War POW camp social networks than we do of twentieth century POW, forced labor, or concentration camp social networks. Even more importantly, by examining the past we can determine whether a phenomenon is transient or long-lasting. By investigating a phenomenon in a different institutional and environmental setting we can reveal "the underlying physiological and psychological mechanisms of the human being."

ACKNOWLEDGMENTS

THIS BOOK EXPANDS THE ARGUMENTS WE HAVE MADE IN previously published work and brings new evidence from original sources as well as from the work of historians, sociologists, economists, psychologists, political scientists, and legal scholars. The book is based on four academic papers on peer effects. These papers were written in the language of statistics; much of their content revolved around estimation issues. Although this book does not repeat any technical estimation details, we still convey the intuition behind the estimation and the various ways we probed the data to be certain that our findings were robust. We present many details about the Civil War and how the army was created because extracting useful information from data required understanding the history of the institution or event under study. It also requires understanding the processes that generated the data, details that we describe in the Appendix.

Our work would not have been possible without the creation of the large, longitudinal dataset described in the Appendix. A description of this data set cannot convey the difficulty of first grappling with the creation of a longitudinal dataset from disparate sources and from the free-form letters, affidavits, and other documents. Creating the Union Army dataset has been a long-term project involving the National Bureau of Economic Research (NBER), the University of Chicago, Brigham Young University, and investigators from various universities and from various disciplines, including economics, demography, and medicine, under the leadership of Robert Fogel (see Wimmer 2003 for a history of the project). NBER first funded the project in 1981 and the first grant proposal was submitted to NIH in 1986. The reviewers said, "An interesting idea, but we are not convinced that you can actually collect these records. When you demonstrate feasibility come back" (Wimmer 2003).

Demonstrating feasibility required completing the collection software, a process that required several years. It also required collecting a pilot sample and analyzing it. The investment paid off. In 1991 the project, entitled *Early Indicators of Later Work Levels, Disease, and Death*, was funded by the National Institute of Aging and the National Science Foundation. It was funded again by the National Institute of Aging in 1995 and in 2002. The data are currently available at *http://www.cpe.uchicago.edu*.

Many people have been involved in the creation of the Union Army samples. Of special note are Larry Wimmer, professor of economics at Brigham Young University, who supervised software developers at BYU, established a team at the National Archives, and set in place data collection procedures; Clayne Pope, also a professor of economics at Brighham Young University, who collaborated with Larry; Noelle Yetter, who still trains inputters, supervises data collection at the National Archives, and uncovers new data sources; Julene Bassett and Sharon Nielsen, who wrote, tested, and re-wrote the most difficult data entry screens, those for medical examinations (Sharon still supervises collection); Nevin Scrimshaw and Irwin Rosenberg, physicians and senior investigators, who provided invaluable help on the creation of the data entry screens for medical examinations; Louis Nguyen, a physician and senior investigator, who helped code the medical data; Janet Bassett, who developed the screens for census collection and trained inputters; John Kim and Dietrich Kappe, who set up the data cleaning and processing systems still used at Chicago; Peter Viechniki and Joseph Burton, past and current managing directors of research at Chicago; and Marilyn Coopersmith, Eveline Murphy, and Veronica Wald, past and current project administrators, who submitted the grants and cajoled faculty and students into writing them. The Union Army project owes a particularly large debt to the National Archives, where the original records are located, and especially to Cynthia Fox and Dr. Kenneth Heger, the branch chiefs in charge of records and customer service, and Dr. Michael Meier, the military archivist Noelle Yetter has relied on since the day she started working at the Archives.

Dora Costa was first involved with the project as a graduate student, when it was still unfunded, and then became a senior investigator and project leader. She has been with the project for more than fifteen years. Bob Fogel has directed the project for even longer. The project would never have been completed without his eternal optimism. Although this optimism led to chronic underbudgeting, no one would have embarked on this project had he known how long it would take to complete the originally proposed sample. But, as Bob has said, "If a project is worth doing, it is worth spending ten years doing it right."

———

The research that produced this book and the papers that underlie it would not have been possible without the support of the National Institution of Aging (NIA) under National Institutes of Health (NIH) grants R01 AG27960 and AG19637 and P01 AG10120, the Robert Wood Johnson Foundation, the Massachusetts Institute of Technology (MIT), and the University of California, Los Angeles (UCLA). These institutions funded data collection and paid for leave time. The book was written at MIT, the National Bureau of Economic Research (NBER), and UCLA.

We especially thank everyone who read and commented on either the entire manuscript or parts of it. Their efforts have improved it immeasurably. These include Leah Platt Boustan, Louis Cain, Stan Engerman, Amy Finkelstein, Claude Fischer, Hank Gemery, Claudia Goldin, Lorens Helmchen, Chulhee Lee, Kris Mitchener, Michael Rothschild, Jesse Shapiro, and Peter Temin. Our editors, Seth Ditchik and Tim Sullivan, provided us with invaluable advice as they pushed us to clarify and sharpen our results.

HEROES & COWARDS

CHAPTER 1

Loyalty and Sacrifice

[In battle] men stand up from one motive or
another—simple manhood, force of discipline, pride,
love, or bond of comradeship—"Here is Bill;
I will go or stay where he does."
—Joshua Lawrence Chamberlain,
The Passing of the Armies

JAMES MONROE RICH LEFT HIS WIFE AND HIS TRADE FOR
the low and irregular pay of a Union army soldier in the
Civil War. He marched through heat and dust, through
torrential thunderstorms and deep mud. He marched
with gear weighing 45 to 50 pounds—guns, cartridges
and cartridges boxes, woolen and rubber blankets, two
shirts and two pairs of drawers, canteens full of water, rations, and trinkets from home. He marched with his comrades even when they "were falling on every side" in a
failed frontal assault where "the lead and iron filled the air
as the snowflakes in an angry driving storm."[1] James was
lucky. He survived the war. Over one-quarter of the men
in his company did not.

Unlike James, George Farrell was well paid to enlist
and take the place of another man who had been called

up. He joined a company that had been re-formed with new men and saw no comrades die. Unlike James, he deserted twice, the second time successfully. Why did James stand up for his comrades while George did not?

War and its aftermath provide the ideal laboratory for exploring the conditions that lead to sacrifice, to co-operation, and to teamwork. Life under pressure brings men's worst or best characteristics to the fore. Choices matter. They determine one's own risk of death and that of one's comrades. The contrasts between decisions become starker once they are removed from the wide array of choices offered in normal, civilian life. Men either stand up or fall back. They can no longer pick which community they will stand up for; their comrades become their community. And when soldiers return home, their wartime choices and experiences continue to shape their lives.

If we want to study men's choices under wartime duress and their outcomes after the war, which soldiers should we look at? More than 42 million men and women have served in our nation's wars.[2] Which soldiers of the more than 42 million should we look at? We should seek soldiers from a war that drew men from all walks of life, so that our soldiers will be a microcosm of the nation. We need a war in which we can easily distinguish the heroes from the cowards and where the stakes were high if a soldier did not do his duty. We also seek a war that allows us to freely examine men's military records and follow them after the war. Only one war meets all these criteria, the American Civil War.

More than 2 million white men and almost 200,000 black men, more than three-quarters of whom were slaves, served in the Union army in the Civil War. Almost two-thirds of all white men of military age served, and in the

North an even greater proportion of blacks served. With the exception of World War II, during which the fraction of men in uniform was even greater, the proportion of military age men in uniform has never been more than one-third.[3]

The Civil War was the deadliest war in U.S. history. Sixteen out of every one hundred Union and twenty-four out of every hundred Confederate soldiers and sailors died in service. By Election Day in November 1864, the number of Union men who had died in combat in three years of war was greater than the number of U.S. servicemen who died in battle in 11 years in Vietnam. The total number of Union deaths from disease almost equaled the number of combat deaths in World War II. The number of Union soldiers imprisoned as POWs was greater than the total number of U.S. soldiers deployed in Iraq and Afghanistan between 2001 and 2006.[4]

This book is about the heroes and cowards of the Civil War. It is about tests of adversity on the battlefield and on long marches and in the POW camps where so many soldiers died. It tells of glory and shame after the war, and of how former slaves made the transition to being free men. What do stories of deserters, POWs, returning veterans, and men throwing off the bonds of slavery have in common? While seemingly unrelated, these stories are connected by a common thread: how men interacted with their comrades, and how these interactions affected their decisions and their outcomes.

Among economists, there is a growing recognition that people are not motivated just by the pursuit of income but that our social environment influences our choices and life outcomes. People care not just about their material well-being but also about their social status in their family, their circle of friends, and their community. People value respect and fair treatment and will punish those who behave unfairly, even at a high cost to themselves. They are willing to sacrifice for family and friends. Parents sacrifice to improve their children's and grandchildren's lives. Spouses care for each other during times of sickness. Some people may try to gain status by purchasing expensive products (such as Rolex watches or fur coats), but others take actions that elicit admiration and respect. It is difficult to sort through all the motives that lead firefighters, for example, to risk their lives extinguishing fires in the homes of strangers. Perhaps they enjoy the challenge. Perhaps they enjoy helping others. Perhaps they feel it is their duty. Perhaps they derive status from standing out as heroes. Willingness to sacrifice for the community explains why towns worry that rising home prices will lead firefighters and policemen to live elsewhere, attenuating the ties that bind them to the community where they work.

Where do altruism, a sense of group identity, and a willingness to sacrifice for the greater good come from? Are these traits hard-wired, or can they be built up between strangers? Sociobiologists have argued that altruism is an evolutionary adaptation to ensure the survival of the species and that it is a behavior that has been passed down across the generations through a gene or combination of genes. Psychologists focus more on the environment, emphasizing that firms, communities, and military units can build altruism and a sense of identification within the group. If firms treat their workers well, then the workers start to care about the firm and become part of the team. If soldiers go through arduous basic training together, they are more likely to care for each other when the going gets rough. Anthropologists and experimental economists have emphasized the role of various emotions among both individuals and community members in inducing sacrifice. Those who betray a community feel shame. Anger leads community members to punish traitors and reward those who are loyal.

Robert Putnam's book *Bowling Alone*, published in 2000, ignited widespread interest in the causes and consequences of vibrant community and popularized the phrase "social capital"—our "stock" of personal bonds and fellowships. A wide range of social scientists, including sociologists, political scientists, and psychologists, have studied PTAs, neighborhood get-togethers, Bible study classes, and bowling leagues to identify the determinants of a "good community" and the consequences of participating in a vibrant community. Economists and other social scientists have investigated what determines social capital by turning to survey data to see who volunteers, to laboratory experiments to see who trusts each other, and to spending data to see which communities invest more in education and welfare.

When are men willing to sacrifice for the common good? We answer this question by examining why men fought in the Civil War. During this war most soldiers stood by their comrades even though a rational soldier would have deserted. Punishments were too rare and insufficiently severe to deter men from deserting. What, then, motivated these men to stand their ground? Was it their commitment to the cause, having the "right stuff," high morale, officers, or comrades? After examining all these explanations, we find that loyalty to comrades trumped cause, morale, and leadership. But loyalty to comrades extended only to men like themselves—in ethnicity, social status, and age.

Sacrifices for the common good are costly. Standing by their comrades raised men's chances of dying. What, then, are the benefits to men of friendship? We can reply by looking at who survived the extreme conditions of Civil War POW camps. We can see the effects of age, social status, rank, camp population, and the presence of one's own officers on survival. We can also see that the fellowship of their comrades helped soldiers survive POW camps, and the deeper the strength of ties between men, the greater the probability of survival. Ties between kin and ties between comrades of the same ethnicity were stronger than ties between other men from the same company.

If loyalty toward one's own kind is admirable, how do communities deal with betrayal? In the Civil War, companies were raised locally, and hometowns were well aware of who was a coward and who was a hero during the war. Some towns were pro-war and others were antiwar. Men who betrayed their pro-war neighbors by deserting moved away, driven out by shame and ostracism. Community codes of conduct are reinforced not just by loyalty but also by punishments.

By examining men's lives during the war, we will see that more diverse communities are less cohesive. Their members are less willing to sacrifice and derive fewer benefits from being part of the community. Are there any benefits to being in a diverse community? When we look at the lives of black soldiers after the Civil War, the tensions between the short-run costs of diversity and its long-run benefits become apparent. Men did not like to serve with those who were different from them, so much so that they were more likely to desert, but in the long run the ex-slaves who joined the Union army learned the most from being in units with men who were different from themselves.

Whether diversity fosters understanding or encourages distrust is a longstanding question in the social sciences that has become particularly timely with rising immigration rates and growing income inequality. The classic study of World War II soldiers, *The American Soldier*, found that white soldiers who had never been assigned to units with blacks opposed the idea of having black soldiers serving in the same platoon with them.[5] But white soldiers who had been assigned to units with black soldiers were much less likely to oppose this arrangement. In the famous Robbers Cave experiment,[6] researchers brought 12-year-old boys to an isolated camp site and divided them into two groups that had no contact with each other. Each group developed its own identity. When the two groups were later brought into contact with each other in competitive situations, the boys became even more attached to their own groups and developed a hearty dislike of all members of the competing group. When researchers subsequently put the two groups into situations in which they had to cooperate to achieve a common goal, tensions between the two groups declined.

The optimistic view of human interactions when brought into contact with the other is belied by studies from many different settings. Researchers have played trust games on college campuses and in developing countries. They bring two players together so that they can observe each one, and then separate the players. For example, in one situation they offer player A money. Player

A can then give player B a certain amount of the money, with both knowing that the researcher will double the amount of money that is passed from A to B, giving this extra money to B. Player B can then pass money back to A. Because the game is played only once, player B should pass nothing back to A and therefore A should pass nothing to B. However, players do pass money to each other, and they are more likely to pass money when they are similar to each other.[7]

Studies outside the laboratory also find that diversity produces distrust. In the United States, people living in more diverse communities are less likely to report that they trust both members of other races and members of their own race. This distrust of others is associated with withdrawal from civic life and social isolation.[8] Within firms, turnover is lower and productivity is higher when workers are of the same age, race, and sex.[9]

A drawback of most survey data, firm studies, and laboratory experiments is that they examine only a point in time, even though short-run and long-run effects could be very different. Diversity may facilitate learning and information transfers. To take an example from business, while in the short run workers who resemble each other might be more likely to get the job done, in the long run the more diverse a workforce is, the more likely workers are to learn from each other and to learn about different segments of the market. Bowen and Bok report[10] that alumni from elite schools pointed to their interactions in college as helping them to relate to members of different racial groups later in life. Our data enable us to examine both the short-run and long-run effects of having been in a diverse environment.

There is a long tradition of looking to the military to

understand social interactions. Stouffer and colleagues' *The American Soldier* examined soldier's combat motivations through questionnaires, spurring the growth of a sociology of the military and influencing the development of organizational theories of the firm. We study social interactions by turning to the records of about 35,000 white and 6,000 black Union army soldiers. We trace their lives from their youth to their death using their army and pension records and census records. Much has been written about the Civil War, and a distinguishing feature of our work is that we are able to tell the stories of men who did not leave a written record and those who preferred to cover up or forget their war records. Almost one-quarter of the letters of enlisted men studied by McPherson[11] were written by professionals and proprietors and less than 5 percent were written by laborers. But, in the army and in our sample of soldiers, less than 10 percent of enlisted men were professionals and proprietors and roughly one-fifth were laborers. Our analytical approach, like that of the authors of *The American Soldier*, is statistical. An advantage of this approach is that it permits us to weigh the relative importance of different motives in men's decisions.

We begin with the stories of nine men who fought in the Civil War. They were ordinary men. They merit no mention in history books. But despite their anonymity, we can reconstruct their lives and the lives of their comrades from administrative and other official records. Their lives can suggest why some communities work while others do not, and why the distinction matters.

The stories of these nine men are referenced repeatedly throughout the book. Some of the men were heroes, remaining with their comrades on long marches and under enemy fire. Others were cowards who deserted. Others were POW camp survivors, and others lost their lives in the camps. Among the former slaves, some returned to tilling the soil and others moved to the growing cities. These men differed in important ways, ways that determined whether they deserted or stood their ground, whether they survived POW camps, and whether they forged a freeman's identity.

NINE MEN

The Heroes

In the darkness, the Thirty-sixth Regiment Massachusetts Volunteers moved quietly into a line of deserted entrenchments, one man at a time.[12] The trees were dripping with moisture, and every drop sounded like a footfall. The enemy on the other side of the line of rifle pits fired at any sound. The assault was set for daybreak, but in the stormy night the tired men could not sleep. For 12 days they had marched late into the night and fought during the day. In the past month they had suffered heavy losses at the battles of the Wilderness and at Spotsylvania, and their numbers had been depleted by disease. Fewer than 200 men out of the roughly 1,000 who had joined in August 1862 awaited the dawn on June 3, 1864.

Sergeant Adams E. French of Company D would carry the national colors, as he had in all previous battles. A mechanic (a shaper of wood or metal), he had enlisted at age 34, leaving a wife and 12-year-old son in Winchendon. Also from Winchendon in Company D was Private James Monroe Rich. Married only two years before, he had enlisted at age 21 with his 54-year-old father, Robert, after his younger brother Jerome had already left the household to enlist at age 19 in the Twenty-sixth Massachusetts Volunteers. All three Riches were mechanics, and over the last 10 years Robert had accumulated enough money to buy land.

Adams, Robert, and James joined a company where brothers served with brothers and fathers with sons. Half of the men in Company D were fellow mechanics and another 17 percent were artisans. The rest were mainly farmers. The men of Company D came primarily from the towns of Royalston, Templeton, and Winchendon in northern Worcester County, and most of them had been born in the county. Worcester County was the northern stronghold of an antislavery movement touched by evangelical fire and the vision of a republican society of equal and independent households. Only by keeping the western territories free from slavery could laboring men like Adams French and James Monroe Rich expect to do business on their own account and acquire just enough wealth to buy land and build a house on it. When these men enlisted, the news from the front was discouraging. The Union army had been defeated near the Chickahominy River, in an unfamiliar terrain of small streams, low ridges, swamps, ravines, and narrow, winding roads. Now the Thirty-sixth was by the banks of the Chickahominy River.

Before dawn, the Thirty-sixth Regiment was taken from the woods and sent to construct a new line of breastworks. Then, weary, hungry, and cold, the men joined the brigade forming for a frontal assault on the entrenched Confederates. The thin line of Union soldiers stretched for six miles; the line of Confederates was even longer. Richmond was five miles beyond the Confederate line.

The brigade crossed the field. As they approached the

woods, the enemy's heavy skirmish line, posted at the edge of the forest, opened fire. The brigade continued to advance under heavy fire. Close to the woods Sergeant Adams E. French fell, wounded. Corporal Stevens of Company K caught the flag from his hands, and the brigade continued to press forward under fire. The Union men drove the enemy across a creek, through a swampy morass, over a ridge, and into their strong entrenchments. The brigade then charged the entrenchments just below the crest and, in front of the enemy's works, received its heaviest losses. To the right, the brigade could not overcome the artillery, and to the left, where the Thirty-sixth Massachusetts Volunteers were deployed, the brigade faced fire from the enemy's entrenched line and cross fire on their exposed flank from the Confederates' longer line. With no support, the regiment could neither advance nor retire. Ordered not to give an inch of ground, and having exhausted their supply of ammunition, they emptied the cartridge boxes of their killed and wounded companions. Men crawled to the rear, and, rolling fallen trees and logs to the top of the crest where the firing was fiercest, they loosened the soil with their bayonets and scooped up the earth with tin cups and plates to form their own entrenchments. Fighting continued until nightfall, but the Confederate forces had successfully repulsed the assault along the whole line.

At the end of June 3, 1864, at the battle of Cold Harbor, Company D sustained the heaviest losses in the regiment. Nine of its men were wounded, four of them severely. Sergeant Adams E. French was pierced by a minié ball in the groin. He survived the jolting wagon drive to a hospital in Washington, D.C., but died there on June 19 of septicemia. James Monroe Rich was wounded in the right elbow.

Both James and his father marched with their regiment in the May 1865 victory parade in Washington and in the June parade in the city of Worcester, where they had enlisted. James and his father returned to Winchendon, and James's daughter Ella was born in 1867. By 1880 James had moved to the city of Worcester, a major manufacturing center and the second largest city in Massachusetts. Factories replaced independent artisans and immigrants displaced the Yankees. Robert worked as a laborer and at his death in Winchendon in 1895 left his widow destitute. James earned a living as a woodworker but was never successful enough to become a home owner. He died in Worcester in 1917 of a stroke.

The Civil War was remembered in Worcester County. Civil War veterans marched in the annual Fourth of July parades. The cities of Winchendon and Worcester built their monuments to the fallen. The Thirty-sixth Massachusetts Regiment held annual reunions in the city of Worcester, commemorating their deeds and recalling the spirit of fraternity and good will that pervaded the regiment. They published a regimental history in which they described themselves as a "compact and homogeneous body of men." The men of Company D could point with pride to their war record: not a single man in their company had dishonored his comrades by deserting.

The Cowards

One out of ten Union army soldiers deserted, a total of roughly 200,000 men.[13] They deserted before their regiments left their training camps. They deserted during marches, before major battles, and in the face of enemy fire. James Horrocks, who fled to the United States from England because of a paternity suit and enlisted as Andrew Ross in the Fifth Battalion New Jersey Volunteers, wrote that before his company left camp, "We have had fifty deserted out of this Company and only three of the number have been caught. Two of these escaped again and the other one has got his head shaved and put to hard labor for only a few months."[14] Most deserters were never caught. Out of the roughly 80,000 men who were caught, 147 were executed. James Horrocks, who intended to "fully desert if I don't get good treatment," could write home that "there have not been any shot except those who have deserted in the face of the enemy."[15]

George Farrell and Daniel Mulholland were among the deserters who were never caught. Both men enlisted in Company B of the Forty-seventh New York Regiment Infantry, the "Washington Grays." The regiment was originally formed in 1861 in New York City, but after three years the soldiers' enlistment terms expired. Only nineteen members of the original Company B reenlisted, and the company was re-formed with new men. Like George Farrell and Daniel Mulholland, most of the men were substitutes, men paid to take the place of those who had been called up. By March 1863 the Conscription Act made all men between the ages of 20 and 35 and all unmarried men between 35 and 45 liable for the draft. Government agents procured a list of names through a laborious house-to-house enrollment. Then a lottery in each congressional district determined who would go to war. Men who either presented an acceptable substitute or paid $300 were exempted. By the fall of 1863, men had formed draft insurance clubs, and factory owners and city political machines either paid for substitutes or paid the commutation fee. New York City had a draft fund of $885,000 by September 20, and on September 28 the county Substitute and Relief Committee announced that only two of the city's 1,093 conscripts had gone to war. The majority of its conscripts had furnished substitutes.

George Farrell enlisted in the Washington Grays in Auburn, the county seat of Cayuga in the Finger Lakes region of New York State. Born in Canada and a molder by trade, he was only 19 when he enlisted in February 1865. Army life did not agree with him. In March 1865 he was listed as a deserter during the occupation of Wilmington, North Carolina. Although his regiment advanced on Kinston and Goldsboro, he either advanced elsewhere or remained in a town crowded with refugees and ravaged by infectious disease. When he was found in May, after the surrender of Lee's and Johnson's armies, however, the military court accepted his claim that he had fallen out because of exhaustion. He was back in service but detached from the regiment, and at the end of June he deserted again, just two months before his regiment was mustered out.

Daniel Mulholland, an Irish-born laborer, enlisted in the Washington Grays in New York City in December 1864. He suffered through the bitter cold, chilly rains, and sheer monotony of the Wilmington campaign only to desert when the city had already surrendered, in March 1865. By mid-1863 the war was deeply unpopular in New York City, particularly among its Irish immigrants. McClellan, the peace candidate in the 1864 election, carried New York City by a more than two-to-one majority and in the heavily Irish Sixth Ward won more than 90 percent of the vote.

After the war, deserters were dishonorably discharged with loss of pay, but there was no attempt to bring them to justice, and the few states that did have laws disenfranchising deserters did not enforce them. George Farrell moved west. He came from Cayuga County, where McClellan had won less than 40 percent of the vote. Daniel Mulholland returned to New York City, a strongly anti-war city, where he lived in an Irish neighborhood, married, and had children.

The POWs

Roughly 1,500 men were camped in Tennessee's Lookout Valley at Wauhatchie Station, a stop on the Nashville & Chattanooga Railroad.[16] The rest of the Union army, including the 141st New York Volunteer Infantry, was camped at Brown's Ferry, three miles away. The Union army aimed to establish a new supply line to Chattanooga, one that was shorter and freer from the raids of the Confederates who occupied Missionary Ridge and Lookout Mountain.

The moon was almost full on the night of October 28, 1863. At about 10:40 p.m., a patrol of 150 men from the 141st New York Volunteer Infantry ran into a skirmish line of the Forty-eighth Alabama, but quiet was soon restored. Shortly after midnight, the camp at Wauhatchie Station was attacked. Brigadier General John W. Geary's men were ready, having slept in the line of battle with their accouterments on and their weapons stacked close by. With clouds drifting over the moon, there was not enough light to see a body of men only 100 yards distant; only the flashes of firearms revealed the enemy's position.

The sound of gunfire roused the men at Brown's Ferry,

and the 141st New York was detached to march with skirmishers and flankers through wooded country and over muddy roads to Wauhatchie. By the time they arrived, at five o'clock in the morning, Geary's men had repulsed the Confederate attack.

Sometime in the confusion of the battlefield, Henry Havens of Company A of the 141st New York and five other men of his regiment were captured by the Confederates. Born in Hector in Schuyler County in 1836, Henry was a farmer. He had already buried a wife, Hannah, and when he enlisted in August 1862 he left behind a second wife, Sarah, and his and Hannah's son, Charles.

Henry was unlucky in the timing of his capture. Not equipped to deal with large numbers of prisoners, the two governments had traded prisoners at frequent intervals, but the system of exchange had stopped in July as the two sides wrangled over terms. Northerners wanted guarantees that black troops would not be enslaved and that their white commanding officers would not be executed as leaders of a slave insurrection.

After having their blankets and shoes appropriated by needy Confederate soldiers, prisoners were shipped by rail in tightly packed open boxcars. Henry was sent to Richmond, which in 1863 held the majority of prisoners. Prisoners of war were first brought to Libby Prison, a brick warehouse, which was so crowded that men had to sleep spoon fashion, head to toe in alternating rows along the floor. Men became covered with vermin shortly after arrival and by 1863 were subsisting on a daily ration of a couple of ounces of meat, a half-cup of bread, and a small cup of rice. After Libby Prison, men might be transferred either to Belle Isle, an island in the middle of the James

River, or to Castle Thunder, formerly a brick factory. Castle Thunder became notorious for beating and robbing men upon arrival and for its punishments of suspending men by their thumbs, floggings of up to 100 lashes, the use of balls and chains, and branding for minor infractions such as insulting guards and for more serious ones such as attempting to escape. Belle Isle was an open compound with a few old, tattered tents for shelter. Because men were not allowed to use the latrines at night, the whole surface of the camp soon became saturated with excrement. The winter of 1863 was unusually cold. The men had no wood to keep warm, were on half rations, and suffered from frozen feet, ears, and hands. Diarrhea, dysentery, typhoid, pneumonia, and smallpox plagued all the Richmond prisons.

Prisoners were rapidly moved out of Richmond in February and March 1864 in response to prison escapes to nearby Union lines and to a (failed) Union raid to free prisoners. Henry Havens and the other men in his regiment were sent to Andersonville, an open stockade in southwest-central Georgia, along a railroad. Andersonville would become the most infamous of all POW camps. When Henry arrived, the emaciated and diseased POWs were left in an open stockade to build their own huts and tents from any scrap wood they could find and from blankets and rags. Few men had cooking utensils for the often uncooked meager rations, which might be reduced even further when attendance was incomplete during a roll call that took several hours as the sleeping, ill, and dead were accounted for.

Henry Havens watched the prison fill up. In May the camp exceeded its capacity of 10,000 men. Prisoners were dying at the rate of twenty per day, their bodies piled up like cordwood in front of the gates to be taken outside in the morning. The attacks of the "Raiders" on their fellow prisoners to rob them of food and other valuables became increasingly brazen.

In May, Lehman Josephson, a German-born peddler who had immigrated only in 1860, entered Andersonville as a private from Company I of the Sixth New Hampshire Infantry. Most of the men of the Sixth New Hampshire regiment had reenlisted when their terms were up, and Lehman was one of the three to four hundred new recruits who were sent to fill up the ranks between December 1863 and March 1864. Lehman was captured in early May at the Battle of the Wilderness, where from the woods his regiment had formed their line of attack in a dense wood, unable to see the entrenched enemy on the opposite side of a swampy ravine. Lehman and his fellow soldiers charged three times at the enemy before the Confederate troops withdrew during the night, and during the retreats the Confederates were able to take quite a few prisoners.

Like most newcomers to the camp, Lehman probably first reacted to the stench of the camp by doubling over and vomiting. The bank of the creek had become a giant swamp, covered in feces. The men he saw were skeletal, ragged, filthy, and black from pinewood fires. In June, Josephson was joined by four other men from his company, captured at Mechanicsville and at Ashland, and by the end of the month the number of prisoners had swelled to more than 26,000. The bank of the creek undulated with maggots and lice. Flies buzzed everywhere, filling the mouths, ears, and eyes of the dead. They were even baked into the corn bread, which together with uncooked cornmeal had become the principal staple of the diet. Men gave up hope of ever seeing their homes again. Private Robert Sneden, a diarist, wrote "everyone was for himself regardless of consequences."[17]

July brought oppressive heat and a prison population that swelled to almost 33,000 men, giving each man roughly the square footage of a grave. Henry Havens, who at six foot one was taller than the typical soldier, could endure no more and died of dysentery on July 23. Only two of the five other men in his regiment would survive Andersonville.

In August, hordes of mosquitoes descended. The prison population still numbered close to 33,000 men. Almost all had scurvy, which loosened their teeth, making the corn bread inedible, and caused their hamstrings to contract, making walking difficult, if not impossible. Scorbutic ulcers became gangrenous, as did any other slight wound, even a mosquito bite.

In September, when Sherman's march through Georgia threatened to bring him close to Andersonville, the prisoners were moved out, first to Charleston or Savannah and then in mid-October to Millen, another open stockade in Georgia. By mid-November only 1,500 men were left at Andersonville. Lehman Josephson was probably in one of the first transports to Charleston. He was exchanged at Charleston in December 1864 and returned to his company at the end of February 1865. He married in 1883 at age 46 and had at least four children. He became a cigar dealer in New York City and died of a stroke in 1906. Two of his four comrades had died at Andersonville, and another had died shortly after leaving Savannah.

The Ex-Slaves

In the summer of 1862, two Union army generals, acting without War Department authorization, formed the first black regiments from fugitive and contraband slaves and from freedmen in Louisiana and the South Carolina Sea Islands.[18] In 1863 the War Department authorized the recruitment of ex-slaves in areas of the South liberated by the Union army and the recruitment of free blacks in the North. By the end of 1865, 186,017 black men had fought for the Union army.

John Nelson Cumbash, born in Frederick County, Maryland, enlisted in his twenties in Company F of the First Regiment of the United States Colored Troops at Masons Island, an island in the Potomac River across from Georgetown, in Washington, D.C. He had been owned by David Best, a landowner in the Monocacy River Valley in Maryland, who had mortgaged him twice (once in 1842 and a second time in 1846) and then in 1860 had sold him and two of his siblings to a neighboring landowner, John Linn. John Cumbash's military service records provide no indication of how he left slavery or how he found himself in a regiment with a significant number of abolitionist officers and a black chaplain. The men in his company were mainly born in Virginia, North Carolina, Maryland, and Washington, D.C., but the regiment also included men born in Canada, Delaware, New York, Pennsylvania, and South Carolina. More than 80 percent of the men were freed slaves.

John was with his regiment at the sieges of Petersburg and of Richmond and at the captures of Fort Fisher and of Wilmington in North Carolina. He sustained a gunshot wound to the right foot and suffered from frostbitten feet and dysentery while in the army. His success as a soldier was mixed, though: he enlisted as a corporal and rose to the rank of sergeant, but was later reduced in rank to private. When the men were discharged in June 1865, Colonel Holman told them they had overthrown slavery and earned the right of citizenship. He warned them that they would face problems with southern whites, and reminded them that as soldiers they had learned industry and forbearance. They must now act as leaders in the black community and teach these qualities to other freedmen.

John returned to Frederick City, Maryland, and in October 1865 married Sarah Jane Hall in Baltimore. In 1870 he was working as a waiter in Baltimore and his wife was supplementing the family income by taking in washing while caring for four-year-old George Elias and six-month-old John. Another child, Emily Blanche, followed in 1874. Sarah died four years later, and in 1883 John married Mary Elizabeth Turner, also widowed. By that time he had moved to Philadelphia, which was experiencing an influx of freedmen, mainly from Maryland, Virginia, and the Carolinas. Brickmakers, teamsters, asphalt workers, and common laborers arrived every spring, worked during the summer, and spent their winters in cheaper, and warmer, quarters in Maryland and Virginia. As a waiter, John was in an occupation commonly held by Philadelphian African Americans, but he was above the class of casual laborers. He learned to write. As the century came to an end, European immigrants increasingly shut blacks out of service occupations. By 1900 John and Mary had moved to Montgomery County, Maryland, and John was no longer working. In 1901 he died of pneumonia.

Joseph Hall's wartime experience was very different. Born in North Carolina in 1821 and sent to Mississippi in 1840, Joseph had several owners. He somehow escaped and enlisted in Grand Gulf, Mississippi, in 1863 in Company D of the Fifty-third United States Colored Troops, worked as a teamster for his regiment, and suffered no illnesses or wounds. His regiment saw some action but no battles, and when he was mustered out in March 1866, he went to Tensas Parish in Louisiana, where he married Melissa Thompson after a year.

Located along the Mississippi River in northeastern Louisiana, Tensas Parish was a land of cotton plantations owned by whites and farmed by African Americans. Joseph farmed rented land in 1870 and had accumulated $250 in personal property, a good sum for an African-American farmer. He had a two-year-old son, Primus, and other children quickly followed. Their childhood, like that of most African-American children in southern farming communities, was spent working the family farm. Joseph died in 1913 in Tensas Parish, having worked land on several different plantations in the parish but never achieving farm ownership. He remained illiterate, and his children were illiterate as well.

OUR QUESTIONS

Why were Adams French, James Monroe Rich, and Robert Rich such loyal soldiers? Given the army's low and irregular pay and the high risk of death, why weren't more soldiers like George Farrell and Daniel Mulholland? Chapter 4 examines why men fought. George and Daniel may have been more mercenary; after all, they were substitutes. As immigrants they may not have felt the same sense of duty to fight in the nation's war. Daniel, coming from a community where the war was deeply unpopular, would have disappointed no one at home with his desertion. He would, however, have disappointed the men in his regiment and company. Because regiments were not replenished with new men after losing men to death or desertion, the men in a smaller regiment would do double duty on the picket line and face the enemy with a thin line. But perhaps George and Daniel did not care about the men in their companies. Their fellow soldiers were not men from their social circles, and the immigrants had very little in common with them.

The risk of death that men faced in army camps or on the battlefield was swamped by the risks they faced as POWs, particularly once the prisoner exchanges stopped. Among those captured after mid-1863, twenty-seven out of one hundred died. Chapter 5 looks at why some survived and others did not. Did Henry Havens die at Andersonville and Lehman Josephson survive because Lehman entered with more friends and with closer friends? Or did Henry die because he arrived at Andersonville weakened by his time spent at Richmond? Perhaps Henry died because he was eight inches taller than Lehman but received the same daily ration. Perhaps Henry was just unlucky.

At the end of the war, 14 percent of Union army veterans were deserters. Ten percent of Union army soldiers had deserted, implying that the best way for a soldier to save his skin was to scarper. Chapter 6 investigates how such large numbers of men could be reintegrated into society when the deeds of the good soldiers were commemorated in magazines and newspapers, in generals' best-selling memoirs, in regimental histories, in annual parades, in songs, and in public monuments. Daniel Mulholland returned home to New York City, whereas George Farrell, who was from upstate New York, moved west. Did George move because his neighbors, unlike Daniel's, would have looked askance at a deserter?

In May 1865, James and Robert Rich and Lehman Josephson marched in the two-day victory parade in Washington, D.C. Black regiments were not allowed to participate. Black veterans later participated in local Fourth of July parades in the North, bringing up the rear guard to remind everyone that blacks had fought for their freedom and sacrificed for the Union, earning the right to citizenship. Some former slaves had fought in units with free blacks. Some had fought in units with abolitionist officers, others had fought under officers indifferent to their welfare. Did the former slaves learn from the free blacks and benefit from having abolitionist officers? After enlisting near Washington, D.C, John Cumbash moved to Baltimore and then to Philadelphia, and learned to read. Joseph Hall, who enlisted in Mississippi, worked as a laborer and farmer in nearby Louisiana until his death and remained illiterate. Why did John move to a large city? Did John learn about Baltimore and Philadelphia from the men in his company who came from those cities? Chapter 7 examines how comrades shaped slaves' becoming freemen.

We can draw few conclusions from the stories of only nine men out of 41,000. Nine different men would have had other stories. The nine men we picked, however, illustrate the themes we uncovered in our analysis. We therefore turn now to the records of all our soldiers. But before we do so, we examine how, throughout history, individuals have interacted with their communities.

CHAPTER 2
Why the U.S. Civil War?

PULITZER PRIZE–WINNING JOURNALIST AND WRITER TONY Horowitz remembers his great-grandfather, who had fled Czarist Russia in 1882 as a teenage draft dodger, poring over a book on the Civil War that he had purchased shortly after his arrival in the United States. Many years later, in *Confederates in the Attic*, Tony Horowitz wrote of Civil War enthusiasts leading the lives of Civil War soldiers.[1] He described men who wore filthy and scratchy homespun clothing, soaked their buttons in urine to give them a more authentic patina, ate a diet of hardtack and salt pork while in the field, talked in antique speech patterns, froze at night under thin blankets, and spent a quarter of their income on their hobby. These men could replicate both the battles and their aftermath in minute detail, even puffing themselves up to resemble the bloated corpses in Civil War photographs.

Almost 150 years later, the Civil War still fascinates. A Google search of "U.S." and "Civil War" yields more than forty million hits. Web sites devoted to the Civil War provide histories of regiments and of battles, diaries and letters, photographs, and help for those searching for a Civil War ancestor. More than 200 histories of the Civil War were published annually between 2000 and 2005. As Confederate veteran Carleton McCarthy noted, "A real good hearty war like that dies hard. No country likes to part with a good earnest war. It likes to talk about the war, write its history, fight its battles over and over again, and build monument after monument to commemorate its glories."[2]

One side fought the war to ensure "that government of the people, by the people, for the people, shall not perish from the earth," and celebrated freeing the slaves as a second American Revolution. The other side seceded over the Republican Party's promise to exclude slavery from the territories, a policy that would make "property in slaves so insecure as to be comparatively worthless" (Jefferson Davis in 1861),[3] and established a nation based "upon the great truth that the negro is not equal to the white man; that slavery, subordination to the superior race, is his natural and normal condition" (Alexander H. Stephens, vice president of the Confederacy).[4] It memorialized the conflict as the "War of Northern Aggression" against "the inalienable right of a people to change their government" (Jefferson Davis in 1881).[5]

While we think of the Civil War as a struggle between North and South, it also divided the North along regional, economic, and religious lines. It pitted slaveholders in the border states against free farmers in New England and the Midwest. It led to talks of secession in western states tied to the South through trade along the Mississippi. It set immigrants in large cities against small-town native-born artisans. Evangelical Protestants rallied to the abolitionist cause, but Anglicans, Lutherans, and Catholics did not.

The Civil War marked the emergence of the United States as an industrial nation, divided between North and South. Northern soldiers grew up in a nation of small farmers and artisans and became old in a land of large industrial enterprises worked by immigrant labor. Southern soldiers left a land of small farmers and large, stately plantations worked by slaves and returned to a region of poor sharecroppers. The Civil War was also a political watershed. The black freedmen of the North became citizens; southern slaves won their freedom and, for a brief time, political rights in the postwar South.

This book is set during the Civil War but, unlike most Civil War books, it is not about its politics, its battles, and its famous men. It is about men's interactions with their comrades under extreme stress. It is based on a unique data source, the computerized life histories of roughly 41,000 men, analyzed with the statistical tools of social scientists. These life histories show who deserted his comrades and who was loyal, who survived POW camps and who did not, and how wartime friends influenced the veterans' later lives.

STUDYING SOCIAL INTERACTIONS: "BY THEIR DEEDS SHALL YE KNOW THEM"

The most famous studies of social interactions have been done by psychologists. In the early 1960s, Stanley Milgram conducted a famous experiment in which volunteer subjects were told they were participating in a study of the effects of punishment on learning.[6] The "teachers" (the volunteers) were ordered to administer what they believed to be electric shocks to the "learners" (who were actors). Twenty-six of the forty teachers continued to administer the realistically simulated shocks up to the maximum level, even after the actor-learners feigned losing consciousness when the voltage meter reached "Danger: severe shock."

Ten years later, in another experiment, Philip G. Zimbardo recruited undergraduate men to play prisoners and prison guards.[7] The guards quickly became abusive, blindfolding and stripping the prisoners, shackling them, and forcing them to wear skimpy hospital gowns. By the fourth day the guards had begun to humiliate the prisoners sexually.

Milgram ran his experiments to see if ordinary people were willing to follow orders and torture others when ordered to do so. Such people on their own would never have harmed their peers, but in the laboratory setting, when a person in authority gave the order, few disobeyed. One of Milgram's motivations was to understand obedience to orders in totalitarian states.

Although much can learned about people by running experiments, serious questions have been raised about the artificiality of experiments. Does a person's choice in an experiment tell us how he would react in a real-world setting? In a laboratory setting, people may sense that "it is not real." Knowing that they are participating in an experiment and being able to guess the goal of the experiment may influence their behavior. Why did Milgram's lab subjects follow the orders of the authorities? What punishment did they fear they would suffer if they disobeyed? If twenty-six out of forty obeyed, does this mean that two-thirds of the general population would torture if placed in a similar social environment?

Today, Stanley Milgram and Philip Zimbardo could never obtain permission from a university to run their experiments. The stakes for decisions made in university labs are now low. But even in the past, no lab researcher could have examined men's life-and-death choices.

Unlike university laboratory researchers, we do examine life-and-death choices. Desertion and POW camp survival strategies were life-and-death choices. Postwar migration decisions were life-altering. Unlike laboratory researchers, we examine real choices made in the field.

Like most historians, we work with dead subjects. Historians (for example, McPherson) have used diaries and letters to understand what Civil War soldiers experienced and why they fought.[8] We see many virtues in using this source of evidence. Diaries and letters personalize the war and provide specific information that humanizes the participants. Historians have used the information contained in diaries to provide compelling portraits of individual soldiers' experiences. Throughout this book, we use diary evidence to provide details. The diaries show clearly that peers played an important role in shaping soldiers' choices.

But relying solely on diaries and letters poses at least two problems for examining the role of peer effects. The first problem is selection bias. Ideally, every soldier would write a diary of his war experiences. If they all had, qualitative historians could choose to read a random subset of these diaries and weave together a narrative of how soldiers lived their war lives.

Intuitively, we know that certain soldiers were more likely to keep diaries than other soldiers. A diarist would need to be literate and have an active interest in keeping a record. Most black soldiers were illiterate, making us often dependent on the letters written by highly educated black soldiers to abolitionist newspapers and on the writings of their white officers. The war survivors who were deserters would have been unlikely to provide a truthful account of their war experience. Even if they kept a diary, we would expect to see an ex post facto rationalization of their actions that might be unrelated to their true motivations at the time they deserted. Diaries written with an eye for a broader audience, and not just for the writer, might slant events to emphasize heroism and downplay cowardice. Men might expect that their families would read their diary if they died in the war. Such expectations might affect and slant how events were recorded as they took place.

Suppose that we are interested in the war experience of all soldiers, but only literate soldiers kept diaries. If we now have a large sample of diaries, can we reconstruct *all* soldiers' war experience? The selection bias problem arises because of missing data. The researcher observes only a subset of the data she wishes she could see, and the subset is not a random sample from the population of soldiers.

Reading numerous soldiers' letters and diaries is useful for generating a long list of explanations for why men fought, how they survived POW camps, and how they lived their lives after the war. We view compiling such a list as the first step, not the last, in conducting research. Rather than simply saying that men were more likely to desert if they didn't like the men in their company, or that they were more likely to desert if men in their company were dying, we seek to make more precise statements.

For a given list of possible drivers of desertion and death during the war and migration after the war, how important is Factor A relative to Factor B? In this book, we make precise statements about the relative importance of each explanation. Our data set provides sufficient information to have a contest between different explanations.

The Civil War provides an ideal setting for studying the effect of social interactions on life-and-death decisions because unlike soldiers today, Civil War soldiers could make these decisions. Desertion was easier in a war fought on U.S. soil and on a nineteenth-century battlefield. Men could, and did, make their way to the rear, often using the excuse of helping a wounded comrade, or, straggling, never made their way to the front at all. Private Wilbur Fisk of the Second Vermont became separated from his regiment and found himself in a crowd of stragglers, "decidedly bad company to be in." Nonetheless, he joined them because "My object was to find a safe place in the rear, and in spite of revolvers, or swords, entreaties, or persuasions, I found it. . . . I should have been ashamed of such conduct at any other time, but just then all I thought of was a cup of coffee, and a dinner of hard tack. . . . My patriotism was well nigh used up, and so was I, till I had had some refreshment."[9]

We examine the influence of social effects on soldiers' choices and outcomes by following individual soldiers from enlistment to discharge and then through the rest of their lives until death. We want to know who the man was and whether he was young or old, married or single, rich or poor. We need to know where he enlisted, where he was born, and what he did for a living. We also need all this information about his comrades. Finally, we want to know which battles his regiment fought in and what losses his company suffered. Fortunately for us, these data exist!

OUR MAIN DATA SOURCE

Ideally, to examine how peers influenced men's behavior, we would like to identify soldiers who fought in companies with high levels of esprit de corps and compare their choices to those made by soldiers fighting in companies where the men cared little for their comrades. We will use our life histories to approximate this ideal. By comparing the actual choices that thousands of similar men made in different peer environments, we can tease out the importance of peer effects. We recognize that such correlations do not tell us why these peer effects were present. In each chapter, we are clear about what we think the most important motivating factors are.

During the war, men interacted mainly with the other men in their company. As we discuss in the next chapter, hometown recruitment of companies meant that many men joined companies where they already knew their future comrades. Because mail was not censored, men wrote home freely about their comrades' behavior in the war. The whole town knew if its men behaved badly. Hometown recruitment, although effective in raising regiments and in building company cohesion, led some communities to bear a disproportionate cost of the war. Winchendon, with a population of only 2,624, provided 237 men, and lost 21 percent of them. Boston, with a population of 177,818, provided 15,887 men and lost 9 percent of them. After World War II, when a small hamlet

HELENA COLLEGE OF TECHNOLOGY LIBRARY
1115 NORTH ROBERTS
HELENA, MONTANA 59601

such as Bedford in Virginia could lose twenty-two of its thirty-five men on D-Day, including one pair of brothers,[10] the military stopped drawing companies locally.

An ongoing research project led by the Nobel laureate Robert Fogel of the University of Chicago has created a longitudinal database for both white and black Union army soldiers from their military service and pension records in the National Archives (for details see the appendix). The military service records provide such basic information as year of muster, age, birthplace, and height in inches, and also information on what happened to the soldier during his military service. Did he desert? Was he arrested? Was he AWOL? Did he become a POW? Did he die during the war? The pension records provide information on later health, residential, and occupational histories at older ages. The white soldiers have been linked backward to the 1850 and 1860 censuses to obtain information on their wealth, marital status, and literacy. (Because the majority of black soldiers were slaves, they were not individually enumerated in those censuses.) Both white and black soldiers have been linked forward to the 1880, 1900, and 1910 censuses to obtain information on their postwar occupations, residences, and family structures.

A novel feature of the Fogel data is its sampling design. More than two million men fought for the North. It would be too costly a task to create a statistical database for all these men. To overcome this hurdle, the Fogel team recognized that men fought in regiments and that regiments consisted of ten companies, with roughly 100 men in each company. The Fogel team randomly selected 331 white and 52 colored infantry companies and then within each company conducted a 100 percent census, collecting information on all the men within that company. Our sample is based on 303 of these 331 white companies and 51 of the 52 colored infantry companies (because collection of the white companies was incomplete when we did our analyses and because one of the black companies was a company of old men who guarded forts).

This sampling design allows us to reconstruct peer groups for each man. In particular, we can know whether an Irish private fought in a company that was 3 percent Irish or 44 percent Irish. If the Fogel team had taken the statistical universe of more than two million men and randomly selected a sample of 30,000 men, we would not have been able to reconstruct each soldier's peer group. The probability that any two men would be from the same company would be much smaller, and the probability of sampling all 100 men from any one company (and thus being able to reconstruct a man's true peer group) would be close to zero. Most data sets used by social scientists sample individuals or households, and therefore, unless the individuals being surveyed are explicitly asked, we do not know who their neighbors or other of their peers are.

From today's vantage point, the Fogel data set is extraordinary. Concern about identity theft and insurance companies using confidential information to cherry-pick healthy and low-risk patients would make it extremely difficult to build a similar data set today. A researcher attempting to build an analogous data set for Vietnam veterans would need to obtain the consent of each man. This requirement would introduce self-selection issues, as many of them would be unwilling to grant permission.

An underappreciated fact about the U.S. Census of Population and Housing is that 72 years after a census comes out, people's names are attached to the micro-data. As we explain in the appendix, this release allows historians to create linked data sets. We know where our Civil War soldiers came from, where they went, whom they lived with, and what they did for a living. For some, we know the value of their property.

Another advantage of the Civil War data is that, as discussed in the appendix, the sample is representative not just of the Union army but also of the northern population of military age in wealth and literacy rates. During the Vietnam conflict, the better-off men received college deferments and found other ways to avoid service. But in the Civil War, 65 to 98 percent of the cohorts born between 1838 and 1845 were examined for military service and 48 to 81 percent of these cohorts served; the remainder were rejected for poor health. Only in World War II were service rates higher.

Like all data sets, the Fogel data have some limitations. One is that, with the exception of the white officers of the U.S. Colored Troops, little is known about commissioned officers who did not rise through the ranks. Another drawback is that postwar income and wealth information is scanty. The 1870 census was the last to have a wealth question, and the pension records rarely provide wealth or income data. We therefore have to assess later socioeconomic status using occupation and home ownership.

WHAT IFS

What do we do with the life records of our soldiers? Each of these men made a choice either to risk death by remaining with his company or to desert and abandon his comrades. We observe this choice. Those unlucky enough to become POWs made a choice either to help each other or to look out just for themselves. We observe who survived. After the war, veterans decided whether to return to their hometowns or to move away, a choice that we can observe. We will compare the choices and outcomes of men in very different companies. Some companies were quite diverse, drawing men of different ethnicities and various occupations, and others were very homogeneous. Some companies were organized in pro-war communities, others were not. Some companies faced intense fighting, others did not. We exploit this variation in the data to study how group characteristics, hometown ideology, war experience, and individual characteristics affected critical choices and outcomes. Cross-company variation in characteristics will be critical in allowing us to test hypotheses. If all companies were the same, we would not be able to test any hypotheses about peer effects.

We can examine the effects of peers on choices and outcomes if we can observe similar soldiers (similar in age and ethnicity) living and fighting in different social environments. To say that serving in a homogeneous company reduces the likelihood that a man deserts is to make a causal statement. But how do we know one causes the other? Ideally, we would like to construct a counterfactual: for men who fought in diverse companies, what would their desertion propensities have been had they fought in a homogeneous company? Although this is an interesting question, it borders on science fiction. Each man lived only one life. How can we infer what his life would have been like in a different social environment?

Constructing counterfactuals is a serious research challenge in the social sciences. Physical scientists can run experiments in their laboratories and randomly assign mice, monkeys, or men to treatment or control groups. The effectiveness of the treatment can then be determined by conducting before and after comparisons of the treatment and control groups.

This method was first outlined in 1836 by Pierre Louis in France: "In any epidemic . . . let us suppose five hundred of the sick, taken indiscriminately, to be subjected to one kind of treatment, and five hundred others, taken in the same manner, to be treated in a different mode: if mortality is greater among the first than among the second, must we not conclude that the treatment was less appropriate, or less efficacious in the first class than in the second."[11] When during a typhoid epidemic Louis compared the effects of bleeding with those of purging and found that fewer died with purging than with bleeding, both his conclusion and his methodology were condemned.

In Pierre Louis's experiments, many patients died regardless of whether they were purged or bled. But even experiments that would be convincing today were not in the nineteenth century. As recounted by David Healy[12] and Morton Thompson,[13] in 1847 Dr. Ignaz Semmelweis noted that in Vienna's obstetric hospital, mortality rates fluctuated wildly but were always much higher in the ward run by physicians and medical students than in the one run by student midwives. He also noted that differences between the wards emerged only in 1841, after courses in pathology were included in medical training. Suspecting that physicians and medical students were infecting women with "cadaveric material" after practicing delivery with corpses, he got them to wash thoroughly with a disinfectant. Death rates in the doctors' ward fell below the rate in the student midwives' ward. His conclusions were rejected, because the current theory stated that puerperal fever was related to milk and was "one of the normal expressions of living and of giving birth."[14]. Semmelweis was driven from Vienna in 1849, mortality rates rose to their previous levels, and the poor doctor died in an insane asylum in 1865, just two weeks after he was committed.

Opponents of the application of numerical methods to medicine condemned them because, as one stated in 1849, "The practice of medicine according to this view is entirely empirical, it is shorn of all rational induction, and takes a position among the lower grades of experimental observations and fragmentary facts."[15] By uncovering the principles of physiology, medicine was to become as predictable as chemistry or physics.

During the two world wars it became clear that the same disease did not always produce the same outcome: some patients recovered quickly, others slowly, and some not at all. The effect of a bacillus depends on where in the body it infects a person, how healthy the person is, how his body reacts, and how confident he is that the medicine will work. A priori a doctor cannot know all these factors and how they interact; a drug given to a healthy person may have a different effect from a drug given to a person in poor health. But a doctor can know the statistical probabilities.

Statistical probabilities can be established from clinical trials, and the development of new drugs required some method to test them. But without very large populations, how could a researcher be certain that he or she was working with groups representative of the target population? Ronald Fisher's analysis-of-variance approach, developed in 1923, allowed researchers to run experiments with smaller numbers, provided there was prior randomization. Ethical qualms about using randomization with people meant that Fisher's method was applied mainly to agricultural studies. The first randomized clinical trial had to await 1946–47, when Austin Bradford Hill, an English medical statistician, tested the effects of streptomycin on tuberculosis by assigning patients to treatment groups by random numbers. Patients who did not receive streptomycin received the next best possible treatment. A radiologist assessed the outcome, a radiograph of the patient's lungs, without knowing who had received the treatment.[16] Randomized clinical trials later became the gold standard of evidence in medicine.

Social scientists have been turning more and more to randomized trials, performing them both in the laboratory and in the field. In a series of laboratory experiments, Smith, Suchanek, and Williams had their subjects trade assets, and watched as price bubbles developed.[17] Laboratory experiments have been criticized for motivating their subjects with small stakes (the first laboratory experiments did not even use real payoffs) and for creating sterile environments. They have also been criticized for leading people to change their behavior. Just knowing they are being studied may make people feel important and improve their performance. People who know the goals of an experiment and want to please the researcher may act accordingly. In contrast, field experiments are done in natural settings, and in some experiments the subjects do not know they are being studied.[18]

The most ambitious field experiments have been social experiments involving a randomized change in the implementation of a government program. One of the first was the Perry preschool project of 1962 which followed 123 black preschoolers in Ypsilanti, Michigan, half of whom were randomly assigned to a treatment that included preschool and home visits. The children were followed until 1993. The program provided the intellectual basis for Head Start, which was begun in 1964 and has served millions of children.[19]

The negative income tax experiments of the early 1970s were another set of extremely influential experiments.[20] When the tests were implemented, welfare provided cash benefits to single-parent low-income families. A recipient who earned an extra $100 had her (most participants were single mothers) benefits reduced by exactly $100 dollars. The experiments tested benefit schedules with different welfare guarantees (but never below the current welfare amount) and different tax rates on extra earnings. It tested these for both single-parent and two-parent households. Single mothers in the control group participated in the existing welfare program and married men and women in the control group received nothing. Knowing that in the experimental welfare program they would not face a 100 percent tax on earnings, families went on welfare. Divorce rates rose, perhaps because unmarried people benefited from the welfare program. Because the tax reductions drew more families to welfare, a comparison of the treatment and control groups showed that lowered tax rates on earnings had no effect on the labor supply.

Federal legislation in the early 1980s encouraged states to conduct social experiments. States received waivers from federal welfare law stipulations to test program reforms and were encouraged to adopt randomized evaluation. Although 1996 reforms that devolved welfare programs to the states meant that the federal government could no longer require randomization before granting a waiver, the federal government has continued to work with states on randomized trials.[21] Private sector policy-evaluation firms implement and analyze the randomized trials.

As the number of randomized social experiments and clinical trials has grown, potential pitfalls have become clearer.[22] Human subjects are not passive participants: some will move themselves out of the control group and into the treatment group. AIDS patients tested the pills they were given and dropped out of the experiment or sought other types of medical care if they were given a placebo or were unhappy with the randomized treatment.[23] Subjects in drug trials are less likely to participate if the trial is randomized.[24] Studies of job training programs found that more than 90 percent of local job training agencies refused to participate in randomized trials, largely because of ethical and public relations concerns about randomization. Because recruitment has to be expanded at participating centers to obtain both treatment and control groups, the client mix at participating sites changes. And even in centers that participate, employees might contaminate the experiment by providing the control group with useful information about job contacts.[25] Another problem is that a randomized welfare reform may not be able to mimic the effect of a system-wide reform. Economy-wide changes in labor supply due to a particular change in welfare policy may affect wages, prices, and unemployment rates, and these will in turn affect labor supply.

The randomized field trials that can be strictly implemented and that leave no space for manipulation tend to be relatively simple. Examples include Duflo and Hanna's study of incentives in increasing teachers' school attendance in remote tribal villages in India.[26] Teachers in the treatment group were given a camera with a tamper-proof time-and-date function and told to take pictures of themselves with their students. They were given a bonus as a function of the number of "valid" days they actually came to school. Teachers in the control group were given the usual flat pay structure and told (as usual) that they could be dismissed for poor performance. In the treatment group, teacher absences fell by almost half and children's test scores increased, because once they were in school, the teachers actually taught. Of course, there is no guarantee that teachers outside this experiment would actually teach.

In our study, all the soldiers are dead. Therefore we cannot randomly assign some men to certain peer groups and other men to other peer groups. Although we cannot achieve the gold standard of random assignment (which even many randomized field experiments cannot achieve), the way companies were formed provides us with the best nonexperimental laboratory we could have for examining the role of peer effects. As we discuss in the next chapter, chance thrust some men into very diverse companies and others into companies composed of men like themselves.

Throughout this book, we make statements about how a soldier's social environment changes the probability of wartime desertion, POW camp survival, or postwar migration for the average man. Civil war companies were thrown together in a hurry, and men had very little idea what type of company they were joining. Some men landed in a company with men like themselves, and others ended up in a very diverse company. If the men who found themselves in the diverse companies were much likelier to desert, then on average, being in a diverse company increased desertion probabilities. Consider the case of POWs. We can determine whether, on average, having friends in camp improved survival probabilities. But even if friends increased a man's chances of survival, some men with many friends still died. Once the war was over, we can see whether, on average, a deserter and a nondeserter behaved the same way. Was the deserter more likely to move away from his hometown? Once the war was over, was there still an effect of wartime peers? On average, were men more likely to migrate to states their peers had come from?

In emphasizing the importance of using soldier-level quantitative data to test plausible social peer effects, we hope that our vocalized criticisms of relying on diaries and letters are not viewed as a dismissal of qualitative research. Instead, we view the small sample of surviving diaries and letters as additional sources of evidence. Without them, it is impossible to know how the men themselves viewed specific actions such as desertion. We need to know that a private from Wisconsin would write, "On my way here I passed within twenty-five miles of where my sisters live. I wanted to stop and go and see them real bad, but could not go unless I wanted to be called a deserter, and I had rather suffer death than be stamped and called a deserter."[27] When desertion is viewed as dishonorable, men will be less likely to desert and, if they do desert, they will want to hide their past.

Our evidence on soldiers all comes from the Union side. Records for Confederate soldiers are often incomplete. Because Union soldiers became eligible for pensions, all of the Union military records were transcribed at the end of the nineteenth century, thus preserving them in Washington, D.C. Analyzing peer effects among Confederate companies would also be harder. Union companies were not replenished, even though a company might be fighting at half-strength. Confederate companies were replenished. The peer group would therefore be changing over time.

We expect that Confederates would have had the same Victorian concepts of honor, duty, and manhood as Union army soldiers. We know that toward the end of the war, their pay was even lower and more irregular than that of Union army soldiers and their provisions of food and clothing were poorer. What we mainly lose by our lack of data on Confederates is that we cannot see how companies disintegrate once it is clear that the war is lost, and how the southern desire to defend a particular way of life led men to fight.

CHAPTER 3

Building the Armies

PATRICK TILLMAN TURNED DOWN A $3.6 MILLION, THREE-
year contract to play football for the Arizona Cardinals in
order to become an Army Ranger, earning a salary of
about $18,000 a year. He joined the army with his brother
Kevin, a minor league baseball player, shortly after mar-
rying his high school sweetheart. After the terrorist attacks of September 11, 2001, he noted in an interview,
"My great-grandfather was at Pearl Harbor and a lot of
my family has gone and fought in wars. And I really
haven't done a damn thing."[1]

Patrick Tillman died in the line of duty in Afghanistan
in 2004, killed by friendly fire. He was the first National
Football League player to be killed in combat in 34 years.

Inducing men such as Patrick Tillman to enlist is one
of the major problems faced by democracies at war. In
summing up the lessons of the Civil War in his *Memoirs*,
Sherman said, "the real difficulty was, and will be again,
to obtain an adequate number of good soldiers."[2] During
the Civil War a draft was not instituted until two years

after the start of war. But even once the draft was instituted men who could easily have bought their way out of
the draft did not. Many of the sons of the New England
elite died leading their troops into battle. Ninety-three of
the 578 Harvard alumni who served in the war died there.
And men like Robert Rich of the Thirty-sixth Massachusetts Volunteers who would never have been drafted because of their age served. What motivated these men to
enlist? Were their motives atypical?

A second problem facing democracies at war is the organizational task of building up a large army. On the eve
of the Civil War, the regular army consisted of only
15,000 enlisted men. By the end of the war more than two
million men had served in the Union army and navy, most
of them in the volunteer infantry regiments organized by
the states. There was no centralized authority to oversee
the process. The federal government was small and the
experience of states was limited to raising local militias.
Administrative chaos and the exigencies of war shaped
companies. These details of how companies were raised
are important to understanding why there was diversity
within companies.

A problem unique to the Civil War was the difficulty of
enforcing discipline on men who felt that they should be
free to come and go as they pleased. When John Beatty,
lieutenant colonel of the Third Ohio, began to court
martial men who left camp without leave, he faced "not
only the hatred and curses of the soldiers tried and punished but in some instances the ill will of their fathers,
who for years were my neighbors and friends." He also
only aggravated insubordination as men extended their
absences, refused to drill, and signed petitions demanding
his resignation.[3]

Enlistment Motives

When the southern states responded to Lincoln's election by seceding, northern reaction was to let the "erring sisters go in peace."[4] The Confederate bombardment of Fort Sumter and Lincoln's subsequent call for 75,000 volunteers to defend the Union united the North in favor of war. "When Fort Sumter was fired into by the Rebels . . . my military spirit along with the rest of the people in the Northern states rose to boiling pitch," wrote Alfred Bellard in his diary.[5] In Boston, "The whole population, men, women, and children, seem to be in the streets with Union favors and flags." In Philadelphia, "The city seems to be full of soldiers, most every other man in the street is in some kind of uniform."[6] States raised more regiments than called for by Lincoln. Lucius Barber, who enlisted in Marengo, Illinois, wrote in his diary that he and his comrades in April 1861 "had little hopes of being accepted under the seventy-five thousand call, so great was the rush of troops. . . . [W]e were accepted as a military company for the State defense, with the understanding that we should be transferred to the United States' service if the President called for more troops."[7] Bellard could not enlist immediately, "being at the time bound down as an apprentice to learn the carpenter's trade. . . . But soon after the battle of Bull Run [July 1861], my boss, thinking perhaps that the war would be carried into our own State, left his ship and started for Canada. This left me free to go for a soldier."[8]

Jefferson Moses, a private in the Ninety-third Illinois Volunteers, developed war fever a year later: "the year the war broke out . . . I was an awful coward. Nothing could get me to inlist and go to war. I was then in my 18th year

Plate 1. The great Union meeting in Union Square, New York City, April 20, 1861 (stereographic image)

and in reading history where they drafted men and put them in the front ranks to keep them from running away. I think if I was put in the front rank I would study how to get out." But "in the spring of 1862 the Battle of Shilow was fought and a numbers of boys were killed and sent home. . . . I got home and told pa and ma I wanted to go to war. I never felt so in my life. I just felt a great duty that I never before thought of. I stayed at home thro the summer. But in August their was a rally at the high school building in Cedarville. I was there and got the fever. To a finish that evening they recruited for a company. . . . This was on the 11th of August and all my comrads or associates inlisted. . . . But I did not want to go till I had the consent of father and mother. . . . All the rest of the boys have inlisted and I want to go along. Finely father said you have our consent to go and may gods blessing go with you. My dear mother stood beside me with her hands to her face crying to most break my heart."[9]

George Richard Browder, a Kentucky preacher and

slaveholder, never served. When drafted, he wrote in his diary, "I am a man of peace. I cannot, I will not fight." Fortunately for him, "My good brother William left home on Thursday morning & has been gone ever since—but he got me a substitute! Such is the anxiety to procure them that 12 & 1500$ are offered, & every effort is made to overreach & dispossess those who bring them up. . . . Friends from every quarter send me pledges of as much money as I needed & urged me to get a substitute at *any price*."[10]

Elijah Marrs, the son of a freedman and a slave woman, belonged, with his mother, to Jesse Robinson, a deacon in the Baptist Church and owner of thirty slaves in Kentucky. After Elijah's conversion and baptism, his master allowed him to learn how to read because he "said he wanted all the boys to learn how to read the Bible." But, "it being against the laws of the State to write,"[11] Elijah taught himself. During the war, former slaves serving in the Union army sent letters to their wives and children addressed in care of Elijah. One day, when he was 24 years old, Elijah decided to join the U.S. Army. He told his friends of his intention, and in the evening he and twenty-seven of his friends, who had elected him their captain, met at the colored church. Armed with twenty-six war clubs and one old rusty pistol, they left for Louisville, taking care to avoid a town where few black men could pass in safety. By eight o'clock on the morning of September 26, 1864, they were at the Louisville recruiting office, where they enlisted in the Union army. As soon as the officers learned that Elijah could read and write, they appointed him duty sergeant of Company L, Twelfth U.S. Colored Artillery.[12]

Why did men enlist? Lincoln enumerated several motives: "patriotism, political bias [ideology], ambition, personal courage, love of adventure, want of employment, and convenience."[13] Historians disagree about the relative importance of each of these motives. Bell Irvin Wiley echoed Lincoln's list, citing "the prevailing excitement, the lure of far places and the desire for change . . . the example of friends and associates . . . the economic motive . . . combination of sense of duty and a fear of compulsion . . . love of country and hatred of those who seemed bent on destroying its institutions."[14] He concluded that "the great bulk of volunteers responded to mixed motives, none of which was deeply felt."[15] James McPherson's analysis of soldiers' letters emphasizes that soldiers' motives were deeply felt and that honor, duty, patriotism, and a commitment to the republican ideals of the American Revolution drove men to enlist.[16] Reid Mitchell pointed to peer pressure from friends and family members who sent them to war with regimental and national flags, exhortations to courage, and brass bands: "To be a good son, a good brother, a good husband and father, and to be a good citizen meant trying to be a good soldier."[17]

We can more easily explain why a man fought once he was in the army than why he enlisted. We do not have a random sample of age-eligible men who did not serve as soldiers, because given a name, age, and state of residence and state of birth in the 1860 census, we cannot determine if a particular man was a soldier. But we can compare the full sample of 331 volunteer infantry companies (containing 39,000 men) with the age-eligible white population in the same states in 1860.[18] We can also examine enlistment rates across Massachusetts towns and infer some of the motives underlying individual enlistment decisions from these aggregate town data.[19] Although data limitations restrict our analysis to Massachusetts, that state included both rich and poor towns, large cities full of pro-Democratic immigrants, and anti-slavery, pro-Lincoln strongholds.

Compared to age-eligible northern white men, the ranks of enlisted infantrymen were especially likely to include artisans. They were less likely to include professionals and proprietors and, if we control for birth year, were more likely to include the foreign-born. Perhaps professionals and proprietors and the native-born were more likely to serve in the artillery or cavalry or as commissioned officers, or perhaps they were not drawn to the service by high bounties. Money, however, could not have been the only enlistment motive. Enlisted men were more likely than the general population to be from pro-Lincoln counties.

Our statistical analysis of the Massachusetts town data shows that, all else being equal, the man who enlisted was from a poorer town (and more likely from a manufacturing town) than the man who did not serve. As seen in our comparison of enlisted men with the general population, an enlistee was also more likely to be from a pro-Lincoln town. Because both he and his neighbors were more likely to have voted for Lincoln, we cannot determine whether his own commitment to the cause or peer pressure from like-minded neighbors drove his decision. Ideology and money were equally important in men's enlistment decisions in Massachusetts. On average, each town enlisted 289 men. A standard deviation increase in the vote for Lincoln would have increased this mean to 302 enlisted men. A standard deviation decrease in the value of town economic output would have increased the number from 289 to 301 men.

We can explain roughly one-third of the variation in town enlistment rates with our measures of ideology and economic status. The remaining two-thirds may reflect variation in adventurousness, patriotism, honor, duty, or even health. The army was not overly fastidious about its men, taking anyone who could march, carry arms and military equipment, hear orders, and shoot a musket. Loss of sight in the left eye did not disqualify a man for military service, but loss of sight in the right eye—the musket eye—did.[20] Nonetheless, one out of five men examined for military service and born between 1837 and 1845 was rejected as unfit, and rejection rates were higher in larger towns.[21]

As the war progressed, towns and states offered large enlistment bounties to entice new enlistees, and the ranks also began to contain draftees and substitutes. The new enlistees were described as "without patriotism" and as having "no interest in the cause."[22] When John Brobst's regiment received an influx of new recruits, he wrote to his friend Mary, "We have our own fun with them, and call them four hundred dollar men [bounty men]. They do not like it very well, but it can't be helped. We do not want them. We wanted to be consolidated with an old regiment and let the new recruits go in a regiment by themselves."[23] When Austin Stearns's regiment received an installment of substitutes, he viewed them as "desperate characters" and "men in form but possessed few of the traits that govern men."[24]

In our sample of white soldiers, the volunteers of 1861 and 1862 were different from the later enlistees. All else equal, they were richer, taller, less likely to be laborers, less likely to be married, and more likely to be born in the United States, Germany, or Ireland than in Britain or other countries. They were no more likely to come from a pro-Lincoln county than other enlistees, but even pro-Lincoln counties had men with no interest in the cause.

The motives that led men to enlist were not necessarily the same as those that kept them in the army. The reality of war quickly dampened both war fever and the attraction of a soldier's pay. In Massachusetts, high town enlistment rates did not lead to low desertion rates. We show in the next chapter that the early enlistees and men from pro-Lincoln communities were less likely to desert, as might be expected from the enlistment data. But wealthier men, who were less likely to serve as enlisted infantrymen, were less likely to desert. Men who enlisted for the sake of money, adventure, or glory could become disillusioned by soldiering. John Voltz wrote to his brother, "I have cursed the day I have enlisted for what benifit will I ever derive from being a Soldier. the common Soldier will not reap the Harvest of Victories but it is some other men that will gain all Praise Honor & Wealth."[25] And as John Brobst pointed out, "There are plenty of ways to get clear of a draft, and make money. . . . Go and hire out for a government teamster or a brakesman on the cars, get thirty-five or forty dollars per month while they are drafting, then quit and go home about your business and it [is] nobody's business."[26] In Massachusetts, high town enlistment rates did not lead to low desertion rates.

It is harder to infer the motives of the slaves who joined the Union army because so little is known of their prior lives. The Federal Writers' Project from the 1930s[27] has at most 100 narratives mentioning a man's enlistment, the enlistment of a family member, or the enlistment of others. (Only thirty-five of the narratives discuss own enlistment.) Fifty-five of the narratives describe how the men or a group of men enlisted. The majority of accounts (thirty-seven) concern men running away from their masters. Ten of the accounts are of men being dragooned into the army, four of the accounts are of men captured while servants in the Confederate army, and the remaining four are of men joining the army on being told that they were free.

Mistreatment by a master motivated some slaves to run away and join the army. According to J. T. Tims, "I don't reckon pa would ever have run off if ol' miss hadn't whipped me and if ol' massa hadn't struck him. They was good till then; but it looked like the war made them mean."[28] But mistreatment was not the only motive. Among the thirty-seven slave narratives that recount a slave running away to join the army, twenty include a description of the master. Half of these describe a good master and half a mean one.

Even men with good masters wanted to be free. Alex Huggins ran away at age 12 with two other boys for this reason: "Twa'nt anythin' wrong about home that made me run away. I'd heard so much talk 'bout freedom I reckon I jus' wanted to try it, an' I thought I had to get away from home to have it. . . . we sho' was after adventure."[29] Although not personally mistreated as a slave, Moses Slaughter explained to the interviewer, "No master was really good to his slaves. The very fact that he could separate a mother from her babes made him a tyrant. Each master demanded exact obedience from his slaves. Negro children were not allowed an education and if they by any chance learned to read and write, they usually had to keep their knowledge a secret."[30] Tom Windham, who grew to like army life after being dragooned into it, concluded, "I think we should have our liberty cause us ain't hogs or horses—us is human fleah [flesh]."[31]

The White Volunteer Regiments

Four out of five white men born in the prime birth cohorts of 1837–1845 eventually served in the Civil War. From April 1861 to July 1862, the army depended solely on volunteers enlisting for low pay.[32] In July 1862, the Militia Act assigned quotas to each state to fill, and states in turn assigned quotas to towns. When patriotic appeals failed, states and towns began offering men bounties to induce them to enlist so the towns could fill their quotas. At the beginning of the summer of 1862 some of the highest town bounties were around $20, but by the end of the summer they had risen to $150, a sum equal to half the yearly wage of an average worker.

In March 1863 the Enrollment Act created a conscription system administered by the federal government. Quotas were assigned to each congressional district and then broken down into subdistricts within each district. When towns failed to meet their quotas, every able-bodied male citizen between the ages of 20 and 45 became eligible for the draft, though married men were less likely to be called. Draftees could hire a substitute to take their place or they could pay a commutation fee of $300 to be exempt from that particular draft, though not from another. Draftees and substitutes were relatively rare, constituting no more than 10 percent of all soldiers. Paying a commutation fee was also rare. Only 87,000 men became exempt in this way. To avoid instituting a draft, towns raised their bounties. By December 1863, town bounties reached $300. Because both states and the federal government also offered bounties, some recruits could expect to receive about $700 for enlisting.

During the Civil War, the federal government did not control the assignment of men to companies. Regiments, the basic unit of the armies, were formed locally. The volunteer infantry regiments consisted of ten companies, each containing roughly 100 men, commanded by a captain and two lieutenants, who were often volunteer officers drawn from state militias, men of political significance, or other prominent men in the community. The newly commissioned officers were responsible for recruiting the regiment. In requesting a military commission, Joshua Chamberlain, a Bowdoin College professor who went on to a distinguished military career, wrote to the governor that "nearly a hundred of those who have been my pupils, are now officers in our army; but there are many more all over our State, who, I believe, would respond with enthusiasm, if summoned by me, and who would bring forward men enough to fill up a Regiment at once."[33]

Sometimes the enlisted men elected their own officers. James A. Garfield helped raise troops for the Seventh Regiment of Ohio Volunteer Infantry but lost the election for colonel to a man who had raised more volunteers. The governor later appointed him colonel of the yet unformed Forty-second Ohio Volunteer Infantry. Garfield first recruited his students at the Western Reserve Eclectic Institute (now Hiram College). His lieutenant colonel and major recruited in their districts, but Garfield still had to scour the countryside for recruits, using revivalist techniques in churches and town halls."[34]

Regiments were typically formed from men who came from the same area. Each company might contain bands of men who had known each other in civilian life.

Company A of Garfield's Forty-second Ohio Volunteer Infantry consisted mainly of Western Reserve Eclectic Institute students. Civil War diaries often recount how men enlisted with a friend or several friends. Rice Bull enlisted with his neighbor and school friend in a regiment organized by one of the county's more prominent citizens.[35] Austin Stearns enlisted with five other men.[36] Alfred Bellard "and some eight Hudson City boys presented ourselves at a recruiting rendezvous in Jersey City."[37]

A company was generally not replenished with new men when disease, military casualties, and desertions whittled down its numbers. After Fredericksburg, one company of the Eighty-eighth New York, part of the Irish Brigade, was down to eight men, and another company had dwindled to one. In such extreme cases, the remaining men would transfer to another company. The Eighty-eighth New York became a regiment of two companies. Federal newsman Charles Coffin compared Union policy unfavorably with that of the Confederate government, which was "not [to] organize new regiments; but put new men into the ranks with soldiers who had been in a score of battles. The new men soon became as brave and steady as they. It was a much better plan than that adopted by the Union Government—the raising of new regiments."[38] General Alpheus Williams agreed, adding, "When regiments fall below a certain number their efficiency is greatly destroyed."[39] Sherman, in his *Memoirs*, described the policy of raising new regiments and letting old ones "dwindle away into mere skeleton organizations" as the "greatest mistake made in our civil war."[40]

Men in the ranks favored preserving existing companies and regiments. Deciding how to fill regiments was left to the states. Some, such as Wisconsin, filled old regiments with new recruits. Because men had no obligation to reenlist when their three-year enlistment terms had expired, other states would reconstitute companies with mixtures of old and new men. In such cases, the veterans complained bitterly about the newcomers. Many years after the war, the regimental history of the Sixth New Hampshire Regiment described their new recruits as "scum of other nations," representing "six or eight nationalities . . . and many of them could not speak or understand a word of English." About half the new recruits deserted.[41] Fortunately for the old veterans, only about one-quarter of all companies mixed old and new recruits.

Company Diversity among White Troops

When we study peer effects in subsequent chapters, we are able to examine how peers affected behavior, because some men ended up in diverse companies and others in very homogeneous companies. Men in the white companies were born in different states and foreign countries, practiced different occupations, and differed widely in age.

Why was there diversity in companies recruited at the local level? At the beginning of the war, men would enlist with one or several friends, but rarely with fifty. And once companies were full, they would take no more men, and friends would need to find another company or regiment. One soldier wrote home, "In regard to our company, it is full. I would very much like to have some more of our boys with us but I guess we cannot take any more at present."[42] The men of Joshua Chamberlain's Twentieth Maine Volunteers came from all corners of the state, most of them excess enlistees in four other regiments.[43] Men's eagerness to get to the front led them to pick regiments thought to be departing soon. Jack Adams, his brother, and his friend "concluded that as company A of the 1st Battalion of Rifles, an old militia company located in West Newbury, and then under arms, would soon be ordered away, we would join it." When the battalion did not depart, it affected the mood: "The company began to get demoralized. Men were leaving every day, going to other States or to regiments that had been ordered to the front. At last we rebelled, and sent our officers to the Governor with a vote passed by the company, that unless we were ordered into camp at once we would disband."[44]

Later in the war, when the new recruits were not so eager, men might enlist in a distant town to receive a large bounty, adding to company diversity. We are able to control for receipt of a bounty. Company diversity also arose when states added new recruits to existing regiments or when regiments were reconstituted with veterans and new men.

The need to travel to recruiting stations increased company diversity. Farmers and farmers' sons had to travel to town to enlist. Small towns could not raise an entire company, so their men would enlist elsewhere. Austin Stearns enlisted in a neighboring town: "My native town failing to raise a company and hearing that Westboro wanted a few more men to make her company full, six of us Bear Hill boys came over and offered ourselves. . . . The company was known as the 'Westboro Company,' but men from Shrewsbury, Southboro, Hopkinton, and Upton were in its ranks."[45] Grant's Twenty-first Illinois Volunteers, organized in Mattoon, "embraced the sons of farmers, lawyers, physicians, politicians, merchants, bankers and ministers, and some men of maturer years who had filled such positions themselves."[46] In large cities, recruits from all over town would flock to recruitment centers.

Some regiments were organized on ethnic lines. They even went into battle with national emblems, the Irish brigade carrying an emerald green flag with a golden harp, the Garibaldi Guard wearing red shirts, and the New York Fire Zouaves wearing baggy pants, braided jackets, fezzes, and sashes. German gymnastic associations were also patriotic clubs, and in Indiana they recruited from all over the state to form the Thirty-second Volunteers, called the "First German." Companies that recruited along ethnic lines would contain men from different occupational backgrounds.

Finding a company that was a good match was partly a matter of luck. One soldier wrote home, "We have a remarkable civil and Religious company. . . . i think it is a providencial circumstance that I enlisted in this company for I hear that there is desperate wickedness in very regiments i came so near enlisting in."[47] Charles Gould was not so fortunate. He reported to his sister Hannah that in his company, "The men here are of the roughest kind, gambling, fighting, and swearing seem to be the principal amusement."[48] He later added, "I however never was so disgusted at the effects of rum before. All the officers were drunk, half of our company were laying about like bruts."[49]

Until the first battle, soldiers could not know whether any of their comrades or officers were good soldiers. The volunteers were all civilians. Nothing in Joshua Chamberlain's career as a college professor would have suggested that he would become a courageous officer. Some men went so far as to argue that good soldiers were found in unexpected places: "As a general thing those that at home are naturally timid are the ones here that have the least fear. [Patrick Cronan] was a sort of street bully as they term it at home. . . . He skulked out of the fight and afterwards was court marshaled and sentenced to wear . . . a wide board on the back with the word coward. . . . Others that it was thought would not fight at all fought the best."[50] No company had the ability to pick the best officers and soldiers.

THE U.S. COLORED TROOPS

Black men had not always been welcomed in the army. When war first broke out, black men in both the North and the South went to war as servants of officers and as teamsters, blacksmiths, and cooks. With rare exceptions, the free black men who sought to enlist as soldiers in the Union army were turned away. The right to bear arms was a privilege of citizenship at a time when the franchise was restricted to white men, and a federal law dating from 1792 barred blacks from serving as soldiers in the U.S. Army. White soldiers often despised blacks. A Civil War surgeon wrote, "You have no idea how greatly the common soldiers are prejudiced against the Negro. An officer can scarcely retain a colored servant. I have seen with pity and indignation [a] poor, unfortunate and inoffensive contraband kicked, cuffed, and maltreated without cause. The soldiers do this because they think the Negro *considers* himself their equal and that before long he will be made so by Congress and the administration."[51] The company commander of an Ohio white regiment who, unusually, had four men of mixed race in his regiment petitioned to have them transferred to a black regiment because "the presence of these men cause great dissatisfaction among the white soldiers and occasion myself a great deal of trouble to keep order and quiet in the company."[52]

The first black regiments were formed in the summer of 1862 in Louisiana, the South Carolina Sea Islands, and Kansas, where the state's brigadier general simply ignored the War Department's repeated protests.[53] After the issuance of the Emancipation Proclamation in January 1863, the War Department authorized Connecticut, Massachusetts, and Rhode Island to form black regiments. Only with the establishment of the Bureau of Colored Troops in May 1863 to regulate and supervise the enlistment of black soldiers and the selection of officers were other northern states authorized to recruit black regiments. At the same time, the War Department expanded its efforts to recruit in the Union-occupied South. Federal law was modified to allow states to add free blacks to the draft pool, but in some states, such as Maryland, this practice began only in the summer of 1864. Both slaves and free men could serve as substitutes. By the end of 1865, 186,017 blacks had enlisted in the Union army, roughly three-quarters of whom were former slaves. Like the white soldiers, the vast majority were volunteers. In our random sample of black soldiers, 91 percent were volunteers (as was true for white soldiers as well), 7 percent were substitutes, and 2 percent were draftees.

When the first black regiments were authorized, in the border states (Delaware, Maryland, Kentucky, and Missouri, so-called because their sympathies were split between North and South), "Union men denounce this measure as odious—monstrous—villainous—say Lincoln & the cabinet & congress ought to be hung—but they will not join with the South in resistance to such tyranny."[54] At first, in the border states, only the slaves of rebellious owners or slaves who had the permission of their owners could enlist. Army recruiters, however, frequently acted without that permission. Recruiters for the Fourth U.S. Colored Infantry (USCI) freed slaves imprisoned in a Baltimore slave pen, many of whom were the property of owners in Washington, D.C., having been transferred to Baltimore when slavery was abolished in the District of Columbia in April 1862. None of the men who enlisted in the Fourth USCI was ever returned to his master, despite owners' protests and proofs of loyalty.[55] Later, when slaves of loyal owners were recruited despite their masters' protestations, the owners were offered compensation of $300, less than one quarter of the price of an adult able-bodied slave in the Confederate South. In February 1864, Congress authorized drafting slaves in the border states, offering slaves their freedom and their owners $100. The draft was soon discontinued because of widespread opposition in the border states.[56]

White officers commanded the black regiments. (Blacks could be promoted to corporal or sergeant, but were still paid the same as privates.) Only one in four applicants for a commission in the U.S. Colored Troops (USCT) received one. Officers were selected on the basis of letters of recommendation and had to pass an oral examination in tactics, army regulations, general military knowledge, history, geography, and mathematics. In contrast, the officers of the white troops were either elected by their men or appointed by state governors.[57]

Many of the men who commanded the colored troops were abolitionists or came from areas where the evangelical revivals of the mid-1820s to 1850s had burned most strongly. Before the war, Thomas Wentworth Higginson was a Unitarian pastor, an unsuccessful Free Soil party candidate, and a rescuer of runaway slaves. He became the colonel of the first official black regiment organized by the federal government and was the most prominent abolitionist in the USCT.[58] Rufus Kinsley, a second lieutenant in the Second Infantry Regiment and the former superintendent of the May Street Sunday School, Negroes, Boston, viewed slavery as a mortal sin. He wrote in his diary, "the terrible harvest we gather; —a nation of graves, and rivers of blood . . . is the legitimate fruit of the seed we have sown."[59] Toward the end of the war, Brevet Major General Alving C. Voris wrote, "Not least among the exploits of which I feel proud is my command of a colored brigade. . . . I am glad the Government is giving them a chance to fight & make men of themselves."[60]

For other men, a commission in the colored troops offered the chance of a promotion. James Horrocks wrote home, "I am expecting in a week or two (see Annie's letter) to get a Lieutenancy in a Coloured Regt. of Infantry. What do you think about it? Chances of being shot greater; Accomodations and comforts generally smaller, but pay much larger than what I have now. No horse to ride but a uniform to wear. And above all—an *Officer*'s real shoulder straps and the right of being addressed and treated as a gentleman, with the advantage of better society, and if I like it, this is a position I can hold for life, being United States troops while Volunteers will undoubtedly be disbanded when the war is over."[61] In our random sample, regiments recruited earlier and regiments recruited in the Union were more likely to have commanders with abolitionist sympathies.

The white officers of the colored troops were responsible for filling the ranks. In the free northern states, black leaders such as Frederick Douglass urged men to enlist, because "Once let the black man get upon his person the brass letter, *U.S.*; let him get an eagle on his button, and a musket on his shoulder, and bullets in his pocket, and there is no power on earth that can deny that he has earned the right to citizenship."[62] Elmo Steele recounted how "When de Civil War broke loose. I was a young man. De war was over here enslaved. I wanted to jine in an' help out, so one day in '65 I says to my pa, 'I wants to go to war.' I never will fergit how he looked at me an' put his hand on my head an' say, 'My son yo' will make a good soldier.'"[63] Roughly 78 percent of age-eligible black men in the free northern states enlisted.

Recruitment in the border states and in the former Confederacy was harder and took several forms. One method was to establish headquarters in a community and have several of the white officers comb the countryside for recruits. The Fourth USCT was to be raised in Baltimore, but soon it became clear that it was not possible to raise an entire regiment in Baltimore alone. Colonel William Birney of the Second USCT, who was in charge of recruitment, and his officers gathered men from all parts of the state of Maryland, actively helping slaves to escape and forcibly removing them from farms, plantations, and slave pens. Local opposition could be quite strong. One of Birney's recruiters was murdered by a slave owner and his son, both avowed secessionists.[64] Another was thrown into a local jail when he enlisted several slaves, and the War Department refused to secure his freedom because it stated that it had no authority in matters involving civilians.[65]

Slaves who wanted to enlist faced many dangers if they had to travel to a recruiting station. Those who were caught were jailed or whipped. Browder described one case in his diary: "His boy *Simon* ran away to the federal army, was caught & returned. Again he ran away & having stolen many things at home was arrested & put in jail where he lay until he was humbled, sick & worn out."[66] Later he wrote, "Found my plantation entirely deserted by negroes—not one left! . . . my brother William came with the rest of the fugitives—looking worn, sad, confounded. They had been overtaken in a few miles of Clarksville. We whipped Jeff & Bob & Lucy, & Ellen made herself sick. . . ."[67] In Kentucky, Missouri, and Tennesseee, southern guerrillas whipped and mutilated slaves traveling to recruiting stations.[68]

The recruitment campaign was less dangerous for both officers and men and was more effective. Large numbers of Union forces, including units from the colored troops, swept through an area and urged the former slaves and the freemen to enlist. Because, as Sherman pointed out, the former slaves, who "were compelled to leave their women in the uncertainty of their new condition . . . cannot be relied on," commanders would often bring both the men and their families to Union lines, sometimes regardless of orders.[69]

The ranks were also filled with runaway slaves who crossed into the border states or to Union-occupied territory. Boston Blackwell told how he ran away with another slave from an Arkansas plantation after being accused of stealing. After two days and nights, the two reached Union lines, and Boston found work as a teamster. William Sherman described how he and his cousin, on hearing that the Yankees were in Robertsville, South Carolina, spread the word to slaves on neighboring plan-

Plate 2. Fugitive Negroes fording the Rappahanok

tations and marched with 500 men to Union lines. In 1863, Henry Buttler's owner transported him and about forty other slaves from Virginia to Arkansas to keep his slaves out of Union hands. Henry escaped alone to federal headquarters at Fort Smith, Arkansas, and enlisted in the army.

Women would also follow the soldiers, as cooks or washerwomen. Susie King Taylor of Savannah, Georgia, and her cousins were brought to Union lines by her uncle. She had several uncles, some cousins, and a husband in the Thirty-third USCT and followed the regiment working as a laundress, teaching the soldiers to read and write when she could.[70]

In recruiting in the South, the USCT could draw only from areas liberated by the Union army. Eleven percent of age-eligible black men in the Confederacy served, the majority enlisting in Arkansas, Louisiana, Mississippi, and Tennessee. In Texas, where Union troops arrived only when the war was over, less than 1 percent of age-eligible men served, whereas in Louisiana one-quarter of them did. In the border states, where recruiting efforts had to avoid stoking the fires of succession, 34 percent of age-eligible black men served. Because most black men were in the slave states, however, one-quarter of the USCT came from the border states or the District of Columbia and half came from the Confederate states.[71]

Participation rates were low even in states penetrated by the Union army early in the war, because the army did not have the manpower to establish a permanent presence in all areas. Some slaves on remote plantations never even saw a Yankee. Other slaves were put to work on plantations. In Louisiana, the federal government used contraband labor on abandoned plantations, paying workers by the month.[72] Were the men who ran away to join the army just lucky that Union soldiers were nearby or that they were not caught while traveling to a recruiting station; or were they somehow different? Bill Simms told an interviewer in the 1930s, "The masters aimed to keep their slaves in ignorance and the ignorant slaves were all in favor of the Rebel army, only the more intelligent were in favor of the Union army."[73] But perhaps he was justifying his own decision. In 1910, 28 percent of black veterans living in the South could write, compared to 25 percent of nonveterans, not a large difference (estimated from the 1910 Integrated Public Use Census sample).

Relatively few black regiments experienced combat, and most black soldiers performed a disproportionate share of garrison duty and fatigue duty during the war, because there were doubts about the ability of black soldiers to fight.[74] Out of 137 black infantry regiments, 35 of them sustained almost three-quarters of the entire loss in action of black troops.[75]

Black companies' wartime experiences differed widely. Regiments formed in the last days of the war spent more time in reconstruction duty or were sent to Texas as an "army of observation" while Mexico was occupied by French troops. Nevertheless, life as a soldier was still dangerous. In our sample, 22 percent of black soldiers died while in the service, a higher service mortality rate than the 14 percent for our sampled white soldiers, mainly because sanitary conditions for black troops were so poor. More than 90 percent of black service deaths were from disease.

Company Diversity among Black Troops

Why was there diversity within companies of the USCT, where diversity is measured by place of birth, slave status, and age? Some companies had few older men, others had many. Some companies were composed mainly of free blacks, others of slaves, and still others were mixed. Some companies drew men from the same state while others drew men from different states.

The recruiters for the USCT did not have the luxury of shaping the ideal company. A regiment that had not yet achieved full strength was not sent into battle, and officers might lose their commissions if they failed to recruit in a timely manner.[76] As with the white companies, once a company was formed it was not replenished and might fight at half-strength after losing men to disease and to battlefield deaths.

The recruiting process and movements of slaves during the war introduced birthplace diversity in companies. In some regiments colonels might request permission to move to different states to recruit more men.[77] Some slave owners from states that were close to the Union, such as Virginia, sent their slaves to Arkansas and Mississippi, thinking that their slaves would be out of reach of the Union army. Slaves working as servants, teamsters, blacksmiths, or laborers for the Confederate army were captured and put in the Union army. Slaves escaping to Union lines would be sent north, where they would enlist or, in some cases, would immediately don a uniform and join a company.

Age diversity was also a byproduct of the recruiting process. Recruiters eager to fill the ranks were not very selective. An assistant inspector general reported that in the Sixty-third USCT, "More than half of the men are old and cripples, both physically and mentally disqualified for being soldiers."[78] With so many former slaves following the army, recruiters may have felt that young men and old men were better off in military service than having to fend for themselves.

Slaves and free blacks would find themselves in the same company when the company was formed in slave states with a free black population, when runaway slaves made their way to Union lines and entered companies that already had free blacks, and when free blacks were sent to serve as noncommissioned officers of southern units. In forming the Fourth USCT, Colonel Birney had always intended to form a regiment using both free blacks and fugitive or liberated slaves.[79] Because few literate noncommissioned officers could be found among the newly freed slaves, Colonel Higginson asked for volunteers among his friends in the free black population of the North. Other commanders were less persuasive, and the Bureau of Colored Troops forcibly picked literate men for promotion and appointment in the South.[80]

STATISTICAL ANALYSIS OF DIVERSITY

Were diverse companies somehow different in ways that would affect our conclusions about the effects of peers on men's behavior? Did they contain the iconoclasts and the outcasts? Although we do find observable differences between men in diverse companies and men in homogeneous companies in our sample of white soldiers, we find no evidence that men's wartime mortality depended on the diversity of their company. All else equal, men from larger cities, draftees and substitutes, nonfarmers, the foreign-born, men who could read and write, and shorter men were more likely to find themselves in a company containing a wide array of men from different birth places and occupations. Men who received large bounties and poorer men were more likely to be in a company of diverse ages.

In our sample of black soldiers, the observable differences between men in diverse companies and men in homogeneous companies are not large. Men in companies with a greater diversity in state of birth were no more likely to die during the war and were similar in height, fighting experience, and enlistment year. Companies with greater birthplace diversity were more likely to have an abolitionist officer, but there was no correlation between a company being led by an abolitionist officer and whether the regiment was a fighting regiment, the fraction of free blacks in the company, or birthplace diversity in the company.

The recruitment process created companies that differed widely. Some companies were diverse and others contained men who were very similar to each other. In the rush to fill the ranks, officers did not discriminate among men. When men enlisted, they had little idea who all of their comrades would be. Austin Stearns lamented, "Life in the army was very different from life at home. In one place we could choose our companions and those we wished to associate with, but in the army how different."[81] As we will show in the next chapter, comrades, both wanted and unwanted, determined whether a soldier was willing to stick it out.

FORMING SOLDIERS FROM CITIZENS

The Union army was not held together by discipline. Men despised the drill, which was designed to inculcate in them unquestioning discipline, even under fire. An enlisted man in the Twenty-seventh Massachusetts wrote, "I like a soldiers duty well enough but I do not like to have a master [and] be drove like a niggar. . . . I think I am just as good as enny boddy."[82] When officers were men soldiers had known all their lives, the men had trouble thinking of officers as their superiors and were slow to follow orders, or simply refused. Mark Twain said of his three-week militia service that the "camps were composed of young men who had been born and reared to a sturdy independence, and who did not know what it meant to be ordered around by every Tom, Dick, and

Harry, whom they had known familiarly all their lives." He went on to describe how when Brigadier General Thomas H. Harris, "the sole and modest-salaried operator in our telegraph office," gave an order, the response was "Oh, now, what'll you take to *don't*, Tom Harris?"[83]

Officers who commanded contempt because of their cowardice or disregard for the welfare of their men resigned their commissions, driven out by their men's ill will. Men who elected their own officers could just as easily dismiss them. Grant was appointed colonel by the governor of Illinois when a regiment refused to enter service with their elected colonel serving in any position. The regiment lost confidence in a colonel who "even went so far at times as to take the guard from their posts and go with them to the village near by and make a night of it."[84]

The army's coercive powers were limited. As the war progressed, the army designated units of provost guards to drive stragglers (men who milled at the rear) into line. Because they were reluctant to shoot soldiers wearing the same uniform, however, they were not always effective. Courage was not for everyone. Lincoln asked, "if Almighty God gives a man a *cowardly pair of legs*, how can he help their running away with him?"[85]

The Union Soldier's Life

The soldiers whose legs did not run away with them could expect boredom and disease in camp and high casualties on the battlefield. During the Civil War the job of a soldier was unskilled, largely consisting of learning the movement of linear formations, obeying orders without hesitation, and mastering the nine steps of loading a musket and firing in the direction of an enemy hidden by the smoke of the battlefield and by vegetation.[86] Rice Bull

Plate 3. Camp scene (22nd NY Volunteers, Lt. J. T. Baldwin), ca. 1860–ca. 1865

wrote that when his regiment first came under fire, "[we] held our fire until we saw the line of smoke that showed that they were on the ridge; then every gun fired. It was then load and fire at will as fast as we could. . . . The smoke was so dense we could seldom see them but we could see the flash of their guns as they advanced yelling."[87] Hess describes the nerve-wracking approach toward the enemy, an approach in which "troops might approach the battlefield on a narrow lane that meandered inside a tunnel of vegetation. Visibility was often limited to a few hundred yards. . . . Deployment from marching columns into lines of battle often meant plunging into a mass of vegetation that swallowed up entire units and severely impeded movement, communication, and combat effectiveness."[88]

Trained soldiers could load and fire the new rifled muskets three times a minute and kill at the previously unheard of range of 1,000 yards, a range that could not be matched by cannon. Soldiers and their officers could be shot at any moment, and bravery meant not flinching under fire. Civil War weaponry combined with Napoleonic war tactics of closed-rank formations, heavy reliance on bayonet charges, saber charges by cavalry, and direct frontal assaults turned men into rifle fodder.

Soldiers responded by digging trenches. The men in Sherman's Army of Tennessee carried their spades with them, rather than keep them in the wagons. Efforts to flank trenches only increased their length, and the only way to overcome the trenches was to close in with opposing forces as rapidly as possible. Men expected high casualty rates. Before Grant's frontal assault on the entrenched Confederates at Cold Harbor, the soldiers ordered to spearhead the attack pinned their names to their clothing so that their bodies could later be identified.

General Alpheus S. Williams described the Civil War battlefield to his daughter by asking her to see and hear

in fancy, the crashing roll of 30,000 muskets mingled with the thunder of over a hundred pieces of artillery; the sharp bursting of shells and the peculiar whizzing sound of its dismembered pieces, traveling with a shriek in all directions; the crash and thud of round shot through trees and buildings and into earth or through columns of human bodies; the "phiz" of the Minie ball; the uproar of thousands of voices in cheers, yells, and imprecations; and see the smoke from all the engines of war's inventions hanging like a curtain between the combatants; see the hundreds of wounded limping away or borne to the rear on litters; riderless horses rushing wildly about; now and then blowing up of a caisson and human frames thrown lifeless into the air; the rush of columns to the front; the scattered fugitives of broken regiments and skulkers making for the rear.[89]

After the battle, the wounded were carried away and the dead were buried. Private Bellard wrote in his diary after one battle,

The firing must have been pretty lively, for in some places the pine trees about 4 inches thick had been cut in two by bullets while others were filled with bullet holes. . . . The dead rebs were still lying where they fell on the second day after the battle, and presented a horrible sight. They had swelled to double their natural size, and as a consequence their clothing had burst thus exposing their bodies to the sun, and turning them as black as ink caused it was said by drinking gun powder and whiskey.

By this time our details were ready to bury them having attended to our own dead men. The were now so far decomposed and made such a horrible stench, that it was as much as we could do to get them under cover. The way we managed it was this. Upon finding a body, a hole was dug about 18 inches deep close to him, two or three pieces of wood or fence rails were placed under the body, and at the word Roll rolled in, the men taking to their heels the instant it went over the edge, for in nearly all cases it burst, upon striking bottom.[90]

Life in camp could be even more dangerous than the battlefield. Rice Bull's friend Spencer Phineas, with whom he had enlisted, came down with typhoid fever before ever seeing action and developed gangrene in both feet. Rice's nursing may have saved his life.[91] Upon hearing that his brother Wesley had joined the army, Charles Gould wrote to his sister Hannah, "I am proud of him as a brother, but, Dear sister, I know the danger through which he must pass & I would to God I were with him to care for him. . . . If any more of the boys [brothers] enlist, be sure to have them with him for there nothen like a friend in these times. Though I do not believe he will be called to fight, still there is a great deal of danger in camp. More die from disease than on the battle ground."[92] Charles died in 1862 of typhoid fever.

A Union army soldier who deserted would have faced only a 40 percent chance of being caught and a negligible risk of death if arrested. Faced with death in combat and death from disease, distance from loved ones, and low and irregular pay, a soldier should have deserted. In the first half of the eighteenth century about 20 percent of the French army deserted, and, though no estimates are available, the leaders of other nations voiced laments about extremely high desertion rates.[93] But more than 90 percent of all Union army soldiers did not desert, and among Union army soldiers whose three-year enlistment terms were up, half reenlisted.[94] What motivated these men to remain loyal to the Union?

CHAPTER 4

Heroes and Cowards

ABRAHAM LINCOLN REPLACED GEORGE MCCLELLAN with Ulysses S. Grant because "he fights." Jefferson Davis replaced the cautious Joseph E. Johnston with John Bell Hood, who promptly destroyed his army attacking Sherman. Both the U.S. president and the president of the Confederacy sought decisive battle, in which two opposing forces meet face to face until one is annihilated or surrenders.

Decisive battle has long dominated Western warfare strategy.[1] During the Peloponnesian Wars, the Spartan general Brasidas told his men about the barbarian tribes of Illyria and Macedonia: "when it comes to real fighting with an opponent who stands his ground, they are not what they seemed: they have no regular order that they should be ashamed of deserting their positions when hard pressed; flight and attack are with them equally honorable, afford no test of courage: their independent mode of fighting never leaving anyone who wants to run away without a fair excuse for so doing." [2] Wars of attrition in which soldiers vanish to live to fight another day were primarily found outside the Western world. Brasidas told his soldiers, "Stand your ground therefore when they advance, and again await your opportunity to retire in good order."[3]

Confederate major general J.E.B. Stuart harked back to myths of medieval knights when he said, "All that I ask of fate is that I may be killed leading a cavalry charge."[4] European knights in the Middle Ages engaged in individual charges, ritualistic fighting, and hand-to-hand combat to display personal courage. The emergence of the gun destroyed the medieval warrior class, and disdain for bullets replaced the courage needed for individualized charges.

The behavior of Alexander Farnese, governor-general of the Netherlands and later duke of Parma, during the siege of Oudenaarde in 1582 foreshadowed this change. The duke had a table set near the trench works so he and his staff could dine in the open air, but

a ball came flying over the table, taking off the head of a young Walloon officer who was sitting near Parma. . . . A portion of his skull struck out the eye of another gentleman present. A second ball . . . destroyed two more of the guests as they sat at the banquet. . . . The blood and the brains of these unfortunate individuals were strewn over the festive board, and the others all started to their feet, having little appetite left for their dinner. Alexander alone remained in his seat. . . . Quietly ordering the attendants to remove the dead bodies, and to bring a clean tablecloth, he insisted that his guests should resume their places.[5]

Soldiers were to stand their ground even if, at Borodino, they had to stand under point-blank artillery fire for two hours, "during which the only movement was the

Plate 4. Gettysburg, PA; battered trees on Culp's Hill

stirring in the lines caused by falling corpses."[6] Clausewitz, a Prussian veteran of the Napoleonic wars, who survived the battles of Jena, Borodino, and Waterloo, later wrote in the most famous book on war,

> The army that maintains its cohesion under the most murderous fire; that cannot be shaken by imaginary fears and resists well-found ones with all its might; that, proud of its victories, will not lose the strength to obey orders and its respect and trust for its officers

even in defeat; whose physical power, like the mus-
cles of an athlete, has been steeled by training in pri-
vation and effort . . . that is mindful of all these duties and qualities by virtue of the single powerful
idea of the honor of its arms—such an army is imbued with the true military spirit."[7]

Winning a decisive battle requires amassing sufficient
numbers of soldiers who will stand their ground. But
throughout history, soldiers have frequently deserted, and
their leaders have had to devote a great deal of attention
to preventing desertions. At Agincourt a large number of
the French cavalry sought refuge from the rain of arrows
in a nearby wood. At Waterloo the Dutch-Belgian and
minor German regiments deliberately stayed out of the
battle which was lost when Napoleon's famed Guard collapsed and fled from the steady musket fire. Wellington
noted of Napoleon, "He just moved forward in the old
style and was driven off in the old style," [8] that is, by an
old-fashioned pounding. During World War I the main
participants all lost their will to fight: more than half of
the French divisions on the Western Front rebelled in
May 1917, the Russian army refused to fight in July 1917,
the Italian Second Army collapsed in November 1917,
the British Fifth Army fell apart in March 1918, and, deci-
sively, the German army in the West refused to continue
the fight in October 1918.

WHY SOLDIERS FOUGHT:
QUALITATIVE EVIDENCE

What motivates soldiers to stand their ground? Few men
would agree with Union general Philip Kearny, who

reportedly said, "I love war. It brings me indescribable pleasure, like that of having a woman."[9] One Civil War diarist wrote of even the most committed volunteers, "Hardly any of us were soldiers by choice."[10] Mercenary armies have been motivated by pay and professional armies by promotions, but what motivates mass armies of citizens? When fighting major wars, countries cannot afford to be generous with pay. Battle police or even men's commanding officers have stood behind soldiers to prevent their running away. During the World War II not only did Stalin's armies have special detachments that formed a second line to shoot at any soldiers in the first line who fled, but the families of all deserters were also arrested.[11] Out of the roughly 35,000 German soldiers tried for desertion by the Third Reich, about 22,750 were executed.[12] Democracies cannot inflict such punishments. Lincoln recognized that "you can't order men shot by the dozens or twenties. People won't stand it."[13]

The first national armies, those of revolutionary France, fought to save the revolution at home and to export it abroad. Pierre Cohin of the Armée du Nord expressed his deep commitment to the cause when he wrote, "The war which we are fighting is not a war between king and king or nation and nation. It is the war of liberty against despotism."[14]

Civil War soldiers' letters and diaries reveal that many Union soldiers viewed the Civil War as a war of liberty against despotism. In the words of two soldiers, losing the war would mean that "all of the hope and confidence in the capacity of men for self government will be lost" and that "the onward march of Liberty in the Old World will be retarded by at least a century."[15] Brevet Major General Alving C. Voris wrote to his wife, "if I should die in battle teach them to respect the memory of a father who did strive to leave them a firm & beneficial Government without which they could not expect to live in security & happiness." Wesley Gould wrote to his sister Hannah, "now is the time to fight for Liberty or Death. If we conquer the South this will be one of the greatest Nations on the face of the earth, but on the other hand if the South conquer us which will never be done unless through treachery on the part of our Generals and peace men, but God forbid that we should ever be ruled by such a Despotic Nation as the South."[16]

Few white soldiers claimed to fight primarily for the abolition of slavery. William Jones wrote to his sister Maggie, "I did not enlist to fight for those black devils."[17] But as the war wore on, many soon echoed the private in the First Minnesota who wrote, "The war will never end until we end slavery."[18]

Black soldiers had different motives. The free blacks of the North fought for citizenship. The slaves of the South fought for freedom. If they surrendered, the Confederates might not be willing to take prisoners, and if captured, they might be enslaved. Colonel Higginson wrote of his colored troops,

> They had more to fight for than the whites. Besides the flag and the Union, they had home and wife and child. They fought with ropes round their necks. . . . when the new colored regiments began to arrive from the North my men still pointed out this difference, —that in case of ultimate defeat the Northern troops, black or white, would go home, while the First South Carolina must fight it out or be re-enslaved.[19]

For many black soldiers, the war was a crusade. Higginson wrote, "It used to seem to me that never, since Cromwell's time, had there been soldiers in whom the religious element held such a place. 'A religious army,' 'gospel army,' were their frequent phrases."[20]

Scholars have downplayed the roles of patriotism and ideology in the nation's twentieth-century wars, arguing that they were negligible even during World War II. A World War II soldier told interviewers, "Ask any dogface on the line. You're fighting for your skin on the line. When I enlisted I was patriotic as all hell. There's no patriotism on the line. A boy up there 60 days in the line is in danger every minute. He ain't fighting for patriotism."[21] Although questionnaires administered to American volunteers in the Spanish Civil War found that ideology was the single most important factor helping men overcome fear in battle,[22] the Americans who traveled to Spain to fight were all committed to the cause.

Basing their arguments in part on questionnaires administered to World War II U.S. soldiers, many sociologists, psychologists, and military historians have said that soldiers' primary motivation for fighting is intense loyalty, to the point of self-sacrifice, to a small band of comrades.[23] One soldier told interviewers, "You know the men in your outfit. You have to be loyal to them. . . . They depend on each other—wouldn't do anything to let the rest of them down."[24] In his study of World War II soldiers, Linderman cites a memorist who wrote, "Men . . . do not fight for flag or country, for the Marine Corps or glory or any other abstraction. They fight for one another." He also cites the antiwar critic Paul Fussell, who wrote that men "will attack only if young, athletic, credulous, and sustained by some equivalent of the buddy system."[25]

Comradeship bolsters loyalty to the group. The nineteenth-century French infantry colonel Ardant du Picq wrote "Four brave men who do not know each other will not dare to attack a lion. Four less brave, but knowing each other well, sure of their reliability and consequently of mutual aid, will attack resolutely."[26] Even with no rational calculations, the brain may code social support as physical safety.[27] Union Captain Frank Holsinger of the Nineteenth U.S. Colored Infantry wrote, "I have always found comforting in battle the companionship of a friend, one in whom you had confidence, one you felt assured would stand by you until the last."[28] Because soldiers live with the same men for so long, endangering the group leads to personal guilt and ostracism within the group. Oliver Wendell Holmes, who served as an officer in the Civil War, wept at not being able to be with his comrades at the battle of Fredericksburg, where his regiment lost more men than in any other engagement of the war.[29] General Alpheus Williams described how "Many of the wounded have come back, some quite disabled but sticking to their ranks. I met one the other day whose left arm was so disabled at Antietam that he could carry only his musket in his right hand. Still he does not ask for a discharge."[30]

Even the most cohesive units will crack under intense pressure. Shils and Janowitz's (1948) classic study of the Wehrmacht during World War II argued that "Once disruption of primary group life resulted through separation, breaks in communications, loss of leadership, depletion of personnel, or major and prolonged breaks in the supply of food and medical care, such an ascendancy of preoccupation with physical survival developed that there was very little 'last-ditch' resistance."[31] Disintegration took the form of group surrender, however, and was widely discussed within the unit beforehand. The British, French, Italian, and Russian armies of World War I cracked when the total number of deaths equaled the number of fighting infantry in the divisions. The Germans cracked later, but only after their armies were no longer victorious.[32]

During the Civil War, soldiers felt intensely both their own victories and those of their distant comrades. Despite their high casualty rate, the soldiers who fought at Gettysburg were elated by their victory. A corporal could write, "Those who a few weeks ago were almost willing to give up everything are now the most hopeful for the future."[33] When word of Gettysburg, Port Hudson, and Rosencrans's Tullahoma campaign in Tennessee reached the Union soldiers besieging Jackson, Mississippi, one of them wrote, "we hardly know how to contain ourselves over the unequalled good news. Everybody is electrified with it—the army is on fire—as irresistible as an avalanche. . . . I never saw such enthusiasm."[34] The many victories of the Army of the West were a powerful tonic; as described by one artilleryman, "We have had so many victories that we do not think there is any such thing as getting whipped; and so when we go into a fight expect to come out the best and are shure to do so."[35] When it was clear that the South was losing the war, soldiers deserted en masse, and desertion rates were highest when company solidarity was highest.[36]

Civil War officers were more likely to discuss honor and duty in their letters than were the enlisted men.[37] Oliver Wendell Holmes could write home early in the war, "I am very happy in the conviction I did my duty handsomely. . . . From a third to a half of our company killed wounded & prisoners."[38] Sergeant Austin C. Stearns concluded his memoirs with, "Of my life as a soldier, I can say that although serving in a humble capacity I was on every march, in every battle and skirmish—never was sick. Always did *my part* whether on drill, fatigue, guard or picket—wherever duty called I was there."[39] The letters of Civil War soldiers echo studies of American soldiers in World War II that found combat performance to be positively associated with social class and education.[40]

Soldiers' combat motivation is not the only force driving armies forward. Military leadership establishes standards, patterns of behavior, and values. General William Tecumseh Sherman wrote, "There is a soul to an army as well as to the individual man, and no general can accomplish the full work of his army unless he commands the soul of his men, as well as their bodies and legs."[41] Victor Hanson has argued that commanders such as Sherman encouraged soldiers' ideological zeal and imbued them with abolitionist fury. One sergeant remarked, "There was never such a man as Sherman or as they call him Crazy Bill and he has got his men to believe that they cant be whipped."[42] Sherman led from the front. Rice Bull wrote, "I never saw General Sherman making for some place in our rear."[43] Sherman could tell his soldiers that "men march to certain death without a murmur if I call on them, because they know I value their lives as much as my own."[44]

Charles Russell Lowell, colonel of the Second Massachusetts Cavalry, also had the "capacity of ruling men."[45] Thirteen horses were shot from under him, and his men "never shrank from following him into any danger after they had seen him in one battle."[46] Risking his life, Lowell led cavalry charges. His men were "ashamed to do anything less than their full duty under his eyes." They had "great confidence in him, wanted to see him among them, and wished for nothing so much as to show him what they dared to do."[47] He died of wounds sustained in a cavalry charge.

Their soldiers' affection in turn sustained commanders. Lowell would watch his men in action "with tears in his eyes."[48] General Alpheus Williams wrote, "I should hardly dare to say these things to anyone but you, but I confess and feel that the love of these men, whom I have taken through snow and rain, [who] have marched thousands of miles for the last year and half under all circumstances that try the temper and disturb the amiability, is worth a great deal. It is my chief support and encouragement amidst the trials and dispiriting circumstances that surround me."[49]

Punishing Deserters

When called to witness an execution for desertion, William Gould wrote to his sister Hannah that "it was one of the [most] painful sights I ever saw."[50] But a deserter's probability of being executed was equivalent to the chance of flipping ten heads in a row with a fair coin. The penalties for desertion, and also for absence without leave, generally ranged from fines and loss of pay to imprisonment (including with hard labor) to performance of the more onerous duties in the company to the social sanctions of men's home communities. Some deserters were shamed publicly. James Horrocks wrote to his parents of a deserter who fled camp before seeing any action: "One of our deserters (we have a considerable number already) was caught a few days since. He lost his bounty or rather what he had left of it, about $200 by Confiscation, his head was shaved and he is placed upon a gun carriage every day with the word deserter on his back in Capitals."[51]

Black and white deserters were equally likely to be captured, but blacks were slightly less likely to be punished for desertion. Forty-nine percent of black deserters were not punished at all, compared to 44 percent of white deserters. Colonel Higginson told of a deserter who returned "after being five days in the woods, almost without food. His clothes were in rags, and he was nearly starved, poor foolish fellow, so that we can almost dispense with further punishment."[52] When soldiers were punished for desertion, however, blacks were punished more harshly. Thirteen percent of all black deserters were sentenced to wearing a ball and chain, compared to 6 percent of white deserters. Punishments were slightly milder in regiments with abolitionist commanders. Colonel Higginson later wrote, "Severe penalties would be wasted on these people, accustomed as they have been to the most violent passions on the part of white men; but a mild inexorableness tells on them, just as it does on any other children. It is something utterly new to me, and it is thus far perfectly efficacious. They have a great deal of pride as soldiers, and a very little of severity goes a great way, if it be firm and consistent."[53] He also emphasized that "in dealing out punishments, we had carefully to avoid all that was brutal and arbitrary, all that savored of the overseer."[54] Nonabolitionists were less paternalistic. One officer stated, "It is useless to talk about being lenient with them for if you give them an inch they will take a mile."[55]

Measuring Loyalty and Its Causes

What motivated soldiers to remain loyal to the Union? It was not punishments. Was it individual attributes, loyalty to comrades, ideology, morale, or leadership? We have cited qualitative evidence on the importance of these causes, but there is no clear consensus in the literature on the relative importance of each of these factors. Does cohesion produce military effectiveness, or does military effectiveness produce cohesion? The armies of different nations have disagreed. The organizational structure of the Israeli Defense Forces, much like that of the Wehrmacht, ensures highly cohesive units. Entire units always have been rotated in and out of combat. In contrast, the U.S. Army emphasized administrative efficiency and rotated individuals in and out of combat during World War II, the Korean War, and the Vietnam War.[56] The army still rotates individuals in South Korea but rotates units during peacekeeping operations and in Iraq.

We quantify the effects of individual attributes, loyalty to comrades, ideology, morale, and leadership on the effectiveness of black and white units. Our primary measure of effectiveness is based on desertion. As General Alpheus Williams wrote, "When regiments fall below a certain number their efficiency is greatly destroyed. The details and daily-duty men oppress the soldier, and their thin ranks discourage and dishearten him."[57] We have also looked at AWOLs and arrests (for reasons other than desertion or AWOL), both individually and by combining them with desertion in one summary measure. We discuss these when there are differences with desertion.

Desertion is the best measure of shirking. It is a more serious offense than AWOL, and because 10 percent of

Union army soldiers deserted, it is also the measure with the largest number of events. Absences without leave were generally due to failure to return from furlough on time or straggling from the company. Although a soldier's AWOL might turn into a desertion, we treat as AWOL only those cases that were not desertions. Arrests that were not for desertion or AWOL were for drunkenness, assault, robbery, insubordination, and sleeping while on picket duty. Arrests for minor infractions depended on officer decisions. Desertions, AWOLs, and arrests were handled by military courts convened in the field.

Our data provide us with detailed information on individual characteristics, company characteristics, ideology, morale, and leadership. Socioeconomic and demographic characteristics of soldiers such as age or literacy may act as proxies for soldiers' productivity (for example, older soldiers may be more disciplined), whereas other characteristics such as social status or birthplace may affect group loyalty because they influence ideas of patriotism, honor, duty, and self-sacrifice and shape soldiers' ideology. In the case of Civil War soldiers, the sense of duty and honor and the potential for public shame were greater among the more socially prominent. Charles Francis Adams, Jr. (the great-grandson of John Adams) enlisted against his father's wishes because "it would have been an actual disgrace had [our] family, of all possible families American, been wholly unrepresented in the field."[58] Oliver Wendell Holmes, Jr., praised the first colonel of the Twentieth Massachusetts for having "taught us more perfectly than we could learn elsewhere to strive not only to acquire the discipline of soldiers but the high feelings and self-sacrifice of chivalrous gentlemen."[59]

Married men may be either more or less motivated to

fight by the thought of loved ones. An Ohio officer wrote to his wife, "When exposing myself to the fire of the enemy, my first thought has always been my family, but the certainty that I had the approval . . . of my dear wife that I should be just where I was, gave my heart courage."[60] Spotswood Rice, a private in the USCT, wrote to his still enslaved daughters in September 1864, "be assured that I will have you if it cost me my life. . . . And I want her [his daughters' owner] to remember if she meets me with ten thousand soldiers she [will?] meet her enemy."[61] But married men also received letters from their families recounting financial and family hardships, and ex-slaves would worry how the families they left behind were treated by their owners.

Immigrants fought for different reasons. Germans who fled the revolutions of 1848 were more likely than Irish or British immigrants who had migrated for economic reasons to view the United States as the best hope for the survival of a form of republican government. Protestant Germans were more likely to be Republican than Catholic Germans or the predominantly Catholic Irish because a large proportion of Republican voters were anti-Catholic Know-Nothings.[62]

A soldier's community was the roughly 100 men in his company. He lived and fought with these men. A World War I German soldier wrote, "The company is the only truly existent community. This community allows neither time nor rest for a personal life. It forces us into its circle for life is at stake."[63] But what makes the company cohesive?

Within a heterogeneous unit, there is less social integration and informal communication. Companies could increase social integration among like-minded individuals because soldiers formed their own groups within companies, ranging from debate societies to Christian associations. Social sanctions may also be less effective in more diverse units.

When we look at white soldiers, we measure cohesion with such company characteristics as diversity in birthplace, social status (as measured by occupation), and age and the percentage of the company of their own ethnicity and occupation. We also investigate other definitions of community, including whether the soldier had a brother, father, or son in the same company and the population size of the city of enlistment. Among Civil War soldiers, feelings of loyalty were compounded by community pressure, because fellow soldiers from the same hometown could and did report on others' behavior.[64] The size of the soldier's town of enlistment provides some indication of whether he faced this kind of community pressure. When we examine black soldiers we are able to measure unit diversity by differences in state of birth, in age, in the percentage of free blacks, and, for slaves, in whether or not there was a soldier from the same plantation.

During the American Civil War, not just the soldier's own ideology but also the ideology of his hometown was an important factor. Soldiers' morale depended not just on good news from the front but also on their families' and communities' support. We can measure ideology for white soldiers using year of enlistment, volunteer status, and percentage of the county voting for Lincoln. Men who enlisted after 1862 were commonly described as being without patriotism, honor, or interest in the cause.[65] We recognize that this variable might be measuring factors other than ideology, such as an influx of inferior recruits or an influx of recruits who did not enlist together.

Nevertheless, we find that our results remain unchanged when we analyze late or early recruits only.

The constituencies voting for Lincoln were diverse, consisting of anti-Catholics, farmers, and land reformers, among others, opposed to slavery on both economic and moral grounds.[66] We cannot, however, distinguish between a pro-Union and an antislavery vote. Soldiers' commitment to the cause may have grown the longer they served in the army. When Lincoln ran for reelection he received 78 percent of the soldier vote compared to 53 percent of the civilian vote, despite some 40 to 45 percent of soldiers having come from Democratic families in 1860.[67] We can test whether soldiers' commitment increased by examining whether desertion rates decrease with time.

Another important determinant of group loyalty is the morale of the troops. Morale will depend on support from the home front, on leadership, and also on the unit's recent fatalities and the entire army's success on the battlefield.

Morale is a dynamic variable. World War I soldiers rebelled when casualty figures became too high.[68] The cost of fighting will appear high if many men in the company have already died. We capture the dynamic aspects of morale by using the company mortality rate and the fraction of major Union victories within each half year that the recruit was in service. Of course, these variables may also reflect the competence of the officers and the troops. In 1865 desertion reached epidemic levels in the Confederate army when it was clear that the Confederacy could not win. In the Union army, desertion reached a high point after the removal of McClellan in November 1862 (despite his procrastination he was respected as a professional soldier), the defeats at Fredericksburg and at Chickasaw Bluffs in December 1862, the rise of the peace Democrats at home, and the controversy over emancipation. Morale revived with victories at Gettysburg and at Vicksburg in July 1863, though continued gyrations were in store for the troops.[69]

We do not have measures of officers' charisma and of their military skills. Nevertheless, we can identify some striking differences in leadership among the officers of the black troops. Some of the white officers who commanded the colored troops were ardent abolitionists who left thriving careers to command the colored troops. Others merely sought a quick promotion and cared little about the welfare of their men. And others had failed as officers of white soldiers. We can measure whether any of the regiment's officers with ranks of colonel, lieutenant colonel, or major were known to be friendly to the abolitionist cause.

We will not be able to examine all of the reasons why soldiers stood their ground. Some reasons might be vague. During World War II, infantry stated that the most important factor that kept them going was ending the task (39 percent)—"getting the war over with to get home again." Nine percent listed duty and self-respect.[70] However, while we cannot measure a sense of duty and self-respect in our data, our socioeconomic variables provide some indication of their roles.

In our samples of soldiers we know, for each soldier, whether he deserted on each day of the war. We also know if he went AWOL, if he was arrested, if he died, if he was missing in action, if he became a POW, or if he was discharged. We use the information on what happened to a soldier to estimate a model of time until desertion controlling for individual characteristics.[71] Intuitively, we estimate a desertion probability model for each day of the war and predict how soldiers' desertion probabilities change under different company characteristics, ideological attributes, and morale conditions. We show how the desertion, AWOL, or arrest probabilities for both white and black soldiers differ with their individual characteristics and circumstances. For example, we can compare the desertion probabilities of otherwise identical white soldiers from pro- and anti-Lincoln counties. We can ask what desertion probabilities would have been if all soldiers had fought in homogeneous units. We can see how war conditions affect soldiers' desertion probabilities. We can determine whether white soldiers were more likely to desert than black soldiers, and whether free northern blacks were more likely to desert than former slaves. We cannot explain why any given soldier was a hero or a coward. Some men may be natural-born heroes or cowards. But we can make statements about the circumstances that make a man a hero or coward.

WHY WHITE SOLDIERS FOUGHT:
QUANTITATIVE EVIDENCE

Adams E. French and James Monroe Rich of Company D of the Thirty-sixth Massachusetts Volunteers fought honorably. George Farrell and Daniel Mulholland of Company B of the Forty-seventh New York Volunteers deserted. Both French and Rich were from highly cohesive companies. They were native-born, early volunteers from a pro-Lincoln county. In contrast, Farrell and Mulholland were both substitutes and were from a diverse com-

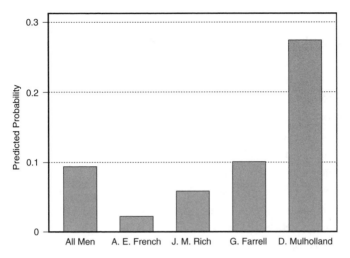

Figure 4.1. Predicted Probability of Desertion

Predicted probabilities are estimated from our statistical model (see note 71 for details). The predicted probabilities are the probability that either French, Rich, Farrell, Mulholland, or a man with the exact same observable characteristics would desert.

pany. Mulholland, who was from New York City, was from a strongly anti-Lincoln area. He was also Irish. Because of these differences between these men, our statistical model predicts that Adams E. French and James Monroe Rich would have a low probability of desertion, that George Farrell would have a slightly higher probability of desertion, and that Daniel Mulholland would have a very high probability of desertion (see figure 4.1). But exactly which characteristics were more important in making Adams E. French and James Monroe Rich less likely to desert than George Farrell and Daniel Mulholland? By seeing how the average probability of desertion would change if we varied a single characteristic for each man while holding all other characteristics fixed we can examine how individual characteristics, company diversity, ideology, and morale affected desertion probabilities.

A good soldier was older. A 20-year-old had a predicted probability of desertion of 10 percent, compared to an 8 percent probability for a 40-year-old. Perhaps only the most dedicated older men became soldiers. A good soldier was also single. Married men were almost one-and-a-half times as likely to desert as single men, and this was true regardless of their wealth, suggesting that financial hardships were not the primary reason. Married men were more likely to receive furloughs to see their families, and these furloughs presented them with the opportunity both to desert and to go AWOL.

A loyal soldier was more likely to be native-born or German-born than Irish- or British-born (see figure 4.2). The Irish- and British-born were 1.4 times as likely to desert as the native-born if we hold fixed differences in socioeconomic characteristics, ideology, company diversity, and morale. They were also twice as likely to be arrested as the native-born. These results persist even when the Irish and British were in the majority in a company. James Horrocks, the Englishman who fled to the United States to avoid a paternity suit, could contemplate desertion and add, "If I was in England or in the English service I should consider that it was a shame and sin to desert but . . . here I am in the land of Yankee doodle and I assure you that what would be considered in England and what I would consider myself disgraceful action is here regarded universally as a *Smart thing*."[72]

Men from a higher social class were better soldiers. The illiterate were more than one-and-a-half times as likely to desert as the literate. The wealthier were less likely to desert. A soldier whose family had no household personal property (as was true for one-quarter of men)

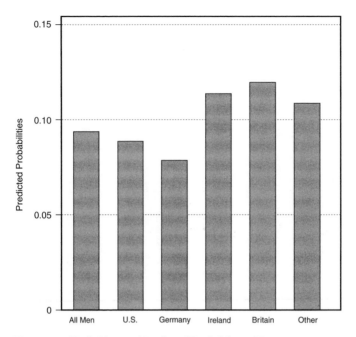

Figure 4.2. Birth Place and Predicted Probability of Desertion

Predicted probabilities are estimated from our statistical model (see note 71 for details). They are the predicted probabilities of desertion if all men had been born in the specific countries.

had a predicted probability of desertion of 9 percent. A soldier whose family had $500 in personal property wealth (one-quarter of the men had that much or more) had a predicted probability of deserting of 7 percent. Farmers were least likely to desert and laborers were most likely, deserting at a rate 1.6 times greater than that of farmers (see figure 4.3).

If an officer could have picked his men on the basis of a single characteristic, he would have chosen either all literate men or all wealthy men. Had all soldiers been literate or had all soldiers been from families with $5000 in personal property wealth, desertion rates would have

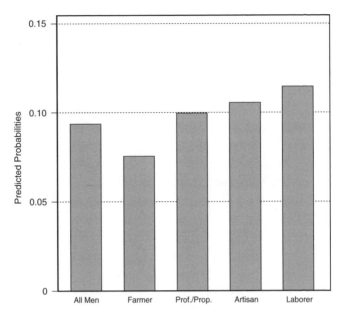

Figure 4.3. Occupation and Predicted Probability of Desertion

Predicted probabilities are estimated from our statistical model (see note 71 for details). They are the desertion probabilities if all men had had a specific occupation. ("Prof./Prop." indicates professional or proprietor.)

been only 7 percent. The next best thing an officer could have done would have been to pick companies of farmers and companies of older men. Desertion rates would have been less than 8 percent if all men had been 40-year-old farmers.

Community characteristics were also important predictors of cowardice and heroism. Men who fought in companies featuring high birthplace, occupation, and age diversity and men who came from large cities were all more likely to desert. Figure 4.4 shows the extent of occupational diversity within companies and predicts what desertion rates would have been for given levels of occu-

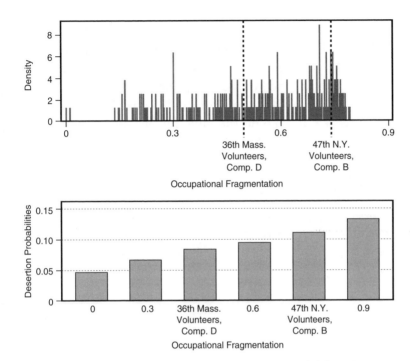

Figure 4.4. Company Occupational Diversity and Probability of Desertion

The greater the occupational fragmentation the larger is occupational diversity. Occupational fragmentation is measured as one minus the share of men in each company in each occupational category, squared. The occupational categories are farmers, higher-rank professionals and proprietors, lower-rank professionals and proprietors, artisans, higher rank laborers, lower-rank laborers, and unknown. The top panel indicates the distribution of occupational diversity within companies in the sample. The density gives the probability that the specified values of occupational fragmentation will occur. The bottom panel gives predicted desertion probabilities if all men had been in companies with a given level of occupational fragmentation (see note 71 for details about the statistical model).

pational diversity, including those prevailing in Company D of the Thirty-sixth Massachusetts Volunteers, the company of James Munroe Rich and Adams E. French, and Company B of the Forty-seventh New York Volunteers, the company of George Farrell and Daniel Mulholland. Figures 4.5 and 4.6 do the same for birthplace and age diversity. The men of the Thirty-sixth Massachusetts Volunteers did not desert despite their age diversity. Their similar ethnic and occupational backgrounds helped hold their company together. James Horrocks, who was in a diverse company and was an Englishman, praised all Englishmen everywhere when he wrote, "Englishmen are kinder, more straightforward and more manly in appearance and character than other people I met."[73] He wrote of the Irish, "Oh how I detest the breed. They are in a strong majority here or else they would get their stinking *posteriori* well kicked by the Englishmen."[74] Men in companies in which birthplace and occupational diversity was high were significantly more likely to be arrested. High company birthplace diversity, but not other company characteristics, led to higher AWOL rates.

James Horrocks wrote of his company, "There are three Englishmen in our tent. I think there are about 20 in the whole company (one fifth) and yet though they are in such small proportion, every sergeant is an Englishman except the Quartermaster Sergeant."[75] Such a situation led to ethnic favoritism. The Irish were significantly more likely to be AWOL if the company had an Irish officer, but we could not determine whether punishments for AWOL were lower in these companies. Both the Irish and the British were more likely to be arrested if the company contained an Irish or British officer, and the British were less likely to desert if the company contained

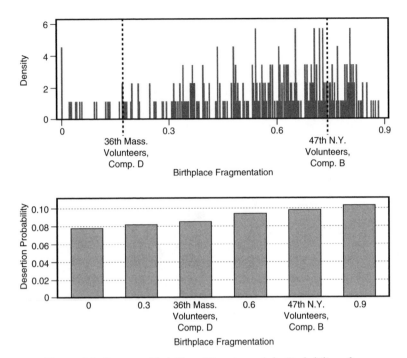

Figure 4.5. Company Birth Place Diversity and the Probability of Desertion

The greater the birthplace fragmentation the larger is birthplace diversity. Birthplace fragmentation is measured as one minus the share of men in each company in each birthplace category, squared. The birthplace categories for the United States are New England, Middle Atlantic, East North Central, West North Central, the border states, the South, and the West. Birthplace categories for men born abroad are Germany, Ireland, Canada, Great Britain, Scandinavia, northwestern Europe (France, Belgium, Luxembourg, the Netherlands), other areas of Europe, and other areas of the world. The top panel indicates the distribution of birthplace diversity within companies in the sample. The density gives the probability that the specified values of birthplace fragmentation will occur. The bottom panel gives predicted desertion probabilities if all men had been in companies with a given level of birthplace fragmentation (see note 71 for details about the statistical model).

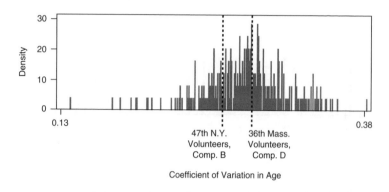

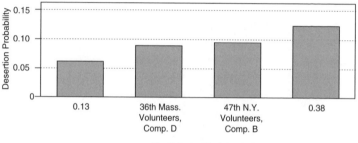

Figure 4.6. Company Age Diversity and Probability of Desertion

The coefficient of variation of age is ratio of the standard deviation of age to its arithmetic mean. A higher coefficient of variation indicates greater age diversity. The top panel shows the distribution of age diversity within companies in the sample. The density gives the probability that the specified values of age diversity will occur. The bottom panel gives the predicted of desertion if all men had been in companies with the specified level of age diversity (see note 71 for details about the statistical model). Strictly on the basis of age, the men of the Thirty-sixth Massachusetts Volunteers should have been more likely to desert.

a British officer. Laborers were more likely to desert and to be arrested if the proportion of laborers in the company was high.

James Monroe Rich and Robert Rich were just one of the many father-and-son pairs who served in the same company in the Civil War. Brothers served together as well. Just before Gettysburg, a Massachusetts soldier worried that his lame brother would not arrive in line before battle began and would be called a "skedaddler."[76] Did having a father, son, or brother in the same company increase or decrease a soldier's probability of desertion? Close kin could agree to desert together, but they might also be more loyal to companies that contained their brothers. Although having close kin in the same company probably had no effect on either desertions or arrests, it decreased the odds that a soldier would go AWOL.

Deserters would often slip away in small groups, varying from five to sixteen or twenty.[77] Sometimes they would run away in large groups. McClellan had roughly 90,000 men at the battle of Antietam, and within two hours after the battle, some 30,000 had straggled and deserted.[78] Colonel Buckland wrote to headquarters after the battle of Shiloh, "We formed line again on the Purdy road, but the fleeing mass from the left broke through our lines, and many of our men caught the infection and fled with the crowd."[79] Among the Union army veterans we studied, we found that when company desertion rates were high, men were more likely to desert. Because company desertion rates were high when many men were dying and when the Union was losing, we might be observing either the effect of morale or the effect of contagion. One of the limitations of our data is that we cannot reconstruct whether mass desertions had any "leaders." We cannot tell who, on any given day, deserted first.

The men we expected to be more dedicated to the cause—the volunteers, particularly those who volunteered early, and the men from pro-Lincoln counties—were less likely to desert. They were also less likely to go AWOL

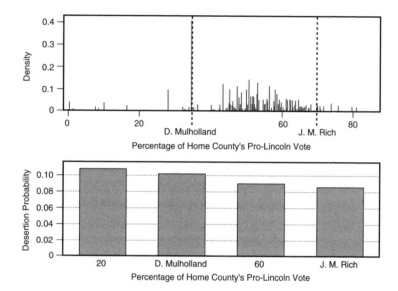

Figure 4.7. County Vote for Lincoln in 1860 and Probability of Desertion

The top panel gives the distribution of the vote for Lincoln in a recruit's county of enlistment. The density gives the probability that the specified values of percent county vote for Lincoln will occur. The bottom panel shows predicted probabilities of desertion if all men had enlisted in counties with the specified share of the vote going to Lincoln (see note 71 for details about the statistical model).

or be arrested. A volunteer's odds of desertion were three-quarters lower than a draftee's or substitute's. A soldier who enlisted in 1861 had a probability of deserting half that of a soldier who enlisted in 1863. Figure 4.7 shows the percentage of the 1860 vote for Lincoln in soldiers' counties of enlistment. James Monroe Rich enlisted in Worcester County in Massachusetts, where Lincoln received 70 percent of the vote. Daniel Mulholland enlisted in New York City, where Lincoln received only 35 percent of the vote. A soldier from a pro-Lincoln county was more likely both to be pro-Lincoln himself and to be shamed by his neighbors if he deserted. As figure 4.7 shows, men from pro-Lincoln counties were less likely to desert. Dedication to the cause may have grown over time: the longer soldiers remained in the army, the less likely they were to desert, even though they were more likely to be arrested or to go AWOL.

Men were more likely to desert when company mortality was high and when the Union was losing. Had the Union always been winning at least two-thirds of all battles, the desertion rate would have fallen to 8 percent. Had it always won only one out of every six battles, the desertion rate would have been 10 percent. Figure 4.8 illustrates the variation in death rates across companies. Arrest rates were higher when the Union was losing. A high company mortality rate reduced AWOL rates—the wounded were furloughed while the remaining men continued to fight.

Among the men who enlisted in 1861 and had already served a three-year term, some men reenlisted for another three years. Approximately half of reenlistees received a bounty on reenlistment. There was no dishonor in not reenlisting. Newton Scott, a private in the Thirty-sixth Iowa Infantry, Company A, wrote to Hannah Cone, "I think it the Duty of Every Able Bodied man If Necessary to Help Defend His country But I think 3 years Sufficient long for one man to Serve while they all take there turns."[80] Generally men reenlisted as regiments or companies,[81] but company characteristics did not predict reenlistment. Older men, men from large cities, and Germans were less likely to reenlist, and men who received a bounty for reenlisting were more likely to reenlist.

So why did the white soldiers fight on? Figure 4.9 shows

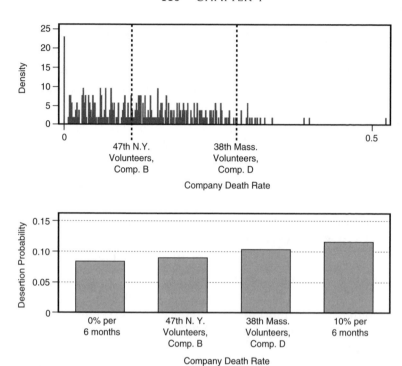

Figure 4.8. Company Death Rate and Probability of Desertion

The top panel gives the distribution of the overall company death rate. The density gives the probability that the specified values of company death rates will occur. The bottom panel shows what desertion probabilities would have been if all men had been in companies with the specified death rates every six months of the war (see note 71 for details about the statistical model).

what desertion rates would have been had morale been high (no deaths and steady Union victories), had all soldiers been ideologically committed to the cause (early volunteers and from a pro-Lincoln county), and had companies been homogeneous in occupation, ethnicity, and age.

Company socioeconomic and demographic diversity was the single most important predictor of desertion.

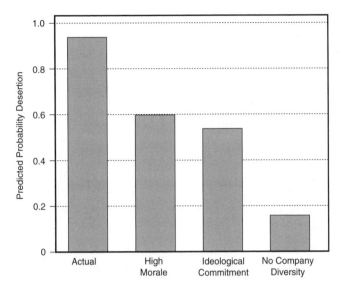

Figure 4.9. Predicted Desertion Rates with High Morale, Ideological Commitment, and No Company Diversity

The predictions show what the desertion probabilities would have been if all men had had high morale (if company death rates had been 0 and if the fraction of Union victories had been 1), had been committed to the cause (if all men were volunteers of 1861 and were from a county where Lincoln received 86.6 percent of the vote, highest share in the sample), and had been in companies homogeneous in occupation, ethnicity, and age (see note 71 for details about the statistical model).

Age and occupational diversity were more important than birthplace diversity. If all companies had been homogeneous, desertion rates would have been only 2 percent rather than 9 percent. Ideology was more important than morale in lowering desertion rates, but even if all soldiers had been committed to the cause, desertion rates would still have been 5 percent. Neither ideology nor morale was as important as having all the right individual characteristics—being literate, being a farmer, being native-born or German-born, being single, and being wealthy. If all soldiers had had these characteristics (and they could not have, because then the army would have had too few men), the desertion probability would have been 3 percent.

Why Black Soldiers Fought:
Quantitative Evidence

Desertion and AWOL rates were lower among black soldiers than among whites. Desertion rates were more than 9 percent among white soldiers but less than 8 percent among black soldiers. Arrest rates were the same. Our statistical models reveal that the odds that a white soldier would desert were one-third higher than the desertion odds of a black soldier of the same age and in a company that was equally diverse in place of birth and age. But many of the colored troops did desert, and we wish to understand why some did and others did not.

Silas J. Coffee was a free black born in Kentucky who enlisted at age 23 in 1864 in Waterford, Pennsylvania in Company G of the Twenty-fifth Regiment of USCT. More than 80 percent of the men in his company were free and more than half of the men in the company were born in the neighboring states of Delaware, New Jersey, and Pennsylvania, but among the remaining men places of birth included such diverse areas as Canada, Ohio, and South Carolina. After less than three months in the service, Silas deserted from Camp William Penn in Pennsylvania and was never heard of again. Charles E. Stoke, age 18 at enlistment and also enlisting in Waterford in the same company, deserted after seven months in the army from Fort Redoubt in Florida by boarding a steamer. He was later captured and spent the rest of his term of service confined to Fort Pickens, Florida, with loss of pay. Fourteen out of 100 men in the company deserted.

The men of Company F of the First USCT, the company of John Nelson Cumbash, the Maryland slave who later moved to Baltimore and Philadelphia, served with greater honor. Only seven out of 100 men deserted. Unlike Silas and Charles's company, which mainly helped with defenses and did garrison duty, Company F of the First Regiment of the USCT was a fighting regiment. Unlike in Silas and Charles' company, only one-fifth of the men were freedmen. The men in John's company were also more alike—70 percent of them were born in the neighboring states of Virginia, Maryland, or Washington, D.C. And unlike Silas's company, John's company had abolitionist officers. Abolitionist sentiment was so strong that the officers of the regiment punished a notorious slaveholder in Virginia for whipping a former slave woman by having a private from the regiment, a former slave on the man's plantation, administer fifteen to twenty lashes, "bringing the blood from his loins at every stroke."[82]

Zack and Harrison, two 21-year-old slaves owned by John Osborne, enlisted in Company I of the 118th USCT in 1864 in Owensboro, Kentucky. Both men were born in Kentucky, and they joined a company of slaves in which 81 percent of the men were born in Kentucky and 12 percent were born in Virginia. Forty-four of the men in the company served with someone from the same plantation. Their regiment participated in siege operations against Petersburg and Richmond and the occupation of Richmond, and, until it was disbanded in 1866, served in Texas along the Mexican border. The company lost only two men to desertion but lost fourteen to death.

Why were some black soldiers deserters and others not? Were Zack and Harrison more loyal than Silas J. Coffee because they were former slaves, because they were fighting together, or because they were fighting with fellow Kentuckians? Was John Nelson Cumbash more loyal than Silas J. Coffee not just because he was a former slave and was in a company that was more homogeneous, but also because his regiment contained many abolitionist officers?

Our statistical model shows that if we control for soldiers' demographic and company characteristics, former slaves were more loyal to their companies than free blacks. The odds that a former slave would desert were less than two-thirds those of a free black. Colonel Higginson may have been right that the former slaves were faced with a choice of either fighting it out or being enslaved. Nonetheless, even some former slaves deserted. In Company D of the Fifty-third Regiment, the company of Joseph Hall, the teamster who later farmed in Tensas Parish, Louisiana, all the men were former slaves, and sixteen out of 100 men in the company deserted.

Black and white soldiers were similar in many ways. Both became more committed to the cause the longer they were in the war. Both were more likely to desert when morale was low—when the Union was losing and when their comrades were dying. Like the white soldiers, black soldiers were more likely to desert if the men in their companies were born in different states. The effects of company heterogeneity and of morale were as strong for black soldiers as they were for white ones. Figure 4.10 illustrates the extent of birthplace diversity among the colored troops. Silas Coffee's Company G of the Twenty-fifth USCT was one of the most diverse units. Zack and Harrison's Company I of the 118th USCT was not. Had all companies been as diverse as Company G of the Twenty-fifth USCT, desertion rates would have been almost 9 percent. Had all companies been as homogeneous

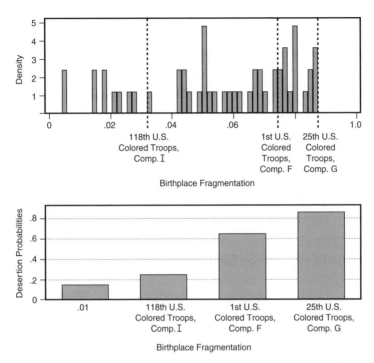

Figure 4.10. Birthplace Diversity among Black Troops and Predicted Probability of Desertion

The greater the birthplace fragmentation, the larger is birthplace diversity. Birthplace fragmentation is measured as one minus the share of men in each company in each birthplace category, squared. The birthplace categories are each U.S. state. The top panel indicates the distribution of birthplace diversity within companies in the sample. The density gives the probability that the specified values of birthplace fragmentation will occur. The bottom panel gives the predicted desertion probabilities if all men had been in companies with a given level of birthplace fragmentation (see note 71 for details about the statistical model).

as Company I of the 118th USCT, desertion rates would have been less than 3 percent. Diversity in age also raised desertion probabilities.

Other sources of diversity within the black companies came from slave status and whether or not the former slaves were from the same plantation. The odds that a former slave who fought with a comrade from the same plantation would desert were one-third the odds when there was no such comrade. If former slaves found themselves in a company with a high fraction of free blacks, they were even more loyal. The free blacks' loyalty did not depend on the slave status of their comrades. Slaves among free men may have felt a greater need to prove their worth.

Former slaves in a regiment where an officer was an abolitionist sympathizer were less likely to desert, but free blacks' desertion probabilities were unaffected by their officers. Having an abolitionist officer meant that the odds that a former slave would desert were two-thirds those of a former slave who did not have an abolitionist officer. Leadership was not as important as the characteristics of fellow soldiers. Figure 4.11 shows that if all of the former slaves had had an abolitionist officer, their probability of desertion would have fallen from 5 percent to 3 percent. But if all of the former slaves had served with a comrade from the same plantation, their probability of desertion would have fallen to 2 percent, and if they had served with men born in the same state and of the same age, their probability of desertion would have fallen to less than 1 percent.

Group Loyalty, Courage, and Survival

What motivated men to risk death in the most horrific war in U.S. history? Civil War veteran John W. De Forest wrote, "The man who does not dread to die or to be mutilated is a lunatic. The man who, dreading these things, still faces them . . . is a hero."[83]

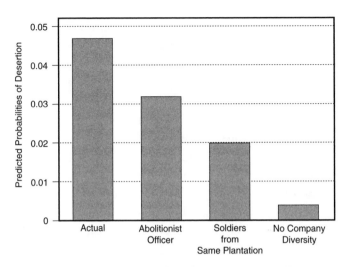

Figure 4.11. Predicted Probability of Desertion among Former Slaves

The predictions show what the desertion probabilities would have been if all men had had an abolitionist officer, had served with a soldier from the same plantation, and had been in companies homogeneous in birth place, age, and slave status (see note 71 for details about the statistical model).

Tales of bravery recounted in books and films are of individual men and their characters. They are of Robert Gould Shaw, son of a prominent abolitionist family and colonel of a black regiment, leading his men into battle at Fort Wagner shouting, "Forward, Fifty-Fourth!" Wounded numerous times, he was killed during the assault. Events after his death gave him heroic status. Confederates denied him an officer's burial. They removed his shoes and buried him in a mass grave with his soldiers, declaring, "We have buried him with his niggers." His father proclaimed that he was proud that his son was buried on the field of battle with the men he had led.[84]

Robert Gould Shaw's burial gave Northerners the moral

high ground. Military historians have reminded us of the importance of a moral crusade in motivating democratic soldiers and of leadership and morale in keeping an army from faltering. Hansen believes that democracies "can produce the most murderous armies from the most unlikely of men, and do so in the pursuit of something spiritual rather than the mere material."[85] Sherman's march to the sea was designed to destroy the morale of the South and uplift that of the North. The destruction of slave plantations, at a minimal loss of Union lives, reminded the North that "we bring the Jubilee," in the words of the popular song, "Marching Through Georgia." Sherman's military successes may have been enough to make his men believe they were crusaders. One private wrote, "if he were Mahomet we'd be devoted Mussulmen."[86]

The American Soldier emphasized the importance of loyalty to a small group in sustaining men's combat motivations, not ideology or leadership. While 14 percent of World War II infantrymen answered that solidarity with the group was the most important reason in making them want to keep going, only 5 percent claimed idealistic reasons, and only 1 percent stated leadership and discipline. However, their officers, either answering from a different vantage point or holding a higher opinion of their own importance, listed leadership as the most important factor that kept their men going in tough times.[87]

Our statistical approach allows us to assess the relative importance of group loyalty, ideology, morale, and leadership in the Civil War. They all mattered, but a tightly knit company, one in which men had much in common and knew each other, was the most loyal company, even in one of our country's more ideological wars. Group loyalty was more than twice as important as ideology and six times as important as leadership. In contrast, during World War II group loyalty was almost three times as important as ideology and fourteen times as important as leadership.

Group loyalty could lead to death. Had Sergeant Adams French deserted before the battle of Cold Harbor, he could have been reunited with his wife and child instead of dying of a wound to the groin. Was there any benefit to the loyal men of being in a cohesive company, or did the army derive all of the benefits? We cannot answer the question whether two companies, one cohesive and one not, would have faced the same mortality if thrust into the same battle location. Because on Civil War battlefields men could make for the rear, the mortality rates of the more cohesive companies were greater than those of the less cohesive companies. But we can investigate the benefits to men of being in a more cohesive company by examining whether men with friends in a POW camp were more likely to survive.

CHAPTER 5

POW Camp Survivors

IN ANTIQUITY, SOLDIERS CAPTURED BY THE ENEMY WERE either killed or enslaved, most likely to die quickly in a mine or galley ship or other lethal place.[1] Medieval writers advocated more humane treatment, echoing Gratian's treatise on canon law, "pity is due to the vanquished or captured."[2] Nobles who could produce a ransom were often treated courteously, but Froissart lamented that the Germans would place even a knight in "chains of iron and throw him into the smallest prison cell they have to extort a greater ransom."[3] The Flemings and Swiss took no prisoners at all. Chivalrous behavior was abandoned when rulers did not have enough men to guard prisoners, ordering them killed, as did Henry V of England at Agincourt. Commoners, because they could not command a ransom, expected no mercy and gave none.[4]

The concept of prisoners of war developed during the seventeenth and eighteenth centuries both because of Enlightenment ideas and because the mercenaries widely used by seventeenth-century armies sought to save their own lives. During the Napoleonic Wars, the first to employ mass conscription, captured troops were often kept in prison camps and later exchanged.[5]

The first total war, the American Civil War, saw the first formal code of conduct for dealing with POWs, drawn up in 1863 at President Lincoln's request. It specified that captured troops had to be imprisoned rather than enslaved, tortured, or killed, and had to be fed and given medical treatment.[6] The Civil War reality, however, did not match the ideals of the code. The death rate for imprisoned POWs was 12 percent in the North and 16 percent in the South.[7] Some prison camps achieved notoriety, particularly Andersonville in the South and to a lesser extent Florence and Salisbury in the South and Elmira in the North. At Andersonville, which at its peak capacity was the fifth largest city in the South, roughly 40 percent of the men who passed through the camp died, and half of the deaths occurred within three months of entry.[8]

How did men survive the horrific conditions of Civil War POW camps? The accounts of survivors of Nazi concentration camps, the Soviet gulag, and Japanese and Vietnamese POW internment camps provide some clues.

After interviewing Norwegian survivors of Nazi concentration camps, Eitinger (1964) concluded that death was random.[9] Schmolling's 1984 study of camp survivors cited several psychological defense mechanisms such as rage, denial of condition, emotional detachment, and a narrowed focus of attention. His list also included belief in God, hope for survival, identification with the aggressor, and, most important, friends.[10] Those without friends might end up with short rations and had more trouble adapting psychologically. At Auschwitz, when non-Jewish civilians provided Jewish inmates with food, they helped their co-nationals.[11]

In Stalin's gulag of the late 1940s, the Ukrainians, Balts, and Poles created their own systems of mutual assistance in the camps where they were in large numbers.[12] Jones's 1980 reading of Vietnamese POW diaries led him to conclude that loyalty to country, idealization of family, maintenance of military bearing, and alliance with fellow prisoners were the keys to survival.[13] One survivor of the Burma-Thailand railway concluded that "men without officers were dead men."[14] Good officers enforced punishment for theft, ensured the accurate division of food, set up funds to pay for food and medicine for the sick, and enforced hygiene regulations.[15] Andrew Carson, a prisoner of the Japanese during World War II, emphasized that "living or dying was often a matter of will power, of determination. . . . It was so easy. Just stop pushing back for an instant, relax and let go, and you could die."[16] Rowley Richards, an Australian doctor on the Burma-Thailand railway, concluded that a variety of factors determined survival: attitude, positive thinking, adjustment of moral values, improvisation, determination, sheer luck, and having friends.[17]

Civil War diaries mention many of the same factors. John McElroy noted that whereas he and some older prisoners "dug tunnels with the persistence of beavers, and . . . watched every possible opportunity to get outside the accursed walls of the pen," others "resigned themselves to Death, and waited despondently till he came."[18] Robert Kellogg would say to himself, "the 'rebs' shall never have satisfaction of carrying my body out upon a stretcher. I will live to spite them."[19] Thomas Newton described "a feeling of bitter hatred . . . against the rebels" and "a determination to live in spite of them."[20] Amos Stearns turned to religion and thoughts of a close friend at home.[21] At Andersonville, the "Raiders," "fledglings of the slums and dives of New York,"[22] grew strong by robbing their fellow prisoners. Other prisoners betrayed tunneling operations for a plug of tobacco or sold their skills as artisans or clerks to the Confederacy, signing an oath not to escape. Robert Knox Sneden survived Andersonville, but after he was transferred to Millen, he concluded that he could not survive another POW camp and became a clerk for the camp physicians, copying Latin invoices.[23] His new position provided him both with more sanitary quarters and with more and better food.

"I have always been blessed with friends, and friends too, of the right sort," wrote John Ransom in his Andersonville diary.[24] Friends in POW camps proffered the moral support necessary to avoid depression, provided extra food or clothing through trade of valuables or from work on prison detail such as the bakery, ensured that none strayed too close to the "dead line," protected against the predations of other prisoners, and tended to the sick. Social attachments may affect health through their impact on the immune and neuroendocrine systems.[25] Chronically high levels of loneliness lead to alterations in the activity of genes that drive inflammation, the first response of the immune system.[26] Lucius Barber noted in his memoirs that "if one was captured alone, put with strangers and became sick, it was ten chances to one he would die unattended by any human being."[27]

How much did friends matter? Civil War diarists and memoir writers often disagreed on the value of friends in POW camps, some arguing that "life at Andersonville was necessarily selfish. Every ounce of food parted with to help a fellow-man was a drop of blood from the giver. . . . That which was necessary to relieve want and suffering was not ours to give. Day after day we were compelled to see a friend, old schoolmate, or stranger sink under the awful pressure."[28] Carson echoed the same sentiments when he wrote of his captivity as a World War II POW of the Japanese, "Every prisoner had to live or die on his own. It wasn't that we didn't try to help one another. God knows, we did. It was simply that that there was very little, almost nothing, a man could do to help."[29] "Why I am sustained is a mystery to me," wrote one Andersonville diarist.[30] Only statistics, not the selected accounts of survivors, can resolve whether friends had any effect on mortality rates.

Confederate POW Camps

An estimated 211,411 Union soldiers were captured during the Civil War. Of these, 16,668 were never imprisoned because they were paroled on the field, but of the remaining 194,743 men, 30,218 died while in captivity.[31] Seven percent of all U.S. Civil War soldiers were ever imprisoned, compared to figures of 0.8 percent for World War II and 0.1 percent for the Korean War.[32] Prisoners who were paroled gave their word not to fight until they were formally exchanged, spending their time in Union camps for parolees.

Even those who were imprisoned, however, were quickly exchanged initially. As early as June 1862, the quartermaster general of the Confederacy stated that "the difficulty of maintaining prisoners is most serious and that the growing deficiency in the resources of the Confederacy, so far as commissary stores are concerned, will render the speedy exchange of prisoners of war or their disposal otherwise absolutely necessary."[33]

By mid-1863, the exchange system had broken down. Confederate president Jefferson Davis denounced General Butler, the Union military governor of New Orleans, and his officers as deserving execution for confiscating property and hanging a citizen who had taken down the U.S. flag. Davis also responded to the Emancipation Proclamation by decreeing that all former slaves captured as Union soldiers and their white officers be turned over to the states, where leading a slave insurrection was a capital crime. Prisoner exchanges stopped as the two sides argued over the terms. General Grant opposed reestablishing a system of exchange as late as August 1864, saying, "If we commence a system of exchange which liberates all prisoners taken, we will have to fight on until the whole South is exterminated."[34] Nearly every Confederate prisoner who was released returned to the ranks, whereas the enlistment terms of many Union prisoners had expired. By 1865 it was clear that exchanges could no longer affect the course of the war. Sick and wounded men were released in December 1864, and in early 1865 exchanges started again.

More than 40 percent of captured men were taken in July 1863 or later.[35] These captives faced ever-worsening conditions as the crowds of prisoners increased. Northern complaints about southern prisons had already begun in 1862. On February 22, 1862, *Harper's* reported, "The condition of our soldiers . . . is indeed fearful . . . covered with vermin . . . half-starved and nearly naked."[36] Fortunately for these men, captured fairly early in the war, they were not imprisoned very long. The mean number of days spent in prison until death or release for men who were captured before mid-1863 was 20, whereas it was 92 for men who were captured after mid-1863. Mortality increased sharply after mid-1863. Only 4 percent of the men captured before July 1863 died in captivity, whereas 27 percent of those captured in July 1863 or later died in captivity. (In contrast, the total wartime mortality rate for our sample of white soldiers was 14 percent.)

POWs suffered from poor and meager rations, from contaminated water, from grounds covered with human excrement and with other filth, from a want of shoes, clothing, and blankets (having often been stripped of these by needy Confederate soldiers), from a lack of shelter in the open stockades that constituted camps such as Andersonville and Millen, from the risk of being robbed and murdered by fellow prisoners, and from trigger-happy guards. Ransom recounted in his diary that when taken prisoner he weighed 178 pounds and when he left Andersonville suffering from scurvy and dropsy he weighed only 95 pounds.[37] Stearns, who was also imprisoned at Andersonville, weighed 90 pounds when he reached home.[38]

Conditions across prisons varied widely, and within prisons they varied widely across time. Andersonville, whose maximum capacity was 10,000 men but which at one point held 32,899, was the most notorious.[39] As crowding increased, so did deaths. The chief causes of death were scurvy, diarrhea, and dysentery.[40] Three months of vitamin C deprivation will lead to scurvy. By June 1864 corn bread and cornmeal were the principal staples of the Andersonville diet, and by August most prisoners were suffering from scurvy.[41]

In contrast to Andersonville, prisoners at Savannah, for example, received better and more plentiful rations.

Andersonville Prison, Ga., August 17, 1864

Plate 5. Andersonville Prison, GA, August 17, 1864, southwest view of the stockade, showing the dead-line

At camps such as Florence and Salisbury, however, food was scarce, and the monthly death rates rivaled those at Andersonville. Florence became notorious for the number of cases of gangrene, brought on by frostbite, that led men to cut off their own putrefying limbs with pocket knives.[42]

Captured men were transferred to a prison by rail, tightly packed in cattle cars; the choice of prison camp was determined largely by time and place of capture. In 1863 the majority of prisoners were held at Richmond, but prisoners were rapidly moved out of that city in February and March 1864 in response to prison escapes to nearby Union lines and to a (failed) Union raid to free prisoners. Andersonville was emptied of men in September 1864 when Sherman's army threatened. Prisoners were then moved to Charleston, Florence (South Carolina), Millen (Georgia), and Savannah, among others. When a November raid by Sherman forced the abandonment of the prison at Millen, prisoners were sent to Blackshear and Thomasville, Georgia. Although a few officers of the colored troops were punished by being sent to Andersonville, the choice of prison largely depended on when the prisoners were moved. About 400 to 700 per day could be moved from one camp to another,[43] But, for example, prisoners could not be sent to Millen until a stockade had been constructed.[44]

Once in a prison camp, the prisoners were responsible for scavenging their own living quarters and digging holes for shelter or constructing tents from sticks of wood and blankets, if the camp was a stockade. Kellogg wrote that at Andersonville, "Eleven of us combined to form a '*family*.' For the small sum of two dollars in greenbacks we purchased eight small saplings about eight or nine feet long; these we bent and made fast in the ground, and covering them with our blankets, made a tent with an oval roof, about thirteen feet long."[45] According to Warren Lee Goss, "The first morning after our arrival [at Andersonville] about twenty pounds of bacon and a bushel of Indian meal was given to me to distribute among ninety men. We had no wood to cook with, when two of my comrades, with myself, succeeded in buying six or seven small pieces for two dollars, and soon got some johnny-cake made. . . . The next day three others with myself formed a mess together; and taking two of our blankets, constructed a temporary shelter from sun and rain."[46]

Prisoners were responsible for dividing any food or firewood given to "squads" and at Andersonville for policing themselves. For the purpose of issuing rations and for roll calls within the camps, newcomers were divided into squads (generally 100 men, but 270 men at Andersonville), which in turn were subdivided into messes (generally 20, but 90 at Andersonville). A sergeant, either elected or a man with the rank of sergeant, issued rations to squads and called roll, receiving an extra ration for his trouble. Goss resigned his position as sergeant after 24 hours because he "had forseen that the position required a great deal of work . . . when men are cut down to very low rations, they are not always discriminating in attaching blame to the proper source, which made the place all the more difficult to fill with credit."[47] Some sergeants took more than two rations, leaving some men without any food and others with reduced rations.[48]

Goss's men were all in the same squad, but units of friends were not necessarily in the same squad or mess. McElroy and his friend Andrews were in the same squads in Andersonville, Millen, and Blackshear but were separated in Florence, where they were put in squads organized by the first letter of the men's surnames. But even at Florence they were together in the same makeshift shelter they had constructed.[49] The Confederates did not deliberately break up units.

Each squad was responsible for its own policing. McElroy described the situation at Andersonville: "Each little squad of men was a law unto itself, and made and enforced its own regulations on its territory. The administration of justice was reduced to its simplest terms. If a fellow did wrong, he was pounded, if there was anybody capable of doing it. It not, he went free."[50] Commissioned officers, except those commanding colored troops, received preferential treatment and were kept either in separate quarters in the same prison or in prisons reserved

Plate 6. Drawing rations; view from main gate. Andersonville Prison, GA, August 17, 1864

for officers.[51] This practice left the enlisted men without leadership. According to McElroy,

> we were a community of twenty-thousand boys and young men, none too regardful of control at best, and now wholly destitute of government. The rebels never made the slightest attempt to maintain order in the prison. Their whole energies were concentrated in preventing our escape. . . . Among ourselves there was no one in position to lay down law and enforce it. Being all enlisted men, we were on a dead level as far as rank was concerned, the highest being only sergeants whose stripes carried no weight of authority.
>
> The time of our stay was, it was hoped, too transient to make it worth while bothering about organizing any form of government. The great bulk of boys were recent comers who hoped that in another week or so they would be out again. There were no fat salaries to tempt anyone to take upon himself the duty of ruling the masses, and all were left to their own devices to do good or evil, according to their several bents and as fear of consequences swayed them.[52]

Successful escapes were rare. At Andersonville there were only 329 successful escapes (out of more than 30,000 men), mainly during the work details.[53] Tunneling and deception (such as hiding among the dead) were favorite means of escape. Prison commanders feared a mass storming of guards and successfully guarded against it by positioning guards and cannons along stockade walls.

Survival and Social Networks

Men's survival depended on their ability to obtain food
and shelter and to avoid disease. The disease environment depended in turn on camp conditions. More crowding led to more diarrhea and dysentery. At Andersonville,
"the dead and dying lie alongside each other," and each
day the corpses "piled up near the dead line . . . nearly all
naked, black as crows, festering in the hot sun all day, covered with lice and maggots" until they were "loaded up in
the ration wagon like cordwood."[54] The creek that ran
through the Andersonville stockade was tainted with re-
fuse from the cookhouse and with runoff from the sinks.
The area around the sinks, established at one end of the
creek, had become a swamp, and many men were too sick
to make it to the sinks. Men dug wells to obtain clean
drinking water, scooping out dirt with half-canteens.[55]

Although Confederate law specified that prisoners
were to be fed the same rations as soldiers (a pound and
quarter of meal daily and either a pound of beef or a third
of a pound of bacon, with occasional small portions of
vinegar, molasses, and salt), problems with procurement,
transportation, spoilage, and skimming by the men detailed to the cookhouse reduced rations.[56] Cornmeal at
Andersonville was delivered with the cob ground up in it
because in rural areas grinding mills were not equipped
with bolting cloth to sift the meal. The prisoners had
no sifters, and the sharp and hard cob irritated the intestines of men suffering from diarrhea and dysentery. Unlike their guards, the prisoners could not forage around
the countryside. They could trade with their guards (a
common but prohibited practice) or, at Andersonville, with
the sutler of the stockade, who brought in vegetables,

fruit, rice, beans, salt, tobacco, and candles, purchased from nearby farmers and sold at a premium. But men who had been imprisoned for long had nothing left to trade except their rations. Those who had lost their teeth from scurvy or who were suffering from diarrhea or dysentery would trade their cornmeal or cornbread for mush or soup. Containers for eating and cooking and firewood were all in short supply.[57] McElroy was "on another plane, as far as worldly goods were concerned," because whereas most prisoners were "absolutely destitute of dishes, or cooking utensils," having to use their pant legs to receive their food, he had managed to find an empty fruit can and had "manufactured a spoon and knife combined from a bit of hoop-iron."[58]

Obtaining food and shelter depended not just on camp conditions but also on the skills and possessions that men brought with them into the camp. At Andersonville, "Each man stood or fell on merits different from those which had been valued by friends at home. . . . He who could make Indian meal and water into the most palatable form was 'looked up to.' He who could cook with little wood, and invent from the mud a fireplace in which to save fuel, was a genius!"[59] Increased numbers of prisoners taxed the camp supply of rations. New POWs had to take the worse land, near the sinks, or pay an older prisoner for his spot.

Men's ability to obtain food and shelter and to avoid disease also depended on their social networks. Both the number of men in a network and the strength of their ties to each other—the "quality" of the network—should affect mortality. A group member could benefit from the extra food or clothing that his friends could provide, from the care his friends provided when he was sick, from moral support, and from protection against other prisoners.

Lawson Carley made a bargain with an Andersonville guard to trade his boots for the guard's shoes and two plugs of tobacco. He then bargained with another guard, trading one plug of tobacco for a vest for his friend, Tibbets, who was ill. Lawson and his friends washed Tibbets, made him blackberry tea, and helped him to the sinks, but, despite their care, Tibbets died of diarrhea.[60] McElroy, while on a work detail, was able to steal soap; both he and his comrades used some, and the rest they traded for onions.[61] Kellogg wrote that his regiment was able beat off the Raiders because "We as a regiment, presented a united front, and were therefore too strong for them."[62]

Although friends helped each other, their close physical proximity increased the risk of disease contagion. Men would share eating utensils. McElroy and four other comrades used a blanket stretched over poles as a tent by day, and by night they lay down on an overcoat and covered themselves with the blanket. "[T]he two outside fellows used to get very chilly, and squeeze the three inside ones until they felt no thicker than a wafer."[63]

Upon entering a camp, a new prisoner can either interact with men he already knows, such as those from the same company, regiment, or hometown, or he can seek new friends. Because he cannot assess the trustworthiness of a stranger and because starvation leads to social withdrawal, a man should have closer ties with his old friends. Of course, some men might form alliances of convenience. Sneden described taking a new "chum" into his Andersonville shanty: because he had "two poles and two pieces of board, with a blanket and two half canteens and knife for cutting large sticks, made it quite an object for me to have to share my shanty."[64]

Prisoners might form "families" with men of their own

kind (such as members of the same ethnic group or same town) because people prefer to be with members of their own tribe.[65] They trust their own kind more and are more willing to help them. At Andersonville the POWs "were strangers to all outside their own little band," sticking with comrades from the same state or group of states.[66] They formed ethnic ghettos.[67] But even prisoners who enjoy being with members of other tribes might need to stick with their own kind, because strangers cannot be trusted. Contracts in POW camps cannot be legally enforced. Trading, both of valuables and of care in sickness, is more feasible in a group that knows everything about its members and that can sanction violators.[68] In addition, if the group exists in civilian life, a prisoner has to worry about his reputation once he returns home. Of course, in the Civil War camps, men who did not believe they would ever see their homes again might not have worried about their reputation at home.

A successful group might need members with diverse skills.[69] A group with a good trader, a good gambler, and a good baker might be more successful than a group of good farmers. When Sneden worked as a clerk, he detailed a skilled gambler as his cook, and the two split the proceeds of his winnings from the Confederate officers at Millen. But the more diverse the group, the greater the difficulty in communication or in agreeing on basic standards of behavior.[70] At Andersonville the men from Ohio, Indiana, Illinois, Iowa, and Kansas "spoke the same dialect, read the same newspapers, had studied *McGuffey's Readers*, *Mitchell's Geography*, and *Ray's Arithmetics* at school, admired the same great men and generally held the same opinions on any given subject. It was never difficult to get them to act in unison. They did it spontaneously, while it required an effort to bring about harmony of action with those of other sections."[71]

Analyzing Survival

The memoirs of POWs provide many insights into prison life. They accurately depict men's reactions to slow starvation. "We thought of food all day, and were visited with torturing dreams of it at night," said one, only to "awake to find myself a half-naked, half-starved, vermin-eaten wretch, crouching in a hole in the ground, waiting for my keepers to fling me a chunk of corn bread."[72] Nevertheless, the memoirs are not analyses of why men survived. Only thirteen of the sixty-three men in McElroy's company survived their imprisonment, and McElroy attributed his survival to his abstention from drinking water.[73]

Bitterness in prison narratives is to be expected, and Civil War prison narratives have often been criticized as being more intent on showing the brutality of their captors than on providing an accurate historical record.[74] The memoirs repeat prison rumors of guards receiving furloughs for shooting prisoners and highlight shootings, even though these were rare events. Our Andersonville database lists six men as "shot by guard" and another man as dying from an unspecified gunshot wound. More than 3,500 men are listed as dying from scurvy and more than 6,000 as dying from diarrhea or dysentery. When McElroy wrote, "There were thousands of instances of this generous devotion to each other by chums in Andersonville, and I know of nothing that reflects any more credit upon our boy soldiers,"[75] was it because he had witnessed these thousands of instances, or was he simply praising Union soldiers?

We investigate the role of friends in survival using data on Union army soldiers from our sample of more than 35,000 white soldiers (relatively few black soldiers became POWs). In our sample (the Fogel sample), we can follow men from first imprisonment to release or death and we can sample from multiple prisons at different points in time. These data also provide us with a wealth of information about the soldiers, including their occupation and their health before capture. We can examine 3,026 cases of captivity for 2,972 men. We know which prison a man entered and on what date, whether he survived or died, and how many men from his company were in the prison with him on any given day. We are not assuming that POWs are a random subset of soldiers. If a subset of men "fight to the death," we would never see them in a POW camp.

We estimate the effect of friends on survival probabilities by looking at time until death, controlling for individual characteristics, the POW camp, and camp crowding.[76] That is, we estimate a survival probability for each day of imprisonment and predict how prisoners' survival probabilities change with different numbers of friends, different camp conditions, and different individual characteristics. We control for camp congestion by using the number of prisoners in camp in each month.

The number of friends varies by month because of death, because the POW was transferred elsewhere, because friends were transferred elsewhere, or because men from the same company were transferred in, either from other prison camps or as new captives. A POW would have been hurt by the death of a friend if his group lost a comrade with valuable skills or if his death led to depression among the survivors.

If we observe men's survival probabilities fall as their comrades die, does this outcome necessarily mean that networks have benefits? An alternative possibility is that dying friends indicate that a POW is sick. We can avoid this reflection problem by looking at the effect of the initial number of friends on mortality, but is this really the variable we want? This variable tells us how "wealthy" in friends a POW was initially and ignores variation in the number of friends resulting from deaths, transfers, and exchanges. Alternatively, we can try to achieve the gold standard of randomization by using the number of net transfers within a camp and whether or not the POW was transferred as an "instrumental variables" strategy within companies. Within a company, newly captured and previously captured men who were transferred because the Union army was threatening a location arguably provide a source of exogenous variation in the number of friends without being related to a prisoner's health.[77] Nevertheless, we discuss only our estimates using the contemporaneous number of friends (the number of friends during each month) because these estimates are very similar to our estimates of the impact of initial number of friends on mortality and are smaller than our "instrumented" estimates.

We control for a rich set of prewar soldier characteristics and for war experience before entering the camp. Our measure of hardships endured in the field is company death rates before capture. Individual characteristics that we control for include age, whether or not the soldier was wounded within ten days before capture, whether the soldier enlisted in a large city (a measure of prior disease exposure), the soldier's occupation at enlistment (artisans and professionals may have had skills that were either marketable in the camp or needed by the Confederacy), his family wealth in 1860 as given in the census (a soldier who could hide money or other valuables could buy food and clothing from the guards or from other prisoners), and his height, which is an indicator both of his health during his growing years and of his caloric needs while in the POW camp. In the next section, we examine how the observable characteristics of POWs with many friends differed from those with few friends.

Despite the richness of our data, there are two drawbacks to looking at our 3,026 cases of captivity. One is that we cannot observe idiosyncratic networks formed outside the company. Men who were in a POW camp with no one else from the same company would have had the greatest incentive to seek out friends from their hometowns or to ally themselves with strangers. We would mistakenly code these men as having no friends. We will therefore underestimate the true effect of friends on survival probabilities. A second drawback is that our sample is too small to examine the effect of the quality of the network (that is, how close individuals are to each other) on survivorship. Nevertheless, we can augment our analysis by looking at the single largest POW camp, Andersonville, which held roughly 17 percent of all men who were ever POWs.

The National Park Service's Andersonville database contains records on 35,323 men and was drawn from such disparate sources as the lists of the dead and published state muster rolls.[78] Although the sample does not cover the entire population of Andersonville (and probably never can, given the lack of complete records), it comes close. An estimated 45,000 men passed through Andersonville.[79] The data provide information on the soldier's name, rank, regiment, and company and on his death date if he died a prisoner, but only incomplete records on camp entry and exit dates. We have inferred town or county of origin from where the regiment was organized and ethnicity from the soldier's last name (see the appendix for full details.) When we exclude men with incomplete company information, we obtain a total of 31,688 men with complete company information in 1,570 regiments and 7,451 companies.

The Andersonville data contain a rich set of social network measures. The measures we use are the number of men in the company, the number of men in the regiment, the number of men of the same ethnicity in the company, the number of men with the same last name in the regiment (a measure of kinship), the fraction of men in the same company with a rank of sergeant or higher (a measure of how well the company's command structure was preserved), and the number of men from the same hometown. We then examine the effect of these social networks on the probability of survival, controlling for rank and ethnicity.[80]

POW Characteristics

A soldier became a POW primarily because of a battle. Soldiers who came from companies with disproportionately higher casualty rates were more likely to become POWs. Men who saw many battles were not a random sample of the population of soldiers, and men who became POWs were more likely to be volunteers, to have enlisted earlier (1862), and to be slightly wealthier than men who never became POWs.

Why did some POWs have many friends at the beginning of captivity and others have few? Men caught on scouting missions and soldiers lost in the haze and smoke of the battlefield were more likely to be caught singly, whereas those who surrendered were more likely to be caught with many comrades (and the surrender decision would be made by the commanding officers).

Diaries and other postwar accounts provide details. Sneden was with the unarmed cooks and clerks in a house guarded by two sleepy men. He "dozed off in a cat nap at 3:45 a.m., and knew nothing more until awakened by a rough tap on the head with a pistol barrel."[81] Stearns was in a company sent out to skirmish with the Confederates when "we run on to them no more than eight feet ahead of us and they took some of our boys prisoners."[82] After helping to guard a wagon train, Ira Pettit reported back to his regiment, which was "in line of battle." He was handed his mail and just had time to read it when "the enemy made a charge on our right flank and captured myself and 12 others of our company." [83] Men who charged ahead of their comrades or those too slow to run away when a retreat was sounded were caught by the Confederates. Men of the Sixth New Hampshire Volunteers were captured at the Battle of the Wilderness, unable to escape during the retreat from the house they had been ordered to hold.[84] An Irishman of the Sixth New Hampshire got "ahead of his company on the charge, was taken prisoner by two rebels where the line gave way a little under a terrific volley of the enemy." Fortunately for him, "the company rallied and charged on," and he was able to take the two Confederates prisoners.[85]

The largest numbers of men surrendering together were the defenders of a fort, not men on the battlefield. The men guarding Plymouth, North Carolina, who were sent to Andersonville were "completely enveloped on every side" and were under constant artillery fire for three days, enduring the "terrible fire . . . without reply, as no man could live at the guns."[86]

Men guarding forts may have been healthier because they had not experienced prolonged campaigning, but they may never have "toughened up." We do not know how most of our more than 3,000 prisoners of war were caught, but we can compare those caught with several friends with those caught with few friends. Men who had three or more comrades from the same company with them were less likely to have been wounded ten days before capture, but we doubt that we observe all of the men who were wounded on the day of captivity. Goss was captured twice during the war. The first time, he was in the camp hospital, ill with a fever, when "[o]ur force had retreated during the night, leaving the whole hospital camp . . . prisoners in the hand of the enemy."[87] The Sixteenth Illinois Cavalry, of which McElroy was a member, was captured when caught in a cul-de-sac. Up against a much larger force, the major surrendered after one-fourth of the men were killed or badly wounded and they were out of ammunition.[88]

Were men who were captured with few friends somehow different? The companies of men caught with three or more comrades did not differ from those of men caught with fewer comrades—the battlefield experience of the companies was the same, as was company diversity. Professionals and proprietors, the Irish, older men, and those from smaller cities were less likely to have many friends, but we can control for all these factors. Because, as we discuss later, those with few friends did not die immediately, we doubt that being captured with few friends indicates unobserved poor health. We also find no evidence of group surrender to become a POW—men who were captured in 1864 were captured with more men, even though they had no hope of a quick exchange.

Once men became POWs, they lost friends to transfers but gained new friends from transfers and from new captures. Lehman Josephson was joined at Andersonville by other men from his company, captured at a later date. McElroy, though captured with many men, was separated from his comrades when he stepped into a different railway car en route to Richmond. He was later reunited with his friend Andrews at Pemberton, because Andrews had been sent there from the hospital. The other men from his regiment (and previously Andrews) had been sent to Belle Isle and arrived at Andersonville after McElroy and Andrews.[89]

Who Survived?

Forty-six years of age and already gray, Private Thomas Withington of Harrisville, Ohio, was sent to Andersonville with at least twenty-seven other men from his company. He had been captured on June 11, 1864, after the Battle of Brice's Crossroads in Mississippi, where Confederate major general Nathan Bedford Forrest routed a much larger Union force. In 1862, Thomas had left behind a wife, two young sons, one young daughter, and a farm worth $4,000. Thomas was lucky. He lived until 1895. His comrades were fortunate too. Only 10 percent of the men in his company died at Andersonville, a camp where the overall death rate was four times as high.

Was Thomas lucky to have been captured with so many of his comrades? Among men who were captured in 1864, survival rates at Andersonville for the first two months of

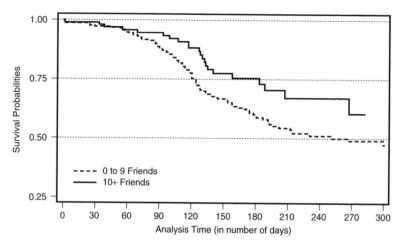

Figure 5.1. Survival Probabilities over Time by Number of Friends at Andersonville Among Men Captured in 1864

The probabilities are estimated from the Fogel data. Analysis time is time in days.

captivity for men captured with ten or more comrades were no different from those of men captured with fewer comrades. After the first two months, survival rates begin to diverge, and after four months, only three-quarters of the men captured with fewer than ten comrades were still alive. After four months about 90 percent of those captured with ten or more comrades were still alive (see figure 5.1).

More comrades from the same company lowered mortality, even when we have accounted for individual characteristics, the POW camp, and camp conditions. Henry Havens, captured during the moonlight battle of Wauhatchie, was sent to Richmond and then to Andersonville with five other men from his regiment but none from the same company. Four of the six men, including Henry, died at Andersonville. Had he had five friends from the same company, he could have increased his probability of survival from 69 in 100 to 72 in 100. Had he had 10 friends from the same company, he could have increased his chances to 74 out of 100. If every man in a POW camp had had an additional 10 friends, the overall survival probability would have risen from 86 out of 100 to 88 out of 100.

Henry Havens would have needed many more friends to make up for the increased disease and malnutrition brought on by crowding. In March the population of Andersonville averaged 7,500 men. In May it averaged 15,000, and in July, when Henry died, the prison population averaged 30,000 men. Adding 7,500 men to every camp at all times would have lowered the overall chance of survival from 86 out of 100 to 56 out of 100. To make up for such an increase, each man would have needed an additional 65 friends.

Henry Havens faced longer survival odds than some men not just because he had few friends, but also because he was a private. A corporal, sergeant, or officer faced odds of death that were half those of a private. Commissioned officers were kept in separate prisons and received better treatment. Some noncommissioned officers received an extra ration for calling roll and dividing up the rations. When the Andersonville prisoners formed a police force at the end of June, the sergeants of the force received an extra ration. Newton, a private imprisoned at Andersonville, described one conversation with a sergeant in which the sergeant said, "If he had one more ration it would be enough of the kind. I asked him how he thought we stood it on one ration. He thought we did not stand it very well."[90]

As a farmer, Henry fared as well as artisans, better than laborers, but not as well as professionals and proprietors, a group whose odds of death were almost half the odds of farmers. Men born in the United States, like Henry, and men born in Germany were more likely to die in a POW camp than those born in foreign countries other than Germany. Although the British, Irish, and other nationalities may have been more inured to hardship, they may also have been more willing to collaborate with the enemy. In October, when his friend Tibbets was dying, First Sergeant Lawson Carley recorded that on the 28th, "[h]ad a special roll call, and all foreigners whose term of service had expired were invited to join the Confederate Army. About 500 took the oath."[91] The Raiders "included representatives from all nationalities, and their descendants, but the English and Irish elements predominated."[92]

Henry was also at a disadvantage because of his height. At six feet one inch (185 cm), he was more likely to die than his shorter comrades because it was harder for him to subsist on the meager rations. Better initial health did not make up for bigger men needing more food. A man younger than Henry would have fared better, but little else mattered for his survival—neither family wealth, literacy, a wife at home, whether he enlisted in the city or the countryside, whether he was wounded ten days before capture, nor how many men in his company had died before capture.

The single most important determinant of camp survival was the number of men in POW camps (see figure 5.2). If everyone had been in a camp holding 7,500 men, survival probabilities would have been less than 60 percent instead of more than 80 percent. With greater camp populations survival probabilities would have been even lower. Another important determinant of camp survival

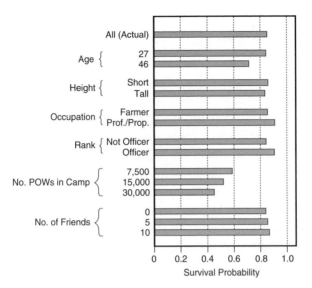

Figure 5.2. Characteristics and Predicted Survival Probabilities

Estimated from the Fogel data. The predictions show what the survival probabilities would have been if all men were age 27 (the age of Henry Havens and Lehman Josephson), age 46 (the age of Thomas Withington), short (166 cm, the height of Lehman Josephson), tall (185 cm, the height of Henry Havens), farmers at enlistment, professionals or proprietors at enlistment, privates or other, and commissioned or noncommissioned officers. The predictions also indicate what the survival probabilities would have been if the total number of men in the POW camp had been 7500, 15,000, and 30,000 (roughly the initial number of men and the maximum population of Andersonville) and if all men had had 0, 5, and 10 friends. See note 76 for details about the statistical model.

was age. Had all men been of Thomas Withington's age (47), only 70 percent of them would have survived. The next most important determinants of camp survival were the number of friends, rank, and height. Men who were not either commissioned or noncommissioned officers fared poorly, as did those with no friends and those of Henry Haven's height.

Adjustment to life as a POW is not easy. In his memoir of World War II imprisonment, Carson reported, "Physically I was able to withstand near anything the Japs could give, but I was totally unprepared for the psychological change. Changing from a combat soldier to a prisoner of war is not like putting on a clean shirt. . . . It took me a while to realize that I was entitled to nothing, that I had no rights, that I lived or died at the whim of my captors, and that I could do absolutely nothing to change this."[93] Civil War soldiers also noted the difficulty of psychological adjustment: "We felt our manhood crushed to the very earth."[94] "There is a certain flexibility of character that adapts itself with readiness to their circumstances. This adaptability to inevitable, unalterable fate, against which it is useless to strive, or where it is death to repine, softens much of the sufferings otherwise unendurable in such a life. . . . It . . . mitigates the mental pains and torments endured by those who are suddenly thrown upon their own resources, amid the acutest sufferings which squalid misery can inflict."[95]

Did men who "soon became conversant with the ways and means of the prison"[96] have a survival advantage, or did all men simply weaken and die after time in POW camps? We find that those who had survived one or two months were less likely to die in the next month than those still in their first month of captivity, but that the advantage of having survived a third month was small, and there was no advantage to surviving a fourth month. Were some men physically and psychologically unable to survive? Such men would die early. Our statistical methods downplay the importance of these factors for camp mortality.

Survival depended on the prison. Among men who were

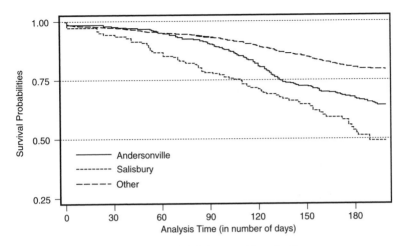

Figure 5.3. Survival Probabilities over Time by Camp among Men Captured in 1864

The probabilities are estimated from the Fogel data. Analysis time is time in days.

captured once exchanges were suspended, one-quarter of those who entered Andersonville were dead after four and a half months. Death at Salisbury was more rapid: it took only three and a half months for a quarter of the men to die. With a capacity of 2,000 men, Salisbury already held 5,500 in February 1864, and by November it held nearly 10,000. Even the wells became fouled when the ground turned into a quagmire from the filth and tread of so many men. At all other prison camps combined, one-quarter of the men died within eight and a half months (see figure 5.3).

Andersonville claimed the most lives because more men passed through it. Thomas Withington entered Andersonville not just with 27 other men from his company but with an additional 221 men from his regiment. His own company contained two sergeants, and except for their youth, the men in his company looked very much like him. Most were farmers. The majority had been born in Ohio, but a few of the older ones, like Thomas, had been born in Pennsylvania. Thomas did not find any other men from his hometown, but others did. When the men guarding Plymouth, North Carolina, were sent to Andersonville, they "retained everything except arms and munitions of war, and freely shared their shelter and conveniences with those of their friends who were less fortunate." W. Frank Bailey had the "good luck to find a company from [his] old home among them, and [he] was not slow in accepting an invitation to make [his] quarters with them."[97] Some of the men who entered Andersonville were brothers or cousins. At the end of July 1864, the dying men around McElroy's tent included two brothers from his battalion.[98]

We use the National Park Service's Andersonville database to examine diverse networks such as those based on hometown or kinship. The stronger the ties between men and the more leadership they had, the higher their odds of survival. Only 60 out of every 100 men in our database survived. An extra three out of 100 men could have survived if any one of the following had been true: (1) each man had had 150 men of his regiment at Andersonville, (2) each man had had 15 men from his company with him, (3) each man had had an additional kinsman with him, or (4) the fraction of the company with a sergeant's rank or higher had quintupled.[99] Among men from smaller towns, the greater the number of POWs from the same town, the more likely they were to live. Had all of the men from small towns found an extra hundred men from their hometowns, an extra two out of 100 men would

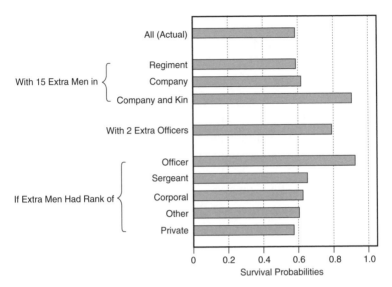

Figure 5.4. Characteristics and the Predicted Probability of Surviving Andersonville

The predictions are estimated from the National Park Service's Andersonville data. The predictions show what the survival probabilities would have been if all men had had 15 extra men in their regiments and in their company and 15 extra men of the same last name in their company (kinsmen in the same company); if all men had had two extra officers with them; and if all men had been officers, sergeants, corporals, private, and of some other rank (teamsters, musicians, etc.). See note 80 for details about the statistical model.

have survived. We do not find any survival differences between companies where men were captured together and companies where they were captured apart—knowledge of camp ways was not the main benefit of friendship.

If all men had had an extra 15 men from their companies with them, overall survival rates would have been slightly higher than if all men had had only an extra 15 men from their regiments with them (see figure 5.4). But survival probabilities would not have been much higher than the actual rate of 60 percent. In contrast, an extra two officers would have raised survival probabilities to 80 percent. If all men had had an extra 15 kinsmen from their company with them, survival rates would have been 90 percent—as high as having all men be officers.

Ties between men of the same ethnicity were strong. Among the Irish and French, 64 out of 100 men survived, and among the Germans, 60 out of 100 men. An additional man in the same company does not affect these odds. But an additional man of the same ethnicity in the same company increased the survival odds of the Germans to 63 out of 100 men and the survival odds of the Irish and the French to about 68 out of 100. If all ethnic groups had had 15 extra men from the same company with them, the effects would have been modest. But if all groups had had 15 extra men of the same ethnicity and company with them, the effects on survival probabilities would have been substantial (see figure 5.5).

The vast majority of POWs held at Andersonville were white. Our database contains only about a hundred black prisoners. Black soldiers were more likely to survive Andersonville than whites—32 percent of them died, compared to 38 percent of white soldiers, probably because blacks were sent to work outside the stockade. The white chaplain of Colonel Wentworth Higginson's regiment of slaves reported that when captured, he adopted a policy of boldness and defiance with his captors, whereas the black soldier caught with him was meek and conciliatory. The black soldier was able to escape after six months, but the chaplain was imprisoned for a year.[100]

What was the best group size? In Japanese POW camps, orders on how many men could congregate at once and the organization of sleeping arrangements led to groups of three to six friends. Four men were not too many to

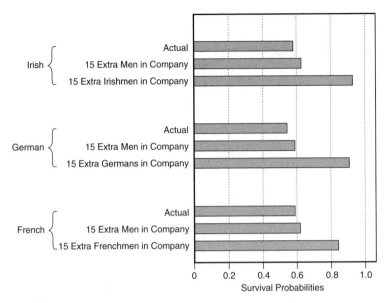

Figure 5.5. Social Networks by Ethnicity and the Predicted Probability of Surviving Andersonville

The predictions are estimated from the National Park Service's Andersonville data for each ethnic group. The predictions show what the survival probabilities would have been if all Irish, German, and French men had had 15 extra men from their companies with them at Andersonville, and if these 15 extra men from their company had been of the same ethnicity. We estimate separate models for the Irish, Germans, and French. See note 80 (pp, 264–65) for details about the statistical models.

split a scrounged can of food and not too few to meet a friend's labor quota when he was sick or to give him extra food when his ration was cut because he could not work.[101] The best group size may have been different in Confederate POW camps. At Andersonville, rations were given to 270 men to divide, and at other camps they were given to 100 men to divide. A large group would be better able to fight off the Raiders. But the shelters the POWs constructed from poles and blankets could rarely hold more than six men. Looking over all POW camps and Andersonville, we find that the effect of a friend on survival was greater for the first two friends than for more than two. At Andersonville, the two largest companies of POWs, two companies of Massachusetts Heavy Artillery that had been guarding Plymouth, North Carolina, suffered unusually high mortality rates. According to McElroy, "They gave up the moment the gates were closed upon them and began pining away."[102] Both of these companies contained well over 100 men.

Having friends and having friends of the right type helped men survive, even in places where "social habits and instincts [were] reduced to silence."[103] We cannot tell whether it was through friends' provision of food, care, or moral support, because we cannot observe daily prison life. But most men simply did not have enough friends to increase their survival probabilities greatly. We can account for less than 10 percent of the variance in survival probabilities. Chance and many things that we cannot observe, including determination, adaptability, skills, and pitilessness, all undoubtedly contributed.

Primo Levi described the social structure of Auschwitz as based on the human law

that the privileged oppress the unprivileged. . . . In the Lager, where man is alone and where the struggle for life is reduced to its primordial mechanism, this unjust law is openly in force, is recognized by all. With the adaptable, the strong and astute individuals, even the leaders willingly keep contact, sometimes even friendly contact, because they hope later to perhaps derive some benefit. . . . [O]f the old Jewish prisoners . . . only a few hundred had survived; not one was an ordinary Häftling, vegetating in the ordinary Kommandos, and subsisting on the normal ration. There remained only the doctors, tailors, shoemakers, musicians, cooks, young attractive homosexuals, friends or compatriots of some authority in the camp; or they were particularly pitiless, vigorous and inhuman individuals, installed . . . in the posts of Kapos, *Blockältester*, etc.; or finally, those who, without fulfilling particular functions, had always succeeded through their astuteness and energy in successfully organizing, gaining in this way, besides material advantages and reputation, the indulgence and esteem of the powerful people in the camp.[104]

COSTS OF SOCIAL NETWORKS

Was there a "dark side" to friendship? Were the most effective groups gangs who robbed and murdered their fellow prisoners? Sneden described the Andersonville Raiders as being "all strong, as they bought food from the sutler and other dealers with stolen money, or robbed some poor prisoner of his whole stock of food."[105] "They had the great advantage . . . of being well acquainted with each other."[106] To fight the Raiders, the POWs, led by Sergeant Leroy Key, an Illinois cavalryman, organized a prison defense force. When a newcomer to the camp was robbed and severely beaten on June 28, 1864, the prison commander armed these "regulators" with clubs and, with the assistance of Confederate soldiers, the hunt for the Raiders within the stockade was on. Once captured, they were held by Confederate guards and then tried by a jury of prison newcomers. On July 11, 1864, six of the Raiders were hanged.[107] Although most diaries note an improvement in crime rates after the capture of the

Raiders, we do not observe any accompanying decline in deaths. (By August, men were complaining about the large rations the regulators drew and the replacement of the Westerners who founded the organization with "the rounders of New York and Brooklyn," men cut from the same cloth as the Raiders.[108]

If bigger groups can steal from stronger groups, a larger group is at an advantage in fighting for a limited set of resources. But our evidence suggests that the first few friends are the most important. Men were not fighting for a limited set of resources within POW camps—there was exchange with the outside world and theft from it.

Social networks imposed costs on their members. One way to survive was to collaborate with the enemy. In the extreme case this meant joining the Confederate army. Sneden commented on one recruitment effort: "If any of us had showed any symptoms of recruiting to the Rebels, he would have been murdered at once by his comrades."[109] Samuel Murdock, in Lehman Josephson's company, was sent to Salisbury, where he joined the Confederate army. At the end of the 1800s he returned to County Down in Ireland, where he lived until 1908. Out of more than 3,000 captives, we observe only seventeen enlistments in the Confederate army, all out of Salisbury. The men who enlisted were more likely to be foreign-born, to be wealthier, to be nonfarmers, and to have been caught with fewer comrades. We find no evidence that the number of friends affected whether an individual was one of the 140 men in our data set (out of 329) who escaped from Andersonville.

Stearns reported that some men remained POWs in order not to abandon their comrades:

> One incident I remember, which occurred at the time we were signing parole papers at Goldsboro'.

There were some of the Fifty-fourth Massachusetts among those who went to sign, and the Rebel officer made them turn back, saying, "We don't parole niggers!" Just behind them, but ahead of Sergeant Bugbee and myself, was Sergeant Jeffs of the Fifty-fourth, who was as white as many of the Yankees—a mulattoe; and when he saw the others turned back, he stepped over the line to go with them. Bugbee said to him: 'Stay in line; they will never suspect you.' But Jeffs replied: "These are my people, and I am going with them"; and he did go. . . . this incident shows how strong an attachment the soldiers had for each other, even among the colored troops.[110]

Aftermath

"Can these be *men*—these little, livid brown, ash-streaked, monkey-looking dwarfs? Are they not really mummied, dwindling corpses?" wrote Walt Whitman of the returning prisoners.[111] If "[w]hoever waits for his neighbour to die in order to take his piece of bread is, albeit guiltless, further from the model of thinking man than the most primitive pigmy or the most vicious sadist,"[112] then both physically and psychologically, many of the survivors were not men. At Andersonville, "[t]wo or three [had sat] around a dying man waiting to grab his blanket, his tin cup or canteen and clothes before life was out of him."[113]

It is easier to trace physical rather than psychological recovery. Lehman Josephson, though hobbled by rheumatism in his old age, lived until age 69, leaving his widow $1,000 in life insurance when he died in 1906. One of his Andersonville comrades survived until 1896, after spending time in a lunatic asylum. But even the survivors of the prison camps of 1864 who were fortunate enough to live

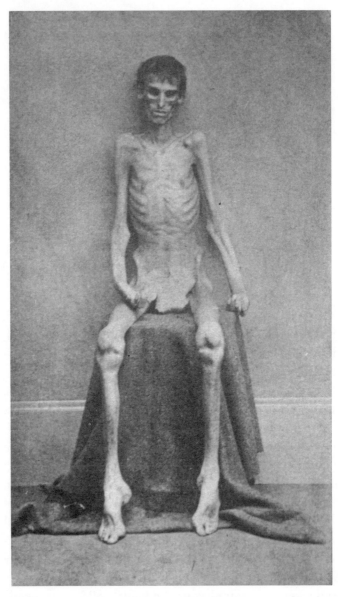

Plate 7. A federal prisoner, returned from prison

until 1900 were scarred—former POWs captured after prisoner exchanges ceased led shorter lives than those captured when the exchange system operated.

How did the survivors attach meaning to their suffering? McElroy celebrated their "unflinching heroism" when "they could read their own fate in that of the loathsome, unburied dead all around them." "They who lie in the shallow graves of Andersonville, Belle Isle, Florence and Salisbury, lie there in obedience to the precepts and maxims inculcated into their minds in the churches and Common Schools of the North; precepts which impressed upon them the duty of manliness and honor in all the relations and exigencies of life; not the 'chivalric' prate of their enemies, but the calm steadfastness which endureth to the end. . . . They died as every American should when duty bids him. No richer heritage was ever bequeathed to posterity."[114]

CHAPTER 6
The Homecoming of Heroes and Cowards

FEW FAMILIES EMERGED FROM THE CIVIL WAR WITHOUT a father, husband, son, brother, or cousin dead or wounded. Of the two million white men who served the Union, almost 325,000 died in the war. Roughly 450,000 of the survivors had been wounded in the war. Thirteen percent of all white men of military age (ages 13 to 43 in 1860) were casualties.

How did soldiers and civilians make sense of so much suffering? Essays from an 1866 penmanship competition for men whose right arms had been amputated emphasized that the writers' "honorable scars" were necessary sacrifices for preserving a self-governing republic of free men and for achieving national salvation: "the widow and the orphan, the empty chair at the fireside, the empty sleeve in the old blue uniform . . . with mute eloquence . . . will remind us through such sacrifices as these are the blessings we now enjoy purchased."[1] The speeches at the first reunion of the Sixth New Hampshire Regiment, held

in 1889, were reminiscences of fallen comrades and re-
minders that Civil War soldiers were the saviors and de-
liverers of the nation, having wiped away the dark stain of
slavery with their blood. "This war was one of the two
which John Bright said were the only justifiable wars in
history since the advent of the Saviour, the other being
the American Revolution."[2]

Some soldiers preferred to forget the war. When invited in 1869 to speak at Gettysburg, Robert E. Lee declined, thinking it "wiser . . . not to keep open the sores
of war, but to follow the examples of those nations who
endeavoured to obliterate the marks of civil strife and to
commit to oblivion the feelings it engendered."[3]

The sores of war between North and South were closed
by a culture of "character." Already in 1874, a Decoration
Day speech in Boston extolled the soldierly virtues of devotion and obedience, regardless of cause, as the "all-sur-
passing reasons for our approval and love."[4] By the 1880s
and 1890s, such discourse was the norm.[5] Soldiers on both
sides had sacrificed equally and embodied the virtues of
manliness and honor. Because of their sacrifices, "the
people of those two sections of the country [North and
South] came to know and understand each other better,
and better state of feeling prevails between the two sections now, than at any former time."[6]

Not all soldiers fought honorably, however. At the first
reunion of the Sixth New Hampshire Regiment, one
speaker said, "If ever men deserved well of their country . . . they are those who sprang to arms from the purest
and most unselfish motives."[7] The men who enlisted late,
receiving bounties, or who were draftees or substitutes
are not even mentioned by name in the history of the
Sixth New Hampshire. Even men such as Lehman

Josephson, who was at Andersonville, were not mentioned. Not only were the motives of bounty-men, draftees, and substitutes less than pure, but their numbers also included deserters.

Loyal soldiers, both Union and Confederate, satisfied Victorian ideals of manhood and self-control and the classical republican ideal of a virtuous citizenry willing to sacrifice for self-government. Union veterans were also God's chosen instruments for saving the Union and sweeping away the curse of slavery, permitting the inauguration of a new era. How were deserters, who were known in their communities to have failed cause and comrades and their test of manhood, reintegrated into their hometowns?

Community social norms should shape soldiers' postwar experiences. Social norms have been cited as explanations for women's labor force participation rates and for their choice of particular jobs. They have been cited as explanations for why some students, eager not to be associated with "nerds," do poorly in school. However, social norms are notoriously difficult to measure. We have a benchmark for community norms, namely, their pro-war sentiment. In chapter 4 we found that pro-Lincoln counties in 1860 produced fewer deserters. But as the war dragged on, some communities turned against it and did not support Lincoln in the 1864 election. How did community support for the war influence the severity of deserters' punishments?

COMMUNITY SUPPORT FOR THE WAR

Not all communities were enthusiastic in their support of the war. We can measure their war ardor using voting variables. The 1864 contest for the presidency between

Plate 8. Civil War Veterans, Fourth of July or Decoration Day, Ortonville, MN, on review in center of town, ca. 1880.

Abraham Lincoln and George McClellan, his dismissed commander of the Army of the Potomac, was a referendum on the war. The 1864 Democratic platform was one of peace without victory, resolving that "immediate effort be made for a cessation of hostilities."[8] Democratic opposition to the war was longstanding. In 1863, Democratic legislatures in Indiana and Illinois sought to take control of state troops from Republican governors, after having passed resolutions calling for an armistice, a peace conference, and a retraction of the "wicked, inhuman and unholy" Emancipation Proclamation.[9]

Secret societies that actively helped northern soldiers desert, which discouraged enlistments, and that resisted the draft were active in such Democratic strongholds as the East North Central region.[10] Democratic newspapers published letters to soldiers, allegedly written by family members, begging them "to come home, if you have to desert, you will be protected—the people are so enraged that you need not be alarmed if you hear of the whole of our Northwest killing off the abolitionists."[11] Armed mobs led by deserters drove away enrolling officers. A mob of 400 men attacked a deputy provost marshal in DuQuoin, Illinois, and freed the deserters he was guarding. An officer of a Pennsylvania regiment, acting on an anonymous tip, found two packages of civilian clothing, one accompanied by a letter of advice on desertion.[12] Antiwar communities also refused to help the families of needy soldiers. Second Lieutenant Charles Conzet of Illinois, who had received no pay for his five months of service, was in January 1863 "induced to abandon his post by letters from his wife begging him to come home and relieve her from her destitute condition, representing to him that the community in which she lived was opposed

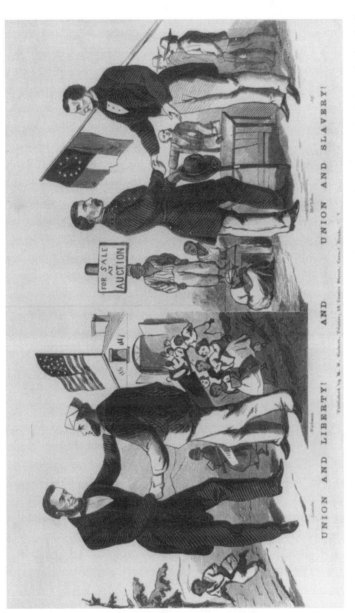

Plate 9. An anti-McClellan broadside ("Union and liberty! And union and slavery!"), showing Lincoln shaking the hand of a free laborer and McClellan shaking the hand of Confederate President, Jefferson Davis

to the war, and would do nothing to relieve her necessities because her husband was in the Army."[13] Convicted of desertion, Conzet was sentenced to death, but Lincoln ordered him dishonorably discharged.

Voting in the United States was even more divided along religious lines in 1864 than it had been in 1860.[14] In the 1860 election Lincoln owed his narrow victory in part to Yankees who were influenced by the religious revival movement that swept the United States in the first half of the nineteenth century and who had migrated from New England to the Midwest.[15] The abolitionists who viewed the war as God's wrath over the curse of slavery were pietists (Methodists, Baptists, Congregationalists, Presbyterians, and Unitarians). The antislavery fervor of the pietists was not found among the liturgical religions (Catholic, Lutheran, and Episcopalian), and some of the members of other religious denominations, such as Quakers, were both antislavery and pacifist. Our analysis of 1864 voting patterns shows that compared to "other" religions, a member of a pietist religion was two-thirds as likely to vote for McClellan and a member of a liturgical religion was almost one and a half times as likely to vote for McClellan.[16]

A vote for McClellan, the peace candidate, was not just an ideological vote, based on religion; it was also a vote based on economic interest.[17] In 1860, displaced skilled native-born workers, well-off farmers in the free states, and anti-immigrant and anti-Catholic members of the former Know-Nothing Party were Lincoln supporters.[18] In 1864, slave-holding counties were more pro-McClellan. Counties in the Middle Atlantic and the East North Central regions were more likely to be pro-McClellan than was New England, whereas counties in the West North Central region were even more anti-McClellan than New

England. In the East North Central region the Civil War severed trade with the South along the Ohio and Mississippi rivers; as a result, local banks, with their holdings of southern bonds, collapsed, further aggravating existing tensions between Midwestern farmers and the Northeast over protective tariffs and high freight rates.[19] Confederate agents even dreamed of an uprising leading to a western Confederacy.[20]

In addition, counties where McClellan received a higher proportion of the vote were poorer, had a lower percentage of their labor force in manufacturing, and had larger foreign-born populations, particularly Irish and German. Catholics, both Irish and German, feared the political ascendancy of New England Puritanism with its emphasis on prohibition and on emancipation, an emancipation that could only lead to competition in the labor market from freed slaves.

PUNISHING DESERTERS

Individuals adhere to community codes of conduct either because of laws and legal punishments or because of systems of informal social control. The community can enforce social norms if it knows who fought honorably and who did not (and this was well-known to all Civil War communities) and if it is willing to punish those who dishonored the community. "An enforcer is on the front line of the system of informal social control. Enforcers observe what actors do and respond by meting out calibrated rewards and punishments."[21] But enforcers are not compensated for their actions, so why would they punish? Communities that were pro-war supplied a disproportionately large number of soldiers who fought and died in the war. Raw emotion and anger at the men who dishonored the community and endangered their comrades would motivate community enforcers.

"We fought with the feeling that we were under the straining eyes of those who had loved us and had sent us forth, whose approval we valued more than life," wrote Ira Dodd of his military experience.[22] "The constant question in our hearts was 'what will the folks at home say about us?' . . . I have known sick men, really unfit for duty, who, when rumours of 'a move' came, would keep out of the surgeon's way, and when their regiment was called into action would shoulder their rifles and drag themselves along with their comrades for fear some report that they had shirked might travel home."[23] A mother could write to a nurse about her wounded son, "I cannot think he is strong enough for the hardships of camp life, but as I have his own honor at heart at least more than my desire to see him again, I hesitate to apply for his discharge."[24]

If deserters left home, it was not because of written laws but because of community mores. Once the war was over, deserters who had not been pardoned during one of the wartime presidential amnesties were dishonorably discharged with forfeiture of pay. They could return home without fear of arrest but were deemed by the federal government to have relinquished their citizenship or right to become a citizen of the United States and therefore their voting rights. Later court interpretations weakened federal law even further by specifying that the requirement could not be desertion alone but had to be a conviction of desertion.[25] Furthermore, because states regulated voting rights, this federal disenfranchisement was widely viewed as ineffectual except in the territories and in the states that passed laws disenfranchising deserters.[26]

Five states, Kansas, Pennsylvania, Wisconsin, New York,

and Vermont, disenfranchised deserters, but only three had strict laws. Pennsylvania's law may never have been codified and was not part of the 1873 Digest of Pennsylvania Laws, and New York's law referred to only one special election of delegates to a state constitutional convention. The three states that had strict laws—Vermont, Wisconsin, and Kansas—were more pro-Lincoln in 1864. In Kansas and Vermont, more than three-quarters of the population voted for Lincoln, and in Wisconsin, Lincoln's share of the vote was equal to his share of the national vote. Lincoln barely carried the states of Pennsylvania and New York.

By 1880 only Vermont still disenfranchised deserters. In Kansas, an 1866 amendment to the state constitution revoked voting rights from those dishonorably discharged as well as from felons and people who had aided in the rebellion, but an 1874 amendment struck dishonorable discharge as one of the listed offenses that led to a revocation of voting rights. Before this amendment, in almost every year after 1868 voting rights were restored to a list of named men by an act of the state legislature. In Wisconsin an 1866 law allowed election officials to block people challenged as deserters from voting, and an 1867 law ordered the distribution of lists of Wisconsin deserters to election officials in each precinct, who were to post a list at every polling place. In 1868 procedures were put in place for an individual to have his name removed from the deserter list, and in 1869 the 1867 law was repealed. In 1873 the 1866 law was repealed.

Deserters and Migration

All veterans faced a decision after the war: should they return to their home communities or move? A deserter's hometown might ostracize and scorn him, and even if it forgave him, he might be too ashamed to face his friends. But in a new community where his war record was unknown, a deserter could escape from his past and reinvent himself. Deserters also could seek out more sympathetic (antiwar) communities. Both deserters and nondeserters moved to seek their fortunes, pulled by the lure of opportunities elsewhere and pushed by dwindling opportunities at home. Nevertheless, the nondeserter faced no shame. Shame can therefore be thought of either as a cost to deserters to staying in the home community or as affecting deserters' expectations of future life in the community.[27]

A deserter who feels no shame may still face community ostracism, and this creates an incentive to migrate away. Community sanctions could be motivated by revenge, by a sense that deserters had not done their fair share, or by the sense that deserters had personally harmed men who served honorably or the cause they had sacrificed for.[28] Even if deserters felt no connection to their home communities and therefore no shame, they could still be harmed by economic sanctions. A pro-war community would be more likely to impose such sanctions. A pro-war community would also be more likely to impose nonpecuniary sanctions, and these would be effective as long as the deserter identified with the home community, in which case he would feel shame.

Although we are not able to distinguish explicitly between shame and ostracism, we are able to distinguish between shame and ostracism on the one hand and economic sanctions on the other, by comparing the occupational mobility of deserters and nondeserters. Economic sanctions should lead deserters to fall down the occupational ladder.

During the war deserters could either remain at large or return to fight again, either willingly or under duress. Roughly a quarter of "returned" deserters (whom we will call "returnees" for short) surrendered voluntarily, including those under presidential amnesty proclamation. The rest had been arrested and sent back to the service.[29] Men should have felt less shame in being a returned deserter, because returnees continued to fight until the end of the war. Cyrus J. Philbrook enlisted in 1861 at age 17 in the Sixth New Hampshire and deserted after one month. He then enlisted in the Twelfth New Hampshire in 1862, was wounded at Fredericksburg, and died of disease in the service. After his death his brother Edwin named his son Cyrus J., not an honor that would have been accorded a deserter. Cyrus had redeemed himself for his youthful lapse.

Once the war was over, a soldier could either move or remain in his home community. Because soldiers had never had the experience of deserting and then returning to their home communities, they could not predict the consequences of their action. Deserters might therefore return home and then move away if they were poorly treated. Until late 1863, before the federal government actively pursued deserters, men who deserted would simply go home. William Howe, an ethnic German who enlisted in the predominantly Irish 116th Pennsylvania Regiment, was sick in a Washington, D.C., hospital and returned home to Frederick Township in Montgomery County, Pennsylvania, during the 1862 Christmas holidays. He continued his life as a subsistence farmer, never hiding his desertion. The majority of his neighbors did not care—McClellan later carried Montgomery County—but bounties for capturing deserters led to a bungled arrest attempt in which the arresting officer was murdered.

William Howe was executed.[30] Returning home had become dangerous for deserters.

After 1863, deserters fled their home communities for less populated areas. They were particularly likely to be found in Canada, the Territory of Wyoming, and the mountainous, wooded, and sparsely settled regions of Pennsylvania. Very few deserters went to the Confederacy.

Once the war was over, local officials in New York, New Jersey, Pennsylvania, Maine, Illinois, Minnesota, and Wisconsin complained that their communities were overrun with deserters who had returned home.[31] Local provost-marshal general's offices wrote that "deserters from the Army and draft . . . are insolent and abusive to soldiers who have endured the hardships and perils of war, and many of whom are crippled by wounds or disease and are entitled to protection" and that "large numbers of these deserters . . . show themselves with impunity in New York and Brooklyn." According to one inquiry "many men drafted . . . who fled to Canada and other parts unknown . . . are now returning home, much to the dissatisfaction of the loyal portion of the community. Desires to know if they are to be arrested as deserters, and if so, what means are to be taken to secure their arrest, as he has no officers and no authority to employ any, and no guards to send in charge of them should they be arrested by citizens." Other inquiries also emphasized the lack of manpower for arrests and some even the lack of legal recourse. The governor of Minnesota "hopes the War Department will take the matter in hand, as the laws of Minnesota make no provision for their punishment."[32]

By using returnees as a control group for deserters, we can recover the causal effect of desertion on migration. Returned deserters resemble permanent deserters. Like deserters they tended to be poorer and were more likely to be illiterate, to be married, and to have enlisted in a large city. (However, deserters were more likely to be foreign-born and less likely to be volunteers or to be farmers than either returnees or nondeserters.) Both returnees and deserters initially deserted. If there was some unobservable characteristic about men who deserted that determined their later behavior, then returnees should look like deserters. But returnees went back to fight and, if they survived, were honorably discharged. If there was stigma to being a deserter, then returnees should be free of this stigma and should behave like nondeserters. We therefore examine how the probability that a veteran left home depended on deserter status, the vote for McClellan in 1864 in his county of enlistment, and the interaction between deserter status and the vote for McClellan, controlling for his individual characteristics and for state of enlistment.[33]

Shame and ostracism also predict that deserters might be more likely to change their names and reinvent themselves, particularly if they are from a pro-war community. We therefore examine what determines the probability that we find a soldier in the 1880 census. Out of more than 20,000 men known to have survived the war, we can find more than one-third of them (more than 7,000 men) in the 1880 census. Because our search uses only name, place of birth, and expected age in 1880, we cannot find men with common names. We are also more likely to find the native-born, those from richer households, and those from more rural areas. But if we control for all observable characteristics and are less likely to find deserters, we can treat this outcome as evidence that deserters sought to hide their past.[34]

Migration

Millions of men advance at once toward the same
point on the horizon: their language, their religion,
their mores differ, their goal is common. They were
told that fortune is to be found somewhere toward
the west, and they go off in haste to meet it. . . . Fifty
years have scarcely elapsed since Ohio was founded;
the greater part of its inhabitants were not born
within its confines; its capital has been built only
thirty years, and its territory is still covered by an
immense extent of uncultivated fields; yet already the
population of Ohio is proceeding westward, and most
of the settlers who descend to the fertile plains of
Illinois are citizens of Ohio.
—Alexis de Toqueville, *Democracy in America*

Although he was writing in 1835, Tocqueville described
both the ante- and the postbellum period.[35] One-quarter
of all 20- to 29-year-olds in 1850 had moved to a different state by 1860, one-fifth of all 20- to 29-year-olds in
1860 had moved to a different state by 1870, and 30 percent of all 20- to 29-year-olds in 1870 had moved to a different state by 1880.[36] Among all northern-born males
aged 33 to 63 years in 1880, 45 percent were living in a
state other than their state of birth.[37]

Union army soldiers joined the westward migration. Al-
bert Horn, son of a farmer in Ripley, Maine, enlisted at age
16, lying about his age. By 1870 he was a prosperous scrap
peddler in Haverhill, Massachusetts, with a son of his own,
and by 1880 he had moved his wife, two sons, and father to
San Francisco, where he was a produce dealer. Forty-four
percent of native-born soldiers moved between their state

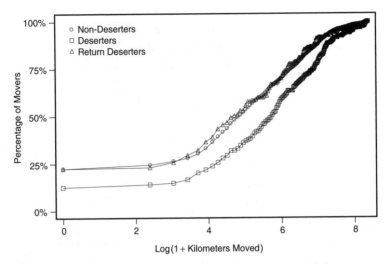

Figure 6.1. Distribution of Migration Distance by Deserter Status

The graph represents the cumulative distribution functions. It gives the percentage of movers who have moved the given distance or less. Migration distance is measured between county centroids at enlistment and in 1880.

of birth and their state of enlistment, and half of them were living in a state other than their state of birth in 1880. Forty-five percent of both native- and foreign-born veterans moved across state lines between enlistment and 1880.

Deserters were more likely to move, and when they did move, they moved farther away (see figure 6.1). Sixty-four percent of deserters moved across states, compared to only 44 percent of nondeserters and 42 percent of returnees. If we measure distance moved across counties in kilometers, deserters were more likely to move farther away than nondeserters or returnees, but deserters who stayed within a state were less likely to move across counties. The migration propensities of nondeserters and returnees were almost identical. These effects persist even

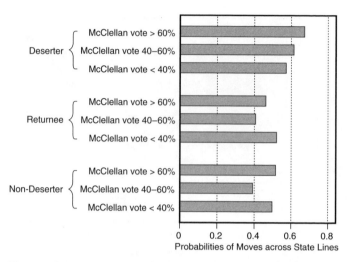

Figure 6.2. Percentage in County Voting for McClellan and Probability of a Deserter Moving across States Between Enlistment and 1880

The top panel shows the distribution in the percentage of the county vote for McClellan. The bottom panel gives the predicted probability that a deserter would have moved across state lines between enlistment and 1880 if all deserters had been from counties with the specified level of the county vote for McClellan (see note 33 for details about the statistical model). George Farrell was from Cayuga County and Daniel Mulholland was from Manhattan.

when we control for individual characteristics and for state of origin.

Deserters were more likely to move if McClellan had received a small share of the home county vote (see figure 6.2). In counties where McClellan received less than 40 percent of the vote, 68 percent of deserters moved across state, compared to 47 percent of nondeserters. But in counties where McClellan received more than 60 percent of the vote, 58 percent of deserters moved across the state, compared to 52 percent of nondeserters. We also observe such differences for the probability of moving at least 350 km. Returnees resembled nondeserters.

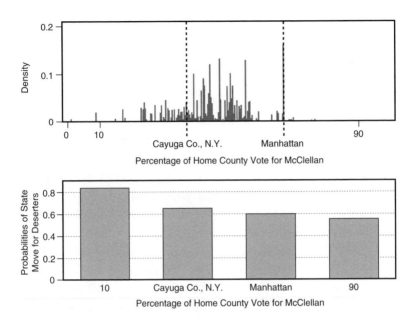

Figure 6.3. Fraction of State Movers by Desertion Status and by Percentage of Home County Voting for McClellan

Moves are moves across state lines. Home county is county of enlistment.

Figure 6.3 (top panel) shows the percentage of the vote cast for McClellan in each enlistment county in our data. McClellan received the largest share of the vote in Green County, Kentucky, which contributed men to both the Union and Confederate armies. Although his smallest share of the vote was in Barton County, Missouri, this county too was divided, and it was devastated by battles between guerrillas and occupying Union troops. Addison County, Vermont, where McClellan received less than 9 percent of the vote, produced his lowest vote in a non-occupied Union state. He received less than a quarter of the vote in Worcester County, Massachusetts, home of Adams French and James Monroe Rich. McClellan received 40 percent of the vote in Cayuga County in upstate

New York, where George Farrell enlisted. Farrell's comrade in the New York Forty-seventh, Daniel Mulholland, enlisted in New York City, where 68 percent of the voters favored McClellan.

Had all deserters been from a county where McClellan received 40 percent of the vote, 65 percent of them would have moved to another state. Had they all been from a county where McClellan received 68 percent of the vote, 60 percent of them would have moved. Had they been from a county where McClellan received only 10 percent of the vote, more than 80 percent of them would have moved (see figure 6.3, bottom panel).

We also calculated differences in the moving propensities of nondeserters, returnees, and deserters by the percentage of the vote cast for McClellan in the 1860 home county. Being in a county where McClellan received less than 40 percent of the vote increased deserters' probability of moving across states by 0.16 relative to nondeserters and by 0.08 relative to returnees. Deserters' probability of moving at least 350 km increased by 0.13 relative to nondeserters and by 0.14 relative to returnees. When deserters did move, the state that they moved to was more pro-McClellan than the state nondeserters moved to, and it was also more distant.

One difficulty in comparing deserters with returnees or nondeserters is that deserters may somehow be different. They may be men who cannot stay still—men who can commit neither to the army nor to a community. Even if they had somehow been prevented from deserting, perhaps they would have migrated anyway. We can still recover the causal effect of desertion. A soldier's propensity to desert will depend on his ideological commitment, but even those highly committed to the cause are more likely to desert when company cohesion is low and when war is particularly horrific. Soldiers might also panic. Company-specific measures of war "horror" and of cohesion therefore provide some exogenous variation in desertion probabilities and can be used as instrumental variables to break the link between deserter status and unobserved factors that may influence the migration decision.[38] When we implement an instrumental variables statistical strategy, we find even stronger effects of deserter status on migration.[39]

Deserters may have sought to hide their past by changing their names. We know what happened to a man if we can find him in the 1880 census. But given only a name, a state or country of birth, and an expected age, we can find only 35 percent of war survivors in 1880. Some men we cannot find because they had very common names. John Andrews, a deserter from the Fifth Connecticut, is lost to follow-up because there are more than eighteen John Andrewses in the 1880 census born in New York State around 1842. Others we simply cannot find despite their distinctive names. Milton Blizzard, married to Margaret and with children Lucinda, William, and Mary, enlisted in the Fiftieth Ohio in August 1862 and deserted in September. We found no record of the family in postwar censuses. Although some of the people we cannot find may have been missed by the census enumerators and others may have died, we are less likely to find deserters than either nondeserters or returnees. When we control for all characteristics, a deserter's probability of being found was lower by 0.10 relative to a nondeserter. Compared to a returnee, a deserter's probability of being found was lower by 0.06. When we interact deserter status with the proportion of the vote for McClellan we find that when we control for county characteristics, deserters from counties where McClellan received a larger share of the vote are more likely to be found.

Does our inability to find two-thirds of the men affect our estimates of migration propensities? No. We can control for selection into our sample by explicitly modeling who enters the sample and then applying a correction factor. One of the pivotal determinants of being in our sample is having an uncommon name. Our correction procedure gives us even larger deserter effects. Returnees remain indistinguishable from nondeserters.

When deserters did move, they sought out a state that was more pro-McClellan compared to those picked by nondeserters or returnees.[40] Although McClellan carried only Kentucky, New Jersey, and Delaware, his share of the vote varied from 18 percent in Kansas to 70 percent in Kentucky. If we control for distance from state of enlistment as measured in miles and in minutes from the enlistment state's latitude, the greater a state's share of the vote for McClellan, the higher were the odds that a deserter would move there. When we control for whether the state had a law disenfranchising deserters and for whether the state was then a territory (in which case federal law was applicable), we find that the odds that a deserter would move to a state with a law disenfranchising deserters were no greater than those of a nondeserter and that the odds that a deserter would move to a territory were 1.28 times greater than those of a nondeserter, but the difference was not statistically significant.

A deserter was also more likely to pick a state of a different latitude, because fewer deserters were farmers and therefore did not have skills that were best used along the same latitude.[41] When we restrict the sample to men who were farmers at enlistment, we find no difference in the latitude attributes of the states picked by deserters and nondeserters. Still, deserters continued to pick more pro-McClellan states. When we examine location choices by region, we find that deserters were not more likely to go to the states of the former Confederacy, but they were more likely to move to a Middle Atlantic or East North Central state. Unlike deserters, returnees were no more likely than nondeserters to pick a pro-McClellan state.

Explaining Deserters' Mobility

Many factors could explain why deserters' migration patterns differed from those of nondeserters, including shame, community ostracism, economic or legal sanctions, and alienation. Or perhaps they were simply more mobile. Although we cannot directly observe deserters' motives, we can rule out the importance of economic and legal sanctions, an inherently greater mobility, economic opportunities, and alienation.

A successful economic boycott of deserters might lead them to fall down the occupational ladder, but we find no evidence that between enlistment and 1880 deserters faced a monetary penalty. Conditional on being a farmer, an artisan, or a laborer at enlistment, statistical tests indicate that the occupational transitions of nondeserters, returnees, and deserters between enlistment and 1880 were the same. Sixty percent of farmers remained farmers and 20 percent of them became laborers. Over 40 percent of artisans remained artisans, and the remaining men became farmers, laborers, or professionals and proprietors in roughly equal numbers. Forty percent of the laborers remained laborers, and for those who did rise up the economic ladder, farming was the most popular occupation. Either communities did not impose economic sanctions on deserters or, by moving to a pro-McClellan state, deserters avoided economic penalties. Nevertheless, among the small group of men who were professionals or proprietors at enlistment, deserters were less likely to remain professionals or proprietors and were more likely to become artisans and less likely to become farmers. Over 40 percent of nondeserters who were professionals and proprietors at enlistment were still professionals and proprietors in 1880, but only a quarter of deserters were still professionals and proprietors.

The data also suggest that the occupational transitions of returned deserters resemble those of deserters, but relative to deserters fewer returnees were laborers and more of them remained professionals or proprietors. When we examine the data by state mover status, we find that only for state movers did the 1880 occupational distribution of former professionals or proprietors differ between deserters and nondeserters, suggesting that professionals or proprietors were differentially hurt by a move because their human and social capital may not have been easily transferable across states. We also find no evidence that strongly pro-war communities imposed economic sanctions on the deserters who did stay. The occupational transitions of deserters and nondeserters from strongly pro-Lincoln counties were the same.

Deserters might simply be highly mobile people, either because of taste or because of their better health. Thirty percent of nondeserters and returnees were wounded in the war compared to 9 percent of deserters, but when we control for whether a soldier was wounded in the war and for length of time served, our migration results remain unchanged. Veterans who migrated between state of birth and state of enlistment arguably have a taste for moving, but when we control for whether a veteran was a previous migrant, our postwar migration results remain unchanged.

Deserters' greater mobility does not reflect legal sanctions in their states or other conditions in the states, counties, or companies they were from. All our regressions include state of origin. When we control for county of origin, we still find that deserters were more likely to migrate out of state than nondeserters. When we control for company, we still find that deserters were more likely to migrate than nondeserters. We find no evidence that state laws disenfranchising deserters influenced their move either away from or to a state.

Deserters' location choice in 1880 does not reflect their efforts to avoid detection during the war. Roughly 75 percent of returnees had been arrested. But McClellan's share of the vote was a poor predictor of which deserters were returnees, suggesting that there was no difference in detection rates in pro-McClellan and pro-Lincoln counties.

Were deserters somehow more alienated from the civilian population? Although this is possible, we would expect alienation where soldiers and civilians disagreed on the war. Soldiers swore in their letters home that they would ostracize or even shoot Peace Democrats. A farmer's son in the Ninety-fourth Ohio wrote to his mother, "I shall never want to see any of my relations that worked against me while I was in the surves." A private in the 114th Ohio expressed his disagreement with his childhood friend's Peace Democrat politics by writing, "I would rather be at home killing Such men as you and Some of your comrades. . . . if I live to get home [you'll see] if I don't Shoot there hearts out So help me God. . . . I tell you that you could Stay about my house no longer than I could raise my foot and kick you out."[42] In Montgomery County, Pennsylvania, the home of William Howe, the soldier executed after the arresting officer was murdered, the soldier vote was 368 for Lincoln and 171 for McClellan. The civilian vote was 6,504 for Lincoln and 7,772 for McClellan.[43] If returning soldiers were estranged from the civilian population, it was not enough to lead nondeserters to leave pro-McClellan states or counties.

Why, then, did deserters move, and why were they more likely to move if they were from a pro-war county? We are left with shame and community ostracism as the only potential explanations. The "action tendency" of shame is to hide or disappear.[44] Ostracism would only reinforce the effects of shame. Shame, like all emotions, is unobservable and therefore rarely studied by economists. We can study it because we can observe whether men hid and disappeared.

Deserters in Civil War Memory

Diaries, letters, and newspaper accounts from the antebellum era have not left a paper trail of how deserters fared after the war. Our unique panel data set allows us to discover that faced with the choice of returning home or of moving and reinventing themselves, deserters moved. Deserters from pro-war communities were more likely to move than deserters from antiwar communities, and when deserters moved they were more likely to move to antiwar states.

Economists rarely rely on psychological theories to explain differences in patterns of behavior. Even with living subjects it is difficult to establish whether, let alone which, specific emotions led to an action. We argue that shame can explain (1) why deserters were more likely to migrate away from their homes than nondeserters and returned deserters, (2) why deserters from pro-war communities were relatively more likely to migrate than deserters from antiwar communities, and (3) why deserters were less likely to be found in the 1880 census than nondeserters and returnees.

It may be no accident that the fate of deserters is not mentioned in contemporary accounts. In countries making a transition to democratic rule, there is a desire to avoid painful confrontations after traumatic national events, particularly if a sizable proportion of the population behaved shamefully.[45] Psychologists have suggested that when current attitudes clash with past attitudes, people will bias their memories by forgetting their original stance and presuming that their opinions have not altered.[46] Transitions are also accompanied by the creation of national epics that provide legitimization for the creation of a new state and national identity.[47] After World War II, all Frenchmen became members of the Resistance and punished collaborators with executions and public humiliations. But at most 2 percent of adult Frenchmen were members of the French Resistance, and one estimate suggests that the number of real resisters was scarcely more than the number who volunteered for the French Gestapo.[48] The East German demonstrations of late 1989 were hailed as leading to the downfall of the communist regime. Although the majority of East Germans had publicly conformed to state policies for 40 years, many began to consider themselves as always having been active opponents of the Communist Party. Even many who had worked as informers remembered their activities as harmless until confronted with their secret police files.[49]

Former Confederate guerrilla leader John Mosby wrote to a member of his battalion in 1902, "Men fight from sentiment. After the fight is over they invent some fanciful theory on which they imagine that they fought."[50] The national myth created after the Civil War was one of sacrifice by both sides, to the "last full measure of devotion." With such myths, Ella Lonn could write in 1928 of her book on desertion, "the few remaining survivors of the struggle, Northern as well as Southern, will be repelled by the very subject of this book; probably the average reader will question the worth-whileness of an exhaustive study of that which seems to record a nation's shame."[51]

CHAPTER 7

Slaves Become Freemen

WARTIME EXPERIENCE CAN RADICALLY ALTER THE COURSE of a person's life. For example, service in World War II and the Vietnam War lowered later earnings because of lost labor market experience,[1] whereas employment during mobilization for World War II permanently raised women's labor force participation rates[2] and lowered both men's and women's wages because of the increase in women's labor supply.

Less is known about the effects of previous wars. Brevet Major General Alving C. Voris wrote that the Civil War "has greatly interrupted my line of business."[3] A white officer of the colored troops wrote,

Entering the army at nineteen, with neither education completed nor trade learned, and coming out at twenty-four without trade or profession or capital, and with a wife to support; with habits of spending formed in the extravagance that prevailed in the army, bringing as almost the sole advantage from those years a sense of self-reliance, I feel increasingly the extent of the sacrifice made by myself and so many thousands of other youth who gave their years of seeding time to their country.[4]

Other soldiers, particularly those who survived with their health intact, may have gained from their Civil War service because it exposed them to a much broader world. This may have been particularly true for black soldiers, most of whom were illiterate ex-slaves. Henry Adams, who later became known as a political organizer, in September 1866 enlisted in the army, where he learned to read and write:

> I could not read a bit. I knowed the letters when I seed them, but I could not put them together under no circumstances. We had a teacher when we were stationed at Fort Jackson, in Louisiana. She was a white lady, Mrs. Bentine, and we had a school for the soldiers, and we had three hours a day to go to the school. I never went all that time, but only part of the time; and I learned to read and write a little in one month's time; and after I quit her I never went only two weeks more. . . . I acquired all the rest myself.[5]

Barney Stone, who ran away from a Kentucky plantation to join the Union army and later became a prominent preacher, told an interviewer,

> I joined that Union army and served one year, eight months and twenty-two days, and fought with them in the battle of Fort Wagnor, and also in the battle of

Milikin's Bend. When I went into the army, I could not read or write. The white soldiers took an interest in me and taught me to write and read, and when the war was over I could write a very good letter. I taught what little I knew to colored children after the war.[6]

In his study of black postwar political leadership in South Carolina, Holt argued that the army served as a leadership school and led veterans to settle in new states:

Twenty-four of the Negro legislators had records of military service, and two-thirds of them were either officers (2) or noncommissioned officers (12). Some of the state's top political leaders in future years— William James Whipper, Benjamin A. Bosemon, Stephen A. Swails—were northern-born Negroes brought to the state by the army. . . . The native ex-soldiers gained other advantages from their military experiences. Some received their first formal education while in the army; others received an education in human relationships that was less formal but perhaps just as important to their personal and political development.[7]

The former slaves and free northern blacks who became political leaders were exceptions. In South Carolina, many of the former slaves who became legislators had been trained as artisans.[8] But only 4 percent of the slaves who enlisted as soldiers were artisans; 90 percent were field hands, and, among the ex-slaves who survived to 1900, most remained in agriculture. Among the free blacks who enlisted as soldiers, almost 90 percent were subsistence farmers or laborers, and by 1900 three-quarters of all surviving free blacks were subsistence farmers or laborers.

The postwar experiences of veterans in many ways mirrored those of the rest of the population. African Americans, both veterans and nonveterans, migrated to large cities, particularly within the South, in the first postbellum wave of black migration. By 1910, 26 percent of veterans living in the South were in an urban area, whereas 22 percent of nonveterans in the same age group were in an urban area. Discrimination and high illiteracy rates hindered movement up the occupational ladder for both veterans and nonveterans. Susie King Taylor and her husband returned to Savannah after the war, and even though he was a "boss carpenter," "being just mustered out of the army, and the prejudice against his race being still too strong to insure him much work at his trade, he took contracts for unloading vessels."[9] Although both Susie King Taylor and her husband were literate, in 1910 only a quarter of Southern blacks of the Civil War generation were able to write. Around 1900, 41 percent of black veterans were farmers and 11 percent were professionals, proprietors, or artisans. Among black nonveterans, 49 percent were farmers and 8 percent were professionals, proprietors, or artisans.[10]

The effect of wartime service on a black soldier depended on who his peers and his commanding officer were and where his regiment traveled. From his comrades and his travels, a man could learn of economic opportunities in states he had never lived in. A former slave who enlisted in Georgia followed his regiment up north and remained there: "Shortly after this our regiment and the Second Minnesota, Col. Uline, went to Pittsburg, then down to Louisville, then to Chicago, where the Indiana regiment was mustered out. I then went with the Second Minnesota to Fort Snelling, where I hired out to E. B. Whitcher, who kept a livery stable in St. Paul."[11] Frank Williams of Arkansas told an interviewer, "Mississippi was my home. I come up here with the Yankees and I ain't never been back since."[12] Peers differed in place of birth, age, and slave status. Slaves brought into contact with free black men might be more likely to learn how to read and might be more likely to forge a new identity by abandoning their slave names. Contemporary observers wrote that former slaves fitted in Union blue were "completely metamorphosed, not only in appearance and dress, but also in character and relations," and that once in uniform "the *chattel* is a *man*."[13]

Black Soldiers after the War

The recorded life of former slaves began with enlistment because slaves were not individually enumerated in the census. The enlistment records provide information about age and place of birth, sometimes the name of the master, and information on wartime experience—illnesses, wounds, promotions, length of service, desertions, AWOLs, and leaves. From official war records we know where a regiment traveled and what engagements it fought in. After the war, pension and census records reveal the life histories of men—where they lived, what they did for a living, when they married, when their children were born, and when they and their family members died. Our analysis is based on information on residence, writing ability, and name changes in the pension records because at the time

Plate 10. Photographs of Private Hubbard Pryor before (*above*) and after (*right*) his enlistment in the 44th Colored US Troops on October 10, 1864

of writing, census information was not yet available. We see writing ability and name changes for anyone who ever applied for a pension. Because most men entered the pension rolls after the passage of the 1890 pension law, we examine men's residential moves between enlistment and circa 1900. We estimate models of the probability of migration, writing ability, and name change, controlling for company and individual characteristics. We then show how our predicted probabilities would change under different company characteristics. We also estimate models in which we predict a soldier's probability of moving to a particular state.[14]

Migration

Comrades might be either sources of information on a new locality or sources of assistance, in the form of housing or jobs, after the war. Accounts of veterans' lives discuss how soldiers formed political networks. Henry Adams and other ex-soldiers formed a committee that organized Republican clubs and advised voters.[15] Less is known about mutual help networks, but at least in the North, the Grand Army of the Republic provided a formal venue. Susie King Taylor's interest "in the boys in blue" never abated, "whether they were black or white." "My hands have never left undone anything they could do towards their aid and comfort in the twilight of their lives." She "helped to organize Corps 67, Women's Relief Corps, auxiliary to the G.A.R." and later became president of the corps.[16]

Company diversity during wartime is associated with postwar migration. Forty-two percent of all black soldiers moved to another state between enlistment and 1900, but men from companies with greater birthplace diversity were more likely to move. In the most diverse company in our sample, Company G of the Twenty-fifth USCT, 61 percent of the men in the sample moved to another state and in Company I of the 118th USCT, where most men were born in Kentucky and a few in Virginia, only 24 percent of the men moved to another state. These effects persist even when we control for other company characteristics and for veterans' individual characteristics. Figure 7.1 shows predicted state migration probabilities for given levels of birthplace diversity. Company G of the Twenty-fifth USCT has the highest predicted state migration levels, and Company I of the 118th USCT, the company of Zack and Harrison Osborne from Kentucky, among the lowest. The men in John Cumbash's company (Company F, First USCT) had relatively high predicted migration rates and the men in Joseph Hall's company (Company D, Fifty-third USCT), most of whom were from Mississippi, had somewhat lower migration rates. Soldiers were more likely to move at least 239 km, the minimum moving distance for the most mobile quartile of state movers, if they were from companies whose birthplace diversity was higher.

Soldiers were more likely to move to a new region if they had traveled through it during the war. Some men simply remained in the state where they were discharged. Hannah Brooks Wright recalled that her father "was a private and mustered out at DeVells Bluff, Arkansas. That is how come my mother to come here [Arkansas]."[17] Abraham Barnett was born in Virginia and enlisted in Company F, First USCT, at Mason's Island, an island in the Potomac across from Georgetown. He was discharged in North Carolina; he and seven other men in his company remained there. Abraham married shortly after

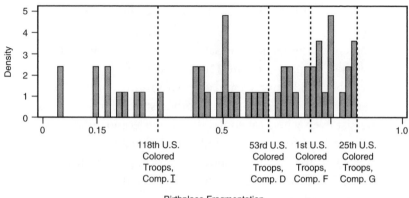

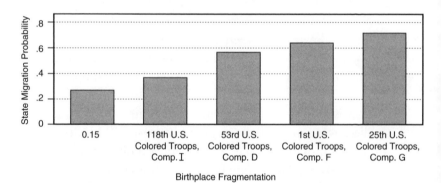

Figure 7.1. Birthplace Diversity and Predicted Probability of Post-war State Migration

The greater the birthplace fragmentation, the greater is birthplace diversity within a company. Birthplace fragmentation is measured as one minus the share of men in each company born in each state, squared. The top panel indicates the distribution of birthplace diversity within companies in the sample. The density gives the probability that the specified values of birthplace diversity will occur. The bottom panel gives the predicted probabilities of state migration if all men had been in companies with a given level of birthplace diversity. See note 14 for details about the statistical model.

discharge and by 1870 had two children. He remained an illiterate day laborer until his death in 1906. On average, traveling to a new region (defined as one of the nine census regions) increased the probability of a move across census regions by 0.13, if we control for individual and company characteristics.

Soldiers from rural areas were more likely to move to a large city if they had traveled to a city during the war or if a larger fraction of the men in their companies had enlisted in a large city. Men from Company G, Twenty-fifth USCT, were scattered in cities such as New York, Washington, Brooklyn, Philadelphia, Detroit, Memphis, Cincinnati, and Indianapolis by 1900. Their company had been to New Orleans during the war. Almost a third of the men in the company had enlisted in a large city, and about half of these men remained in one. But even among the men who had not enlisted in a large city, one-quarter had moved to one by 1900. The move to large cities occurred even among men who had had no experience of city life and who had had no comrades with experience of city life. Nevertheless, the frequency of moves was lower. No one in Company D, Fifty-third USCT, enlisted in a large city, and the regiment remained in predominantly rural areas. Roughly one-fifth of the men moved to a large city later. When we control for individual and company characteristics, travel with the regiment to a large city increased the probability of a subsequent move to a large city by 30 percent, and a standard deviation increase in the fraction of the company enlisting in a large city increased the probability of such a move by 12 percent.

Push factors may also have influenced soldiers' migration decisions. Black former soldiers and their families were targets of mob anger in the South because, in the words of one former black chaplain, he was "looked upon as a runaway 'nigger' who has been fighting against his old master and now returns full of impudent notions of a freeman."[18] Rhoda Ann Childs was raped and beaten, and one of the men "Swore they ought to Shoot me, as my husband had been in the 'God damned Yankee Army,' and Swore they meant to kill every black Son-of-a-bitch they could find that had ever fought against them."[19] Henry Adams was discharged in Shreveport, Louisiana, in 1869. He reported, "After we had been there [Shreveport] a few months the white people began saying they were going to kill us; to kill all the discharged negro soldiers; that these discharged men were going to spoil all the other negroes, so that whites could do nothing with them."[20] When Susie King Taylor traveled to Shreveport in 1898 to care for a dying son, the city was calmer, but she "met several comrades, white and colored, there, and noticed that the colored comrades did not wear their buttons. I asked one of them why this was, and was told, should they wear it, they could not get work."[21]

Whites responded to the extension of suffrage to blacks with organized campaigns of violence. A widow recounted, "They made me and my children wrap our heads up in bed-quilts and come out of the house, and they then set it on fire, burning it up, and my husband in it, and all we had. . . . They killed him because he refused to resign his office as constable to which he was elected on the Republican ticket."[22] In Natchitoches Parish, Louisiana, in 1878 badges marked "voted the Democratic ticket" were pinned to black voters to protect them from roving mobs who attacked those who had not "voted right."[23] With the removal of Union troops from the South in 1877, violence was greatest in areas where there was a large black Republican constituency—the Deep South, particularly South Carolina, Alabama, Mississippi, and Louisiana, but also areas of North Carolina and Texas.[24] The threat of violence extended to white employers who hired "Republican" blacks. When Henry Adams lost his job, his boss told him, "Adams, I think a heap of you as a man; I know you are a true man, and that you will do what you promise to do, but under this order [from the White League] I cannot employ you. . . .You are a good old Republican, and I cannot employ you because you are a Republican. I cannot employ you no more."[25]

African Americans escaped Klan-style vigilantism by moving to cities or different states, or by seeking the protection of a large planter. Henry Pyles's step-father, Jordan, a veteran active in Republican Party politics in Tennessee, was "tied with a rope and walked along on de ground betwixt two horses" by "'bout 20 bushwhackers in Sesesh clothes":

> Old Master knowed all of then. . . . "Whar you taking my nigger!" Old Master say . . . "He ain't your nigger no more—you know that," old Captain Taylor holler back. "He jest as such my nigger as that Taylor nigger was your nigger, and you ain't laid hand on him! Now you jest have pity on my nigger!" "Your nigger Jordan been in de Yankee army, and he was in de battle at Fort Piller and help kill our white folks, and you know it!" Old Captain Taylor say, and argue on like that, but old Master jest take hold his bridle and shake his head. "No. Clay", he say, "that boy maybe didn't kill Confederates, but you and him both know my two boys killed plenty Yankees, and you forgot I lost one of my boys in de War. Ain't that enough to

pay for letting my nigger alone?" And old Captain Taylor give the word to turn Jordan loose, and they rid on down de road. That's one reason my step-daddy never did leave old Master's place, and I stayed on dere till I was grown and had children.[26]

Violence, disenfranchisement, lack of civil rights, and low levels of spending on education and welfare led to the dependence of blacks and poor whites on the white, rural elite.[27]

The majority of southern blacks remained tied to the white rural elite until the Great Migration of the 1940s, but some of them moved to other states or cities. Blacks calling themselves "Exodusters" moved west to Kansas and Indiana. After 1889, when suffrage restrictions were further tightened and funding for black schools declined, blacks migrated to Kansas, Arkansas, Texas, and Oklahoma.[28] J. C. Embry, an elder in the African Methodist Episcopal Church, who had moved to Kansas from Mississippi wrote to Senator Blanche K. Bruce, "I shall return to the south in a few days. Whether I shall stay there till after the campaign & election will depend upon the attitude of the administration towards us in that section. If those fellows are to be allowed to arm and persecute us at pleasure as they have done the past season [1875], we must all of necessity soon abandon the state & the south entirely."[29] Assassinations of prominent black political leaders and violence in Louisiana parishes led to black leaders moving to New Orleans.[30] In large cities, Klan vigilantism was less common. In the countryside blacks lived in relatively small groups on plantations and farms and could not defend themselves.[31]

The Republican Party was the party of Reconstruction. According to one black politician in South Carolina, "The condition of the south made it as natural for the Negro to be a Republican as for the young of animals to follow their parents."[32] In states with large white majorities such as Texas, the Democrats regained control of the state simply by mobilizing white voters in 1873. In other states, fraud, voter intimidation, and violence ended Reconstruction. In Alabama in 1874, armed bands prevented blacks from casting their votes. In 1875, Mississippi was "redeemed" after a campaign of violence in which black leaders, including schoolteachers, ministers, and local Republican Party leaders, were murdered. When the Republican governor asked for federal troops to quell the violence, President Grant refused because "The whole public are tired out with these annual autumnal outbreaks in the South . . . [and] are ready now to condemn any interference on the part of the government."[33]

In South Carolina, the Democrats hoped to split the black vote along class lines—in Charleston (as was true in New Orleans) the elite free mulattoes had been slave owners and had lost both property and status with Union victory.[34] By 1876, South Carolina, Louisiana, and Florida remained the only states under Republican rule, and both parties claimed to have carried these states in the 1876 election. The Democrats agreed not to contest the election of Republican Rutherford B. Hayes if Hayes recognized the Democrats' control of the South and did not interfere in southern affairs. In 1877, Hayes withdrew federal troops from the South, and the Democrats seized control of the governorships of Louisiana and South Carolina.[35]

We find some support for the hypothesis that blacks were pushed out of some states. Republican strength in

1880 is a measure of black enfranchisement without the support of federal troops. James Garfield, the Republican presidential candidate (and election winner), did not carry any states in the former Confederacy, but he received more than 40 percent of the vote in Florida, North Carolina, and Tennessee and got at least 35 percent of the vote in Alabama, Arkansas, Louisiana, and Virginia. Among men who enlisted in the former Confederacy, those who enlisted in states where Garfield received a larger share of the vote in 1880 were less likely to move across state lines. A one percentage point increase in Garfield's share of the vote lowered men's probability of migration by four percentage points. Veterans were more likely to leave states where they were harassed.

What determined the state a veteran moved to? Conditional on moving across states between enlistment and 1900 (as was true for 891 men), veterans were more likely to move to a state where they had traveled during the war or where a large fraction of the men in their company had come from. A veteran's odds of moving to a state was 1.4 times higher if his regiment had passed through that state than if it had not. An increase of 0.1 in the fraction of men in the company from a particular state increased the odds that a veteran would move to that state by 0.3. A higher black population share increased the odds of a veteran moving there, but not at the level of statistical significance. Veterans were more likely to move to a nearby state.

The effect of the fraction of men in the company from a state on the probability of moving to that state was smaller if the veteran could write, perhaps because veterans who could write were less dependent on their comrades for information about localities. For the illiterate, an increase of 0.1 in the fraction of men in the company from a particular state raised the odds of moving to that state by 0.32. In contrast, for the literate such an increase in the fraction of men in the company from a particular state raised the odds of their moving to that state by 0.29. Both the illiterate and the literate were more likely to move to a state with a larger black population, but the effect was slightly greater for the illiterate. Networks of friends may have been more important for the illiterate. In contrast to the literacy results, there were no differential effects by slave status.

White soldiers' migration decisions were also affected by their wartime service. The farther in the South a veteran had traveled while in the service, the higher the probability that he would migrate to the South. Among migrants to the South, veterans who had been to a state while in the service were more likely to move to that state.[36]

Literacy

The newly freed slaves were for the most part illiterate. John Ogee, who had been a slave in Louisiana, told a WPA interviewer, "I nevah fin' any nigger befo' d' war dat coul' read."[37] Most of the former slaves remained illiterate. J. T. Tims, a 12-year-old servant in the Union army during the Civil War, went to school in Natchez, Mississippi, after the war, but "I didn't get no further than the second grads [grade]. I stopped school to go work when the teacher went back to Chicago. After that I went to work in the field and made me a living."[38] More than 85 percent of southern-born black men and women of the Civil War generation were illiterate in 1870. Illiteracy rates for the free blacks of the North were considerably lower, on the order of 40 percent, but still much higher than the 10 percent observed among whites.[39] A sergeant of the Fifty-fifth Massachusetts Infantry wrote to The Liberator, "I find that there are not a few in the regiment, who, although never having been slaves, are unable to write their names, and many are unable to read."[40]

The sergeant of the Fifty-fifth Massachusetts went on to add, "A year's experience in the army has shown most of them the disadvantage of being dependent upon others to do their writing and reading of letters; and they are now applying themselves assiduously with spelling book, pen, ink, and paper." In his regiment, "Two large tents have been erected and floored adjoining each other, making a room some 45 by 25 feet, with suitable desks and benches for furniture. Evening schools have been established. The valuable accessions to the reading matter of the regiment, recently received from Massachusetts, have given us quite a library."[41] In Col. Samuel C. Armstrong's camp (Eighth USCI), school was open four hours a day. Col. Thomas Morgan, organizer of the Forty-second and Forty-fourth USCI, established "in every company a regular school, teaching men to read and write."[42]

Education in camps was haphazard and depended on the support of officers and the initiative of the soldiers. Officers set up schools to prepare men for life in the liberated South, to turn them into socially responsible citizens, to make them better Christians, and to increase military effectiveness. Soldiers had to rely on their often faulty memories to establish who was a member of each relief party for guard duty. Without literate noncommissioned officers who could act as clerks for routine tasks such as writing out the company sick list, officers had a greater administrative burden.[43] Col. Charles Francis Adams, Jr., hoped that the Union army would "become for the black race, a school for skilled labor and of self-reliance as well as an engine of war."[44] Rev. Samuel Colt, corresponding secretary of the General Assembly of the Presbyterian Church of the United States, offered President Lincoln aid from his church to open "camp schools during the winter for the freedmen soldiers" to turn them into "better soldiers and better men" and to "fit them to become safe and useful members of the community after their military service honorably ceases."[45] Jonathan J. Wright, a black northern minister sent to the South, not only taught reading, writing, arithmetic, and geography but also gave lectures titled "You are no longer slaves, but freemen, show it to be so," "Arise and shine for your light has come," and "Avoid the great *evil* intemperance." [46] Chaplain Charles Buckley viewed the ability to read the Holy Scriptures as "the basis of an intelligent Christian faith."[47]

The camp teachers were chaplains, sympathetic officers, officers' wives, Yankee "schoolmarms" who taught black children by day and soldiers by night, delegates from the U.S. Christian Commission, and literate black soldiers and their wives. Nearly every northern church helped support Christian missionaries and teachers, generally white men and women.[48] Jonathan J. Wright, assigned to the 128th Regiment, described his days: "I have three hours each day to teach in my regiment, the rest of the day is spent among the people teaching them, how to do business, and sustain themselves. Three evenings of the week are spent teaching a class of adults at my room. Thursday evening I lecture at the AME [African Methodist Episcopal] Church."[49] Susie King Taylor "taught a great many of the comrades in Company E to read and write, when they were off duty. Nearly all were anxious to learn. My husband [a sergeant] taught some also when it was convenient for him."[50] But, as Col. Thomas Wentworth Higginson noted, "the alphabet must always be very incidental business in a camp."[51] School was for leisure hours. Fatigue and camp duties kept soldiers occupied, and during military campaigns formal schoolhouses had to be abandoned.

Officers without abolitionist tendencies did not look upon schooling sympathetically. Chaplain Corydon Millerd complained to the U.S. adjutant general that he could not provide his men with an education because all the soldiers' leisure time was spent building comfortable quarters for officers.[52] Col. Lauriston Whipple closed the school in his camp because the teachers, "persons not assigned by law to the organization," could make the men "feel that their duties are irksome and needless."[53] Even in the abolitionist Fifty-fifth Massachusetts, Lt. Col. Charles Fox became very closely involved in the management of the school lest it interfere with military discipline because "the old proverb about giving an inch and taking an ell grows more true as education less perfect, and judgement less acute."[54]

Literate soldiers may have been the most effective teachers, because they shared a common background with their pupils. They assisted northern teachers in a formal setting—one assistant established four schools at Hilton Head, South Carolina, before joining the Union army. Literate soldiers also provided one-on-one tutoring during routine duties and during leisure time. Soldiers kept their spelling books attached to their belts and would study them while on fatigue, picket, or even guard duty.[55] Sgt. Milton Harris praised the teaching of sympathetic officers but pointed out that educational attainment in one company "improved a great deal by the teaching of the sergeant of that company, Lewis Willis."[56] Wilson argued that most "of the learning that took place went on outside the classroom while the soldiers were performing monotonous military tasks, such as picket and fatigue duty, or during off-duty hours."[57] Glatthaar, however, viewed the "military structure as providing a good atmosphere for instruction, and although other duties sometimes upset the academic schedule, the desires of black soldiers and the commitment of their white officers more than compensated for the interference."[58] Both Wilson and Glatthaar based their assessments on their readings of letters and memoirs, but letters and memoirs do not necessarily represent the experiences of a random sample of the population. We therefore turn to the evidence from our random sample of companies.

The former slaves in our random sample were more likely to be able to write after the war if they were in a company with a large fraction of free blacks. Zack and Harrison Osborne were in a company (Company I, 118th USCI) where only 1 percent of the men had been free. They never learned to write, and only 16 percent of the former slaves in their company ever did. In Company G of the Twenty-fifth USCI, 81 percent of the men were free, and 30 percent of the former slaves learned to write. Half of the former slaves in Company F, First USCI, learned to write, and 17 percent of the men were free. The percentage of a company that was free was not the only factor in learning to write. Controlling for all individual and company characteristics, we predict that if in all companies 17 percent of the men were free, 23 percent of the former slaves would know how to write after the war, and that if 81 percent of the men were free, 28 percent of the former slaves would know how to write (see figure 7.2). A standard deviation increase in the fraction

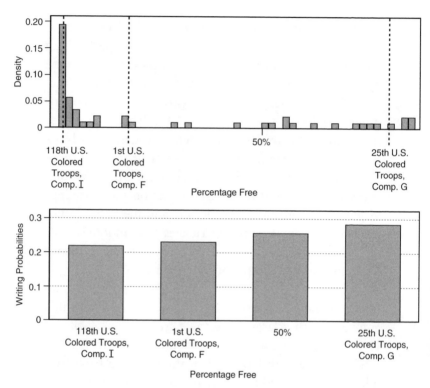

Figure 7.2. Percentage of the Company That Was Free and Predicted Probability of Writing Ability

The top panel indicates the distribution of the percent free within a company in the sample. The density gives the probability that the specified values of percent free will occur. The bottom panel gives the predicted probabilities of writing ability if all men had been in companies with a given level of percent free. See note 14 for details about the statistical model.

of the company that was free increased the probability that a veteran could write by 0.28, an increase of 108 percent. This is probably an underestimate of the true effect; if charitable organizations focused their efforts on slave units, we would expect that slaves would benefit from being with other slaves. Because free blacks were more likely to be able to write, comrades may have been a valuable educational resource for slaves. Former slaves were more likely to be literate if they served longer. An additional hundred days spent in the army increased the probability that a veteran could write by 0.21.[59]

Whether or not any commanding officer in the regiment had abolitionist tendencies (as assessed by our reading of primary and secondary sources) had no effect on the literacy of slaves. In contrast, for the free blacks, having an abolitionist officer increased postwar writing ability.

For illiterate slaves, writing was a sign of a new identity. Soldiers who could sign the payroll rather than making the "slave's mark" were civilized and self-reliant men. Another way for a soldier to form a new, freeman's identity was to abandon his slave name.

A New Name

Slaves generally enlisted under their master's last name. Owned by John Osborne, Zack and Harrison enlisted as Osborne and remained Osborne until their deaths in the late 1910s. Abraham, owned by Bob Pendleton and Thomas Murden, used both masters' names while in the service but later took the last name of his father, Barnett. Most slaves who changed their names took those of their father, even if their father's name was the name of his master, because freemen inherited their fathers' names.[60] There were exceptions. Abbie Lindsay told a WPA interviewer,

> My father was named Alec Summerville. He named himself after the Civil War. They were going around

letting the people choose their names. He had belonged to Alec Watts; but when they allowed him to select his own name after the war, he called himself Summerville after the town Summerville (Somerville), Alabama. His mother was named Charlotte Dantzler. She was born in North Carolina. John Haynes bought her and brought her to Arkansas. My father was an overseer's child. You know they whipped people in those days and forced them. That is why he didn't go by the name of Watts after he got free and could select his own name.[61]

Even free blacks sometimes changed their names. Omelia Thomas's father, a free black in a slave state, "was George Grant. . . . My father has said that he was really named George LeGrande. But after he enlisted in the War, he went by the name of George Grant. There was one of the officers by that name, and he took it too."[62]

In our ex-slave sample, a larger share of free blacks in the company led the former slaves to abandon their slave names, if we control for individual and company characteristics. Zack and Harrison Osborne were in a company where only 1 percent of the soldiers were free blacks. Abraham Pendleton or Murden, later Barnett, was in a company where 17 percent of the men were free. When we examine the 576 former slaves who had a last name that was the name of their master and for whom we have fairly complete records, we find that 32 percent of them changed their last name after the war. Seventeen percent of free blacks changed their names, but company characteristics did not predict name changes among free blacks. For the small set of men whose fathers' names were mentioned in the pension records, we are able to determine that most men who changed their last names took their fathers' surnames. Name changes were not statistically significant predictors of either postwar migration or writing ability. Even so, the magnitude of the coefficients suggests that former slaves who had rejected their masters' surnames were more likely to migrate across states and were more likely to write.

Remembering the Civil War

In black memory, the Civil War remained a war for freedom. African-American soldiers had "washed the blood scars of slavery out of the American flag, and painted freedom there; they snatched black lies out of every false star upon its folds and set in their stead the diadem of liberty. . . . They tore the Dred Scott decision from the statutes, and wrote there, 'All men are equal before God.'"[63] Christian Fleetwood, winner of a Congressional Medal of Honor and someone who "led an active social life, always in the best society,"[64] lamented white America's "absolute effacement of remembrance of the gallant deeds done for the country by its brave black defenders."[65] By the 1930s, this effacement led WPA interviewers to search for black Confederates. It also led to edited versions of interviews that deleted comments such as those of Ann Edwards, a minister's wife and the adopted daughter of a Reconstruction Congressman, "I knew there was a conflict taking place and a war waging that was taking thousands of lives, and that my race was the main cause, and I knew that the outcome of the conflict would determine the status of the negroes,"[66] because the

Plate 11. Negro Grand Army of the Republic (G.A.R.) veterans parading, New York City, May 30, 1912

historiography of the time no longer viewed slavery as a cause of the Civil War.

Was the Civil War a war for freedom only for the black elite? Arey Lemar who enlisted at age 15 and then "went back and stayed 45 years on the Lambert place," told a WPA interviewer that "I aint seen but mighty little difference since freedom."[67] For a former slave, a dramatic, observable life change would be abandoning one's slave name, a change in residence, and becoming literate. Because we have the full life histories of men and because men in each of the fifty-one companies in our data set experienced a different set of peers and because each of the thirty-nine regiments in our data set had a different set of leaders and traveled to different places, we are able to demonstrate that the Civil War was a catalyst for change. War experiences changed the lives of both ex-slaves and free blacks. Although we found in chapter 4 that soldiers, whether white or black, deserted when in companies with men who did not look like them, in the long run they benefited from being in a diverse company.

Participation in the Civil War may have both magnified the initial differences between slaves and free blacks and created the necessary conditions that allowed the descendants of slaves to catch up to the descendants of free blacks. It took two generations for the descendants of slaves to catch up in literacy, occupation, and children's school attendance.[68] The majority of northern free blacks had served, whereas only a fraction of blacks in the former slave states had been in military service. Free blacks therefore disproportionately benefited from knowledge of migration opportunities learned from comrades or from travel and from educational programs set up by abolitionist officers. Still, the war exposed some former slaves to new social interactions, allowing them to learn of migration opportunities, to learn how to write, and to adopt a free black's identity. Slaves who had served in the Union army in turn may have paved the way in turn for other ex-slaves, by helping them to adjust to freedom and to migrate from rural to urban areas.

CHAPTER 8

Learning from the Past

"I MYSELF AM AS BIG A COWARD AS ENY COULD BE," wrote a survivor of the Battle of the Wilderness, Spotsylvania, Cold Harbor, and Petersburg, "but me the ball [bullet] before the coward when all my friends and comrades are going forward. Once and once only was I behind when the regt was under fire, and I cant describe my feelings at that time none can tell them only a soldier. I was not able to walk . . . but as soon as the rattle of musketry was heard and I knew my Regt was engaged I hobbled on the field and went to them."[1] Sergeant Jeffs of the Fifty-fourth Massachusetts remained with his men in a prison camp even though he could have passed as white and been paroled. When Sergeant Charles L. Sumbardo of the Twelfth Iowa and other prisoners were to be exchanged, "every man that could walk responded. One prisoner carried his friend, who was a living skeleton, on his back; when changing cars we could see that faithful friend carrying his invalid companion. At Columbia, S.C., we must have marched nearly two miles from one road to another . . . amid the constant displays of selfishness he seemed to me the true hero of our prison days."[2]

Our analysis of the records of more than 40,000 Union army soldiers has shown that social networks affected men's desertion decisions during the war and their migration choices after the war. Social networks helped men survive the horrific conditions of POW camps and increased their literacy rates. There were no desertions from Company D, Thirty-sixth Massachusetts, the company of Adams E. French and James Monroe and Robert Rich, in large part because it was "a compact and homogeneous body of men." Henry Havens might have survived Andersonville if he had not entered the prison alone. After deserting from the army, Daniel Mulholland returned to his hometown of New York City and George Farrell left upper New York State partially because Daniel's home community was antiwar and George's was prowar. John Nelson Cumbash moved to Baltimore and then to Philadelphia after enlisting near Washington, D.C., perhaps because he had learned about these cities from men in his company who came from them. Almost a fifth of the men in his company were free blacks, and they taught their ex-slave comrades to read and write.

The study of social networks dates to the late 1800s.[3] Empirical work on social networks began in the early twentieth century. In the 1930s J. L. Moreno pioneered the study of social interactions through observation in small groups such as classrooms and work groups. Work by Warner, Mayo, Roethlisberger, and Dickson on the Hawthorne plant of the Western Electric Company in Chicago in the 1920s began as a study of how alterations in the physical conditions of work such as lighting, heat-ing, and rest periods affected worker productivity. (They argued that any change led to higher productivity perhaps because workers enjoyed the attention.) This work turned them into anthropologists of the firm, and they simply watched and observed how social interactions between workers affected productivity. In the 1950s and 1960s British anthropologists such as Elizabeth Bott and Max Gluckman examined kinship and community networks in Africa, India, and the United Kingdom. Also in the 1950s Coleman, Katz, and Menzel found that doctors who had lots of friends were more likely to adopt tetracycline (an antibiotic) and to adopt it earlier. The 1960s and 1970s saw additional studies of how information diffuses through social networks. In 1969 Lee found that a woman searching for an abortionist (when abortion was illegal) had to ask only three people to find one. In 1974 Granovetter's surveys showed people obtained jobs through accidental contacts with others, mainly acquaintances.

There is still great interest in the impact of social networks on our lives. Research on terrorist organizations indicates that friends and relatives join together and work together. By one estimate, roughly three-quarters of *mujahedin* joined the global Salafi Jihad (of which Al Qaeda is a part) either as a group with friends or relatives or as men with close social ties to members.[4] Seventy percent of captured Italian Red Brigade terrorists had joined a friend who was in the terrorist organization—a next-door neighbor, a school friend with whom he or she had spent vacations, or a cousin who belonged to the same voluntary association."[5] Social bonds, not a shared terrorist ideology, drove the decision to join. The ideology came later.[6] In the case of suicide bombers, this loyalty to individuals is used by organizations to cultivate a mutual commitment to die. The video testament seals this social contract.[7] As the father of a candy seller linked to the 2004 Madrid train bombings said, "It's the problem of friends. If you're friends with a good person, you're good. If your friend is a pickpocket, you become a pickpocket."[8]

There is now greater recognition of how hard it is to identify the impact of social networks. The early research on social networks was observational and not the product of controlled experiments. Early adopters of tetracycline might be more energetic individuals and more energetic individuals may also have more friends. It has become harder to identify the impact of social networks in the modern economy. Researchers examining peer effects today face the challenge of identifying who a person's peers are. When the car has become the dominant mode of transport and much communication is through the Internet, next-door neighbors are no longer necessarily peers. People can pick and choose their peers. A unique feature of our work is that we can identify men's networks—during wartime the company was the community, and except for a few furloughs, men lived with their comrades 24 hours a day.

Researchers studying peer effects today have had to resort to great creativity to avoid confounding genuine peer effects with the effects of like sorting with like. Random assignment of first-year roommates at Dartmouth College demonstrates that peers determine levels of academic effort and decisions to join social groups such as fraternities or sororities.[9] The employment outcomes of roommates are correlated, and students networking with fraternity and sorority members and alumni are the most likely to obtain high-paying jobs.[10] Students at a large state university who were randomly assigned a roommate who drank before entering college were more likely to have lower grades.[11] Korean-American adoptees who as infants were randomly assigned to American families are as likely as their nonadopted siblings to develop the drinking and smoking habits of their parents.[12] Grocery-store cashiers work harder when they are observed by co-workers, particularly those with whom they frequently overlap.[13] When rainfall is low in a Mexican village, the number of migrants to the United States from that village rises and these migrants earn higher wages than those who cannot rely on a large network for information and assistance.[14] An experiment done at Harvard University showed that when a randomly chosen person from a department was induced to show up at a benefits information fair by a monetary award, all employees in that department were more likely to enroll in a tax-deferred retirement plan.[15] Welfare use rises when the potential recipients are surrounded by others who speak the same language and are from a high-welfare-using language group, even when researchers control for the local area and for the language group.[16]

How do friendships form? Psychologists have emphasized similarity and status—for example, sex, race, and achievement.[17] Geographic proximity and race, in particular, but also common interests, majors, and family background were determinants of email communication between students and recent alumni at Dartmouth.[18] William Daryl Henderson has argued that unit cohesion in the military does not occur spontaneously, and that a common religion, race, ethnic group, age, socioeconomic standing, or sex enhances cohesion by facilitating communication.[19] In prison, according to one former Hispanic inmate, "You hate to say it, but just like on the outside people tend to help people who are like them—and Hispanics and blacks are the majority in there."[20] Union army soldiers, whether in prison camps or in the field, were loyal to men who looked like themselves—of the same ethnicity and occupation, from the same state or hometown, of the same age, and related by blood.

Not all scholars agree that social ties between soldiers lead to stronger unit cohesion. Studies of army combat exercises have not found that units where members socialize off-base perform any better than units where there is no such socialization.[21] But men do not sacrifice their lives for their fellow soldiers in combat exercises. By examining desertion and POW camp survivorship during the Civil War, we are able to analyze the effect of peers in a high-stakes setting, and in that setting peers mattered.

The same types of social network variables that determined who deserted from the Union army and who survived POW camps predict commitment to organizations in civilian life today. Organizational membership is lower in metropolitan areas with greater racial and ethnic diversity and higher income inequality.[22] In counties with higher levels of ethnic diversity, the rate of response to the 2000 census was lower, suggesting either greater distrust of the government or reduced willingness to provide information that would help the community receive federal funds.[23]

Studies of public expenditure in the United States today echo our findings on diversity and loyalty. Support for income redistribution is higher when the aid recipients are from the same racial group.[24] Researchers have found a similar result for public education, reporting evidence of a "Florida effect" in states' public school expenditures.[25] In Florida the "average" taxpayer is a white senior citizen, whereas the typical public school student is Hispanic. In this diverse environment, there is less support for public school expenditures than in states where the students and taxpayers are of the same ethnicity. A similar pattern prevailed in the past—racial, ethnic, and religious diversity and income inequality are associated with lower state educational expenditures.[26]

Data from U.S. cities, metropolitan areas, and urban counties show that the share of spending on such productive goods as education, roads, sewers, and trash pickup is inversely related to the area's ethnic diversity, even when researchers control for other socioeconomic and demographic characteristics.[27] Not only are participation and expenditure lower in more diverse settings, but so is trust. Self-reported levels of trust and experimental evidence document that when Americans interact with people who look like them, levels of trust in the community are higher.[28]

Researchers studying developing countries have also found that social capital is higher among more similar people. School funding is lower in communities that are more ethnically diverse.[29] Income inequality lowers civic participation and community expenditure.[30] In Peru, cultural similarity within the community of micro-finance loan recipients lowers default rates. These loans are an important source of funds for the poor. If there is strong social capital within the group providing and receiving loans, then default is lower as well, because altruism, peer pressure, and social sanctions enforce repayment.[31]

Our work emphasizes the importance of ethnicity, state of birth, occupation, age, and kinship for the formation of social ties in the past. We are not claiming these were the only factors that influenced the formation of social ties among Union army soldiers. Nor are we claiming that these factors are as important now as they were in the past. Race and ethnicity no longer predetermine friendships and marriages. For example, in the nineteenth and early twentieth century, Asians were viewed as "forever foreigners,"[32] but marriages between whites and Asians have become increasingly common. About one-third of Japanese-, Filipino-, and Korean-American wives have white husbands, as do 14 percent of Chinese-American wives.[33] Although black-white intermarriages are still rare, they are increasing steadily.[34] Even religion has become less important. In the 1950s, low contemporary and historical rates of intermarriage between Protestants, Catholics, and Jews led scholars to argue that immigrants were not assimilating along religious dimensions.[35] Rising rates of interfaith marriages have recently led to a discussion of the "vanishing Jew."[36] Like still marries like, but like now means someone of the same educational level. In 1960 the odds of a husband and wife having the same educational level were 0.78, but by 1990 the odds of being married to someone with the same level of schooling were 1.03.[37]

Racial and ethnic diversity still affect community participation, but they have become less important relative to income. In the United States today, rates of volunteering, membership in nonchurch organizations, and trust among 25- to 54-year-olds are lower in more diverse communities, particularly those in which wage inequality is high, but also in those with high country of birth and racial diversity. For Americans older than 64, community birthplace diversity, not community income diversity, was the single most important predictor of their volunteering, joining groups, and stating that most people can be trusted.[38]

Although not all surveys that we examined showed declines in volunteering, memberships, and trust, overall this type of participation has declined slightly since the 1970s.[39] Memberships declined sharply in the early 1980s relative to the 1970s, precisely mirroring the sharp increase in income inequality. The rise in married women's labor force participation can explain some of the decline in volunteering among women, but not in memberships. Income inequality was a particularly important predictor for membership in sports, youth, church, literary, and hobby clubs, but not in professional organizations, suggesting that when interpersonal contact is high, people prefer to be with others like them.

What explains declines in community participation? In examining who participates in a community today, Alesina and La Ferrara emphasize the role of racial diversity[40] and Putnam focuses on ethnic diversity.[41] We have stressed the role of income inequality. Race, however, cannot explain the decline in community participation. Communities in the United States have become more fragmented by income, ethnicity, and race since the 1970s, but racial diversity peaked in 1980, then declined. Rising diversity in ethnicity and, especially, in income explains much of the decline in community participation among 25- to 54-year-olds. However, among older Americans, both membership and trust have declined, with the largest declines in membership occurring in the 1980s, thus coinciding with increases in immigration. Rising diversity in both income and ethnicity explains roughly two-thirds of the decline in membership among older Americans.[42]

Why does income inequality matter? *New York Magazine* interviewed five friends who were trying to live similar lifestyles in New York City on vastly different budgets.[43] Liz, a doctoral degree candidate in neuroscience at

Rockefeller University, was receiving a $23,000 annual stipend; Sara was working in finance and earning a "low to mid" six-figure salary; Alex and Michelle were working in advertising, earning "mid to upper" five-figure salaries, though Alex had student loans to pay off; and Miss X, who came from serious money and was making serious money, paid $1.5 million in cash for an apartment. When the friends met, their visits meant consuming, whether in shopping outings, restaurants, or vacations. As Michelle recounted, "Last year, she [Miss X] wanted to go to the Dominican Republic and was like, 'If you can't afford it, just ask your parents for Christmas.'" By encouraging the friends to discuss money, the writer of the story hastened the end of the friendships. Liz later told the writer, "I'm closer now with my friends who live in Brooklyn and don't have any money. We come from a similar background, and that's who you want to be friends with—the people you relate to."

Although people want to be friends with others they can relate to, they may learn the most from those who are different. In recent Supreme Court cases a brief filed by eight universities emphasized that students educate each other, that cross-racial learning takes place, and that this learning is valued by students and by the labor market. Nevertheless, few large-scale studies actually measure the benefits of diversity in either a university or an employment setting. Campus newspaper accounts suggest large amounts of racial self-segregation. When Harvard began randomized assignment to undergraduate residence halls, minority residence tutors argued that this change had destroyed a "supporting and nurturing community . . . [in which] students of color felt comfortable, academically, socially, personally."[44] One study found that white students at a large state university who were randomly assigned a black roommate were more likely to endorse affirmative action and view a diverse student body as essential for a high-quality education. They were also more likely to say they have more personal contact with, and interact more comfortably with, members of minority groups. White students assigned a wealthy roommate were less likely to support redistribution.[45] At Dartmouth, however, white students were less likely to interact with a black roommate than with a white one, and if assigned a black roommate, they were no more likely to interact with black students outside their room, hall, or dormitory than a student assigned a white roommate.[46]

Like college students, Civil War soldiers preferred to interact with others who looked like them. For white Union army soldiers, similar men were those of the same ethnicity, occupation, and age group. For black soldiers, similar men were those from the same state or even plantation and from the same slave or free background. But, in the long run (and studies of college roommates have never been able to examine the long run), Union army soldiers benefited from their interactions with men who were different. Free blacks taught the former slaves to write and helped them forge a freeman's identity. Zack and Harrison Osborne were in a company where only 1 percent of the men were free. They never learned to write, and kept their slave names. Abraham, owned by Bob Pendleton and Thomas Murden, took the last name of his father, Barnett. He was in a company where 17 percent of the men were free and where half the former slaves learned to write. Both slaves, such as John Nelson Cumbash, and free blacks first learned of new cities and states from their comrades who had come from those places.

There is increasing interest in building "good" communities today. The World Bank, on its social capital Web site, writes, "Increasing evidence shows that social cohesion—social capital—is critical for poverty alleviation and sustainable human and economic development."[47] This social capital has both positive and negative consequences. Union army deserters were never reintegrated into their communities, not because of possible legal punishments but because of shame and ostracism. In Ghana, members of the same clan are held responsible for each other's actions, and the children of parents who default on a loan are punished. These social sanctions enable Ghanaians to receive below-market rates. They also encourage lending, because people who lend more expect that they or their children will receive more loans in the future.[48] The neighborhood of Howard Beach in New York City's borough of Queens is one where "a large segment of the population is multigenerational" and residents can say, "Not only do I know my neighbors, but I know their families."[49] But community cohesiveness can produce suspicion of outsiders and Howard Beach has suffered from well-publicized racial incidents.

We have highlighted the tensions between cohesion and diversity. A community of similar people is likely to be cohesive and its members are likely to sacrifice time, effort, and even their lives for each other. But in a diverse community members can learn from one another.

APPENDIX

Records and Collection Methods

ROBERT FOGEL'S UNION ARMY SAMPLE BEGAN WITH TWO lists of companies and regiments drawn from Frederick Dyer's *A Compendium of the War of the Rebellion*. Units were assigned a random number and the lists were ordered by that random number. One list was of the white volunteer infantry units. Another list was of U.S. Colored Infantry units. Information on the men in these companies was then collected from the "Regimental Books" stored at the National Archives in Washington, D.C. (record group 94.2.2).[1] These books were created by clerks during the Civil War and provide the name, birthplace, rank, personal description (such as height, hair color, and skin color), age at enlistment, occupation at enlistment, and place of enlistment for the recruits in each company. If the book for a company was missing, the book of the next company was entered until the two samples consisted of roughly 1.6 percent of all whites and 1.6 percent of all blacks mustered into the Union army.

This procedure yielded a sample of almost 40,000 white men in 331 companies in 284 regiments and 6,000 black soldiers in 52 companies in 40 regiments. The black sample includes the records of the white officers commanding the U.S. Colored Infantry companies. The white sample contains no commissioned officers except those who rose from the ranks. Although the North Central region is somewhat overrepresented and New England is somewhat underrepresented, on the whole, the white sample is representative of white Union army soldiers in height, foreign birth, and desertion rates.[2]

The analyses in this book used roughly 35,000 white men in 303 companies (linkage to additional records had not yet been completed at the time of analysis) and almost 6,000 black soldiers in 51 companies (one company of old men who were guarding forts was omitted). These men are the observations in our data. Because information was collected on all of the men in a company, we also used these data to construct variables describing company characteristics.

The men in the white and black samples were linked to their army records, stored in the National Archives. These records consist of compiled military service (record group 94.12.2) and of cards containing medical records and vital statistics ("carded records," record group 94.12.3). The military service records were compiled on cards after the war from muster rolls, monthly returns, descriptive books, and similar records to verify pension applicants' claims. They record a soldier's muster-in and muster-out information, his promotions and demotions, his furloughs, AWOLs, and desertions, and his capture, wounds, illnesses, and death. The carded medical records are records of any hospital admissions.

Once men's military service and carded medical records were entered into our database, their pension records were collected from the National Archives (record group 15.7.3). The pension record files contain veterans' and widows' applications, supporting information in the form of affidavits from friends, neighbors, and former comrades, physical examinations by the board of surgeons, reports of Pension Bureau investigators, Pension Bureau rulings, information on family members, and copies of death certificates.

The Union army pension program was the most widespread form of assistance to the elderly before Social Security. It covered 85 percent of all Union army veterans by 1900 and 90 percent by 1910, and benefited an estimated one-quarter of the population older than 64 whether as a couple consisting of the former soldier and his wife, the single or widowed veteran, or the widow of a veteran.[3] The program began in 1862, when Congress established the basic system of pension laws, known as the General Law pension system, to provide pensions to both regular and volunteer recruits who were severely disabled as a direct result of military service.[4] The Union army pension program became a universal disability and old-age pension program for veterans with the passage of the act of June 27, 1890, which specified that any disability entitled the veteran to a pension. Even though old age was not recognized by statute law as sufficient cause to qualify for a pension until 1907, the Pension Bureau instructed the examining surgeons in 1890 to grant a minimum pension to all men at least 65 years of age unless they were unusually vigorous. Veterans, however, had every incentive to undergo a complete examination, because those with a severe chronic condition, particularly if it could be traced to wartime experience, were eligible for larger pensions.

Both white and black veterans were eligible for a pension for war-related injuries, but because relatively few blacks were in fighting units, most African-American veterans could not claim a war-related injury. Before 1890, the Pension Bureau admitted 81 percent of white applicants onto the pension rolls but only 44 percent of black applicants. Among all men who identified themselves as Union veterans in the 1910 census, 86 percent of the white veterans and 79 percent of the black veterans can be found in the pension records. Soldiers who survived the war were less likely to have a pension if they were deserters (and therefore ineligible), if they had never been injured in the war, if they had never been promoted, and if they were from a regiment that saw little fighting. Black soldiers were also less likely to have a pension if they had been born in the Confederacy, if they were free men at enlistment, and if they were dark-skinned. Among pension applicants under the 1890 law, 74 percent of blacks applying between 1890 and 1899 had their applications approved by 1899, compared to 82 percent of whites. Pension awards under the 1890 law ranged from $6 to $12 per month, and the mean pension award was 80 cents higher for whites than blacks.

After the pension records for a soldier are collected, the soldier is linked to the various manuscript censuses. On average, linking a soldier to all available censuses requires an hour. White soldiers are linked to the 1850, 1860, 1880, 1900, 1910, 1920, and 1930 censuses. (We cannot link to the 1890 census because most the original manuscript schedules were destroyed in a fire.) Black soldiers are linked to the same censuses except for 1850 and 1860 because slaves were not recorded by name in the slave schedules. Black soldiers have also been linked to 1870, and there are plans to link all white soldiers to 1870 as well.

Linkage rates to the censuses are quite high. With the new electronic indexes, such as those created by ancestry.com, the Fogel team can achieve linkage rates of 75 percent to the 1850 and 1860 censuses. In linking to the census, the Fogel team used information from the pension records because these records provide information on family members. Because deserters were ineligible for pensions, we created the "Costa-Kahn" sample by linking men to the 1880 census using only information on name and date and place of birth, that is, information available in only the military service records.[5]

We linked to the 1880 census 36 percent of all men searched for. The single most important factor predicting whom we found was an uncommon name. Nevertheless, some personal characteristics mattered. The men we linked were less likely to be foreign-born, particularly Irish, and they were less likely to be laborers than farmers, professionals and proprietors, or artisans. We were also more likely to find those who lived in households with higher total personal property wealth in 1860. Census enumerators may have been less meticulous in accurately recording the names, places of birth, and ages of the poor and foreign-born and in enumerating them and the foreign-born and the poor may have given census enumerators less accurate information. In addition, if mortality rates were higher among the foreign-born and the poor, we would be less likely to find them. In searching for a veteran, we knew only whether he died during the war, not whether he died between 1865 and 1880. To our surprise, men who enlisted in counties with higher percentages of foreign-born and of workers in manufacturing and with a large city of at least 50,000 people in the county were less likely to be found. We suspect that in such counties either individuals or census enumerators in 1880 were less careful, or else we are measuring an urban mortality penalty.

Table A.1 shows which subsets of the Union army sample are used in each chapter. In chapter 3 we examined who served in army by comparing the characteristics of the 39,000 white soldiers from the Regimental Books with the population as a whole, and we analyzed company diversity by examining the army records of both white and black soldiers. Chapter 4 used the army records of both white and black soldiers. Chapter 5 utilized the army records of white soldiers, but restricted the analysis to the cases of captivity. Chapter 6 limited the sample of white army soldiers to war survivors and to men linked to the 1880 census. Chapter 7 used the army records of black soldiers linked to their pension records and, in analyzing residential moves, restricted the sample to those alive in 1900. We did not use the records of the examining surgeons that are part of the pension in our analyses but describe them below.

Example of Collection Procedures

The records of John Nelson Cumbash show how an individual soldier's life history is reconstructed. John's compiled military service record consists of one company descriptive book card, one company muster-in roll card, fifteen company muster roll cards, one detachment muster-out roll card, and one company muster-out roll card. The company descriptive book card gives his name as "John Comebash" of Company F, First Regiment USCI, and lists him as 23 years of age, five feet seven inches in height, dark-complexioned, born in Frederick County, Maryland, and a farmer at enlistment. It shows where he enlisted and provides a brief synopsis of his military career—the promotion to sergeant (recorded incorrectly

TABLE A.1
The Use of Robert Fogel's Union Army Sample

Chapter	Main data source	Subsample used
3: Building the Armies	39,622 white soldiers from Regimental Books 35,570 white soldiers linked to army records and to the 1850 census 5,673 black soldiers linked to army records	
4: Heroes and Cowards	35,570 white soldiers linked to army records and to the 1860 census 5,673 black soldiers linked to army records	
5: POW Camp Survivors	35,570 white soldiers linked to army records and to the 1860 census	3,026 cases of captivity
6: The Homecoming of Heroes and Cowards	35,570 white soldiers linked to army records and to the 1860 and 1880 censuses	20,301 war survivors with good information 7,224 men linked to 1880 census
7: Slaves Become Freemen	5,673 black soldiers linked to army records and to pension records	2,790 men linked to pension records 1,515 men linked to pension records and alive in 1900

as 1864 instead of 1863), his demotion, and his hospitalization at Goldsboro, North Carolina, on May 26, 1865 (see figure A.1). The company muster-in roll lists his name as "John Cumbash" and his age at enlistment as 22. The July and August 1863 company muster roll shows him on recruiting service in Baltimore (see figure A.2). The November and December 1863 company muster roll records his promotion to sergeant on November 8, 1863. The September and October 1864 company muster roll records that he was absent because he was sick since October 28, 1864 and was in the hospital at Point of Rocks. Later muster rolls indicate his demotion on February 28, 1865. His detachment muster-out roll shows he was owed $6 per month in pay from enlistment to February 29, 1864, and transportation to Mason's Island from Goldsboro, and that he owed $25.97 for clothing, $1.25 for equipment, and $14 for goods purchased from the sutler while a patient.

John Nelson Cumbash had eight medical record cards. On November 15, 1864, he was admitted to a field hospital; he was sent on to a general hospital on November 18. The next day he was admitted to the base hospital at Point of Rocks, Virginia, suffering from debility. He returned to duty on December 20, 1864. On January 27, 1865, he was again admitted to the Point of Rocks hospital suffering from fever. He returned to duty February 9, 1865 (see figure A.3). One day later he was admitted to the post hospital at Bermuda Hundred, Virginia, suffering from chilblains (ulcers resulting from exposure to cold or humidity), and he was transferred to Point of Rocks hospital February 12, 1865. From there he was sent on February 15, 1865, to the general hospital at Fort Monroe, Virginia, where the diagnosis was "frozen feet."

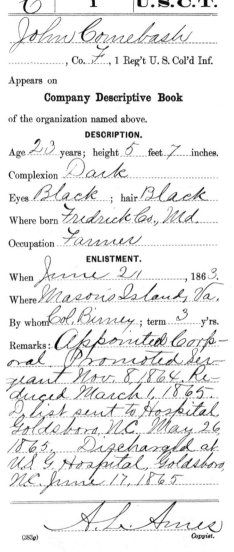

Figure A.1. Military Service Record, Company Descriptive Book

Source: Compiled military service record of John Nelson Cumbash, Company F, First USCI, National Archives Record Group 94.12.2.

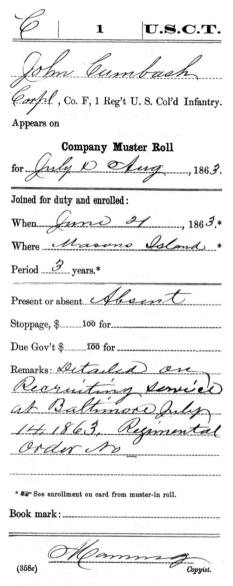

𝒞 | 1 | **U.S.C.T.**

John Cumbash

Corpl , Co. F, 1 Reg't U. S. Col'd Infantry.

Appears on

Company Muster Roll

for *July & Aug* ....., 186*3*.

Joined for duty and enrolled:

When..... *June 21* ...., 186*3*.*

Where ..... *Masons Island,* ..*

Period ....*3*.... years.*

Present or absent..... *Absent*

Stoppage, $....100̄ for........

Due Gov't $.....100̄ for.......

Remarks: *Detailed on Recruiting service at Baltimore July 14, 1863, Regimental Order No*

---

* ☞ See enrollment on card from muster-in roll.

Book mark:..........

(858c)   *Copyist.*

Figure A.2. Military Service Record Company Muster Roll Indicating Absence for Recruiting Services

Source: Compiled military service record of John Nelson Cumbash, Company F, First USCI, National Archives Record Group 94.12.2

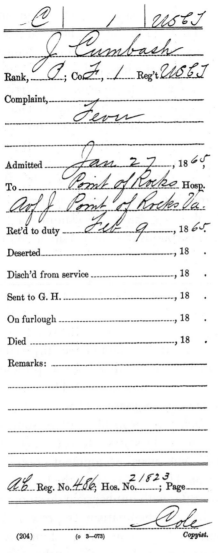

Figure A.3. Medical Record Card Indicating Complaint ("Fever")

Source: Cards containing medical records and vital statistics ("carded records"), John Nelson Cumbash, Company F, First USCI, National Archives Record Group 94.12.3.

He returned to duty March 20, 1865, but on May 27, 1865, he was admitted to the post hospital at Goldsboro, North Carolina, suffering from chronic rheumatism, and was discharged from the hospital.

John Nelson Cumbash's pension file (certificate number 979856) is roughly three-quarters of an inch thick. He first filed for a pension in 1887 because he "was Disabled by Exposure to Cold which settled especially on his Bowels and produced Chronic Dysentery or Chronic Inflammation of Large Intestines and its Results." He further stated that since leaving the service he lived in Baltimore and Philadelphia as a waiter. His claim for a pension was rejected on the grounds that he had no disability since he filed the claim.

In 1890 John filed again, this time under the act of June 27, 1890, for chronic diarrhea, rheumatism, and disease of stomach. Again his claim was rejected on the grounds that he had no notable disability. The report of the examining surgeon stated, "Moderately healthy well nourished colored man. He has no diarrhoea at present. Tongue clean, skin, rectum & anus normal. There are no signs of dysentery nor of inflammation of intestines; nor of disease of stomach. He probably suffers somewhat with chronic diarrhoea as he states. Heart & lungs normal. All joints normal. Muscular development good, no impairment of motion. He has plaster on the back for lumbago, & appears to suffer with lumbar pain on stooping. Except for this he has no rheumatism at present. Otherwise sound." John filed again in 1893, asking for a careful medical examination, and according to the examining surgeon was "well nourished, healthy looking" and did not merit a disability rating. John filed again in 1896 and was rejected again.

John filed again in 1897 for "rheumatism, heart trouble, disease of stomach, and rupture of right side [a hernia]." This time he received a high disability rating, particularly for his hernia but also for his rheumatism, and until his death February 4, 1901, he received $6 per month. According to the physician's affidavit, his death was from pneumonia, "its rapid course and prompt termination was the result of neglect of treatment in the early stage of the disease."

In 1898 the Pension Bureau asked John about his family, in case his wife or children were later to claim a pension as dependents. He listed his first wife, Sarah Hall, who died in Baltimore in 1876, his children, George Elias and Emily Blanche, and his second wife, Mary E. Turner, whom he had married June 25, 1880 (see figure A.4).

Upon John's death Mary applied for a widow's pension. She was "perfectly blind in one eye and almost blind in the other" and "perfectly destitute." She stated, "those who care for me have no legal right [obligation] to do so. . . . I am in such a bad way and in such needy circumstances, and my friends are poor themselves and I feel that I am a burden on them." Most of the pension file consists of correspondence between the Pension Bureau and Mary and affidavits and investigator reports about her pension claim.

The Pension Bureau investigated Mary's claim. On July 1901, the record says, "she is unable to furnish record proof of her marriage as there is neither public nor private record in existence: that the affidavits of two persons who were present and witnessed the ceremony is the best evidence on this point that she can submit: that the minister who performed the marriage ceremony is deceased and she has ascertained that he left no records to furnish

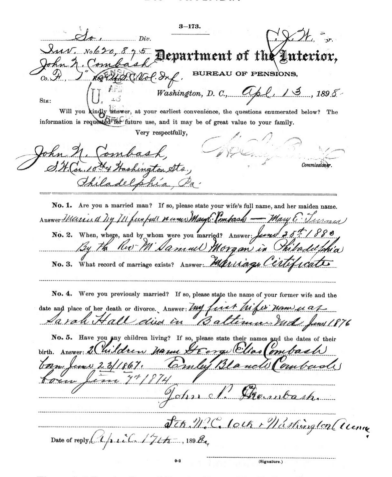

Figure A.4. Pension Record, Pension Bureau Family Questions, 1895

Source: Pension of John Nelson Cumbash, Company F, First USCI, National Archives Record Group 15.7.3, Certificate No. 979, 856.

record proof of her husband's death as no records are kept where she lives." With her June 20, 1902, statement Mary produced the marriage certificate given to her by the minister, but never recorded in the public records, and recounted some more of her history. She stated that she had always been free, that her husband John had belonged to a man named David Bess [Best], and that she had known John when they were children. She also stated that her maiden name was Mary E. Turner. She said that John lived on the Best farm "until after John Brown came through" (Brown's raid on Harpers Ferry took place in October 1859) and was then sold. John and Mary met again about five years before their marriage.

Witness accounts led the Pension Bureau to investigate whether Mary was the Lizzie Lucas who had married Jerry Lyles, a freeman, around 1858. Mary denied that she had ever known anyone by the name Lizzie Lucas and in August and September of 1902 stated that her maiden name was Mary E. or Lizzie Turner and that she "was never married to Jerry Lyles and only lived with him a year or two without marriage." She left Lyles because she "could not get along with him and just left him and come straight to Baltimore," probably some time in 1862. Jerry Lyles subsequently married Sylvia Fisher.

In the afternoon of September 22, 1902, Mary corrected her morning statement. Her maiden name was Mary Elizabeth Lucas. She still stated that she had never married Jerry Lyles, even though witnesses recalled being present at the marriage, and reported that she had married Wallace Turner before the close of the war. They lived in Baltimore for about a year and then Wallace left her and never returned. About a year after he left her he sent her a "bill of separation" from New York. Mary lost the paper after a couple of years. She also stated that she had thought Jerry Lyles was dead when she married John.

Pension Bureau investigators could find no record of Mary's marriage to Turner, but they did find a record of marriage on March 1864 between Samuel Tighlman and

Eliza Lucas, whom they believed to be Mary. They also discovered that Lyles had died in January 1895, 15 years after Mary's marriage to John. They could find no record of Turner or Tighlman. Mary abandoned her pension claim.

As the details of John Cumbash's files suggest, creating a man's life history from his army and pension records is a time-consuming task. Collecting information from the military service records, the carded medical records, and the free-form pension records for a single veteran requires an average of two hours of a trained data entry clerk's time, with half the time spent collecting the records of the examining surgeons. This estimate does not account for the fixed costs of data entry. Training a data collector to input the reports of the examining surgeons requires almost a year and supervisor time. Supervisors need to be available to answer the inevitable questions that come up during data entry and to perform quality checks on the data. Once the data are collected at the National Archives, they need to be cleaned and processed (a task done at the University of Chicago). The data are in the form of strings, and the spellings of words need to be standardized and variables need to be coded.

The data entry process continues with the census records which provide valuable socioeconomic, residential, and family information. From John Cumbash's 1870 census record we learn that he was a waiter in a hotel, that his wife took in washing, and that he had two boys. John, six months of age in 1870, was not listed as a surviving child in 1898.

ENDNOTES

Preface

1. Larry Wimmer, 2003, "Reflections on the Early Indicators Project: A Partial History," in Dora L. Costa (Ed.), *Health and Labor Force Participation over the Life Cycle: Evidence from the Past* (Chicago: University of Chicago Press for the National Bureau of Economic Research), 1–10.

Chapter 1
Loyalty and Sacrifice

1. Captain Maginnis, quoted by Gordon C. Rhea, 2002, *Cold Harbor: Grant and Lee, May 26–June 3 1864* (Baton Rouge: Louisiana State University Press), 333.

2. U.S. Department of Veterans Affairs, 2006, "Fact Sheet: America's Wars" (http://www1.va.gov/opa/fact/amwars.asp).

3. U.S. Department of Veterans Affairs, 2006; Robert William Fogel, 1993, "New Sources and New Techniques for the Study of Secular Trends in Nutritional Status, Health, Mortality, and the Process of Aging," *Historical Methods* 26(1): 5–43.

4. U.S. Department of Veterans Affairs, 2006; Maris Vinovskis, 1990, "Have Social Historians Lost the Civil War? Some Preliminary Demographic Speculations," in Maris A. Vinovskis (Ed.), *Toward a Social History of the American Civil War* (Cambridge: Cambridge University Press), 1–30.

5. Samuel A. Stouffer, Arthur A. Lumsdaine, Marion Harper Lumsdaine, Robin M. Williams, Jr., M. Brewster Smith, Irving L. Janis, Shirley A. Star, and Leonard S. Cottrell, Jr., 1949, *The American Soldier: Combat and Its Aftermath*, vol. II (Princeton, NJ: Princeton University Press).

6. Muzafer Sherif, O. J. Harvey, B. Jack White, William R. Hood, and Carolyn W. Sherif, 1961, *Intergroup Conflict and Cooperation: The Robbers Cave Experiment*. Norman: University of Oklahoma Book Exchange (http://psychclassics.yorku.ca/Sherif).

7. Edward L. Glaeser, David I. Laibson, Jose A. Scheinkman, and Christine L. Soutter, 2000, "Measuring Trust," *Quarterly Journal of Economics* 115(3): 715–1090; Dean S. Karlan, 2005, "Using Experimental Economics to Measure Social Capital and Predict Financial Decisions," *American Economic Review* 95(5): 1688–99.

8. Robert Putnam, 2007, "*E Pluribus Unum*: Diversity and Community in the Twenty-first Century. The 2006 Johan Skytte Prize Lecture," *Scandinavian Political Studies* 30(2): 137–74.

9. Jeffrey Pfeffer, 1997, *New Directions for Organization Theory* (New York: Oxford University Press).

10. William G. Bowen and Derek Bok, 1998, *The Shape of the River: Long-Term Consequences of Race in College and University Admissions* (Princeton, NJ: Princeton University Press).

11. James M. McPherson, 1997, *For Cause and Comrades: Why Men Fought in the Civil War* (New York: Oxford University Press), 182.

12. Our accounts of the heroes are based on our data and on Henry S. Burrage, 1884, *History of the Thirty-Sixth Regiment Massachusetts Volunteers, 1862–1865* (Boston: Press of Rockwell and Churchill); John L. Brooke, 1989, *The Heart of the Commonwealth: Society and Political Culture in Worcester County, Massachusetts, 1713–1861* (Cambridge: Cambridge University Press); Patrick McDonald, n.d., "Opportunities Lost, The Battle of Cold Harbor" (http://www.civilwarhome.com /coldharborsummary.htm); Rhea (2002), and Roy Rosenzweig, 1983, *Eight Hours for What We Will: Workers and Leisure in an Industrial City, 1870– 1920* (New York: Cambridge University Press).

13. See Gerald F. Linderman, 1987, *Embattled Courage: The Experience of Combat in the American Civil War* (New York: Free Press), 176.

Our account of the cowards is based on the data and on Iver Bernstein, 1990, *The New York City Draft Riots: Their Significance for American Society and Politics in the Age of the Civil War* (New York: Oxford University Press); Chris E. Fonvielle, Jr., 1997, *The Wilmington Campaign: Last Rays of Departing Hope* (Mechanicsburg, PA: Stackpole Books); and Edward K. Spann, 1996, "Union Green: The Irish Community and the Civil War," in Ronald H. Bayor and Timothy J. Meagher

(Eds.), *The New York Irish* (Baltimore: Johns Hopkins University Press), 193–209.

14. A. S. Lewis (Ed.), 1982. *My Dear Parents: An Englishman's Letters Home from the American Civil War* (London: Victor Gollancz), 23, 39.

15. Ibid., 23, 29.

16. Our account of the POWs is based on the data and on Steven E. Woodworth, 1998, *Six Armies in Tennessee: The Chickamauga and Chattanooga Campaigns* (Lincoln: University of Nebraska Press); Capt. Lyman Jackman and Amos Hadley, 1891, *History of the Sixth New Hampshire Regiment in the War for the Union* (Concord, NH: Republican Press Association); William Marvel, 1994, *Andersonville: The Last Depot* (Chapel Hill: University of North Carolina Press); and Lonnie R. Speer, 1997, *Portals to Hell: Military Prisons of the Civil War* (Mechanicsburg, PA: Stackpole Books).

17. Robert Knox Sneden, 2000, *Eye of the Storm*, edited by Charles E. Bryan and Nelson D. Lankford (New York: Free Press), 229.

18. Our account of the ex-slaves is based on our data and on Ira Berlin, Joseph P. Reidy, and Leslie S. Rowland (Eds.), 1998, *Freedom's Soldiers: The Black Military Experience in the Civil War* (Cambridge: and New York: Cambridge University Press); Joseph T. Glatthaar, 1990, *Forged in Battle: The Civil War Alliance of Black Soldiers and White Officers* (New York: Free Press); National Park Service, 2007, "Other Slaves at Monocacy" (http://www.nps.gov/mono/historyculture/ei_others.htm); Greta de Jong, 2002, *A Different Day: African American Struggles for Justice in Rural Louisiana, 1900–1970* (Chapel Hill: University of North Carolina Press); Theodore Hershberg (Ed.), 1981, *Philadelphia: Work, Space, Family, and Group Experience in the Nineteenth Century* (New York: Oxford University Press); and W.E.B. DuBois, 1967, *The Philadelphia Negro: A Social Study* (New York: Schocken Books; first published 1899).

Chapter 2
Why the U.S. Civil War?

1. Tony Horowitz, 1998, *Confederates in the Attic* (New York: Pantheon Books).

2. David W. Blight, 2001, *Race and Reunion: The Civil War in American Memory* (Cambridge, MA: Harvard University Press).

3. James M. McPherson, 2007, *This Mighty Scourge: Perspectives on the Civil War* (Oxford: Oxford University Press), 3.

4. Ibid., 3.

5. Ibid., 4.

6. Stanley Milgram, 1963, "Behavioral Studies of Obedience," *Journal of Abnormal and Social Psychology* 67: 371–78.

7. C. Haney, W. C. Banks, and P. G, Zimbardo, 1973, "Study of Prisoners and Guards in a Simulated Prison," *Naval Research Reviews* 9: 1–17.

8. McPherson, 1997.

9. Earl J. Hess, 1997, *The Union Soldier in Battle: Enduring the Ordeal of Combat* (Lawrence: University Press of Kansas), 85–86.

10. Alex Kershaw, 2003, *The Bedford Boys: One American Town's Ultimate D-Day Sacrifice* (London: DaCapo Press).

11. David Healey, 1997, *The Anti-Depressant Era* (Cambridge, MA: Harvard University Press), 83.

12. Ibid., 84–85.

13. Morton Thompson, 1949, *The Cry and the Covenant* (New York: Garden City Books).

14. Ibid., 170.

15. Quoted in Healy, 1997, 83.

16. Ibid., 88–89.

17. Vernon L. Smith, Gerry L. Suchanek, and Arlington W. Williams, 1988, "Bubbles, Crashes, and Endogenous Expectations in Experimental Spot Asset Markets," *Econometrica* 56(5): 1119–51.

18. Glenn W. Harrison and John A. List, 2004, "Field Experiments," *Journal of Economic Literature* 42(4): 1009–55.

19. Joshua D. Angrist, 2004, "American Education Research Changes Tack," *Oxford Review of Economic Policy* 20(2): 198–212.

20. Robert A. Moffitt, 2004, "The Role of Randomized Field Trial in Social Science Research: A Perspective from Evaluations of Reforms of Social Welfare Programs," *American Behavioral Scientist*, January.

21. Ibid.

22. James J. Heckman, 1992, "Randomization and Social Policy Evaluation," in Charles Manski and Irwin Garfinkel (Eds.), *Evaluating Welfare and Training Programs* (Cambridge, MA: Harvard University Press), 201–30.

23. Joseph Palaca, 1989, "AIDS Drug Trials Enter New Age," *Science Magazine*, Oct. 6, 19–21.

24. Michael S. Kramer and Stanley Shapiro, 1984, "Scientific Challenges in the Application of Randomized Trials," *JAMA* 252: 2739–45.

25. Heckman, 1992.

26. Esther Duflo and Rema Hanna, 2005, "Monitoring Works: Getting Teachers to Come to School," NBER Working Paper No. 11880 (Cambridge, MA: National Bureau of Economic Research).

27. Margaret Brobst Roth (Ed.), 1960, *Well, Mary: Civil War Letters of a Wisconsin Volunteer* (Madison: University of Wisconsin Press), 113.

Chapter 3
Building Armies

1. Bob Glauber, 2004, "Ex-NFL Player Dies in Combat" (http://www.SpokesmanReview.com, April 24).

2. William T. Sherman, 1876, *Memoirs of General William T. Sherman* (New York: D. Appleton), 386.

3. Linderman, 1987, 41.

4. Horace Greeley, quoted by William Livingstone, 1900, *Livingstone's History of the Republican Party* (Detroit, MI: Wm. Livingstone; digitized 2006 by Google), 119.

5. David Herbert Donald (Ed.), 1975, *Gone for a Soldier: The Civil War Memoirs of Private Alfred Bellard* (Boston: Little, Brown), 3.

6. McPherson, 1997, 16.

7. Lucius W. Barber, 1894, *Army Memoirs of Lucius W. Barber, Company "D," 15th Illinois Volunteer Infantry, May 24, 1861, to Sept. 30, 1865* (Chicago: J.M.W. Jones Stationery and Printing Co.), 10.

8. Donald, 1975, 3.

9. Jefferson Moses, 1911, *The Memoirs, Diary, and Life of Private Jefferson Moses, Company G, 93rd Illinois Volunteers* (http://www.ioweb.com/civilwar).

10. Richard L. Troutman (Ed.), 1987, *The Heavens Are Weeping: The Diaries of George Richard Browder, 1852–1886* (Grand Rapids, MI: Zondervan Publishing House), 185–86.

11. Elijah P. Marrs, 1969, *Life and History of the Rev. Elijah P. Marrs, First Pastor of Beargrass Baptist Church, and Author* (Miami, FL: Mnemosyne Publishing Co.), 15.

12. Ibid., 9–21.

13. Quoted in Godfrey Rathbone Benson, Lord Charnwood, 1917, *Abraham Lincoln* (Garden City, NY: Henry Holt), 373.

14. Bell Irvin Wiley, 1952, *The Life of Billy Yank* (Indianapolis: Bobbs-Merrill), 37–38.

15. Ibid., 39.

16. McPherson, 1997.

17. Reid Mitchell, 1990, "The Northern Soldier and His Community," in Maris A. Vinovskis (Ed.), *Toward a Social History of the American Civil War* (Cambridge: Cambridge University Press), 1–30.

18. Comparisons are based on the 1860 Integrated Public Use Census Sample (http://www.ipums.umn.edu).

19. We combined data on town enlistment rates obtained from the American Civil War Research Database (http://www.civilwardata .com) with Dale Baum's *Electoral and Demographic Data, 1848–1876: Massachusetts*, obtained from the Inter-university Consortium for Political and Social Resarch as study number 8242.

20. For more details on criteria, see U.S. Provost Marshall General, 1866, U.S. Provost Marshall General, *Final Report*, United States House of Representatives, Executive Document No. 1, 39th Congress, 1st Session (Series Numbers 1251, 1252, 1866), 284–87.

21. See Table 7 in Fogel (1993) and Dan Smith, 2003, "Seasoning Disease Environment, and Conditions of Exposure: New York Union Army Regiments and Soldiers," in Dora L. Costa (Ed.), *Health and Labor Force Participation over the Life Cycle: Evidence from the Past* (Chicago: University of Chicago Press for the National Bureau of Economic Research).

22. McPherson, 1997, 9.

23. Roth, 1960, 39.

24. Arthur A. Kent (Ed.), 1976, *Three Years with Company K: Sergt. Austin C. Stearns Company K 13th Mass. Infantry (Deceased)* (Cranbury, NJ: Associated University Presses), 214–15.

25. John Voltz, 2/10/1865, University Libraries of Virginia Tech (http://spec.lib.vt.edu/voltz).

26. Quoted in Roth, 1960, 5.

27. Works Progress Administration, Federal Writers Project, 2000, *Slave Narratives* (on-line database) (Provo, UT: Ancestry.com). Original data from Works Project Administration, Federal Writers Project, *Slave Narratives: A Folk History of Slavery in the United States from Interviews with Former Slaves* (Washington, D.C.: n.p.).

28. Ibid.

29. Ibid.

30. Ibid.

31. Ibid.

32. See Herman M. Hattaway, 1997, "The Civil War Armies: Creation, Mobilization, and Development," in Stig Föster and Jörg Nagler (Eds.), *On the Road to Total War: The American Civil War and the German Wars of Unification, 1861– 1871* (Cambridge: German Historical Institute and Cambridge University Press); Benjamin Apthorp Gould, 1869, *Investigations in the Military and Anthropological Statistics of American Soldiers* (New York: Hurd and Houghton, for the United States Sanitary Commission); and U.S. Provost Marshall General (1866) for a detailed discussion of the organization of the Civil War armies, and Linderman (1987); Thomas R. Kemp, 1990, "Community and War: The Civil War Experience of Two New Hampshire Towns," in Maris A. Vinovskis (Ed.), *Toward a Social History of the American Civil War* (Cambridge: Cambridge University Press), 1–30; Mitchell (1990); and McPherson (1997) for discussions of soldiers and their communities.

33. Edward G. Longacre, 1999, *Joshua Chamberlain: The Soldier and the Man* (Conshohocken, PA: Combined Publishing), 53.

34. Allan Peskin, 1999, *Garfield: A Biography* (Kent, OH: Kent State University Press), 86–94.

35. Jack K. Bauer (Ed.), 1977, *Soldiering: The Civil War Diary of Rice C. Bull, 123rd New York Volunteer Infantry* (San Rafael, CA: Presidio Press), 2.

36. Kent, 1976, 9.

37. Donald, 1975, 3.

38. Richard Wheeler (Ed.), 1976, *Voices of the Civil War* (New York: Thomas Y. Crowell), 250.

39. Milo M. Quaife (Ed.), 1959, *From the Cannon's Mouth: The Civil War Letters of General Alpheus S. Williams* (Detroit: Wayne State University Press and the Detroit Historical Society), 239.

40. Sherman, 1876, 387–88.

41. Jackman and Hadley, 1891, 205.

42. Aida Cragg Truxall (Ed.), 1962, *"Respects to All": Letters of Two Pennsylvania Boys in the War of the Rebellion* (Pittsburgh: University of Pittsburgh Press), 5.

43. Longacre, 1999, 60.

44. Capt. John G. B. Adams, 1899, *Reminiscences of the Nineteenth Massachusetts Regiment* (Boston: Wright, Potter Printing Co.; http://sunsite.utk.edu/civil-war/Mass19.html).

45. Kent, 1976, 9–10.

46. Ulysses S. Grant, 1996, *Personal Memoirs of U.S. Grant* (Lincoln: University of Nebraska Press), 145.

47. Letter of David Close, Nov. 4, 1862, 126th Ohio Volunteer Infantry, Company D (http://www.frontierfamilies.net/ family/DCletters .htm).

48. Robert F. Harris and John Niflot (Eds.), 1998, *Dear Sister: The Civil War Letters of the Brothers Gould* (Westport, CT: Praeger), 1–2.

49. Ibid., 3.

50. Quoted in McPherson, 1997, 8.

51. Paul Fatout (Ed.), 1961, *Letters of a Civil War Surgeon*, Purdue University Studies, Humanities Series (Lafayette, IN: Purdue Research Foundation), 53.

52. Berlin et al., 1998, 25.

53. For a history of black soldiers in the Civil War, see Berlin et al. (1998); Hondon B. Hargrove, 1988, *Black Union Soldiers in the Civil War* (Jefferson, NC: McFarland); Howard C. Westwood, 1992, *Black Troops, White Commanders, and Freedmen During the Civil War* (Carbondale: Southern Illinois University Press); and Jack D. Foner, 1974, *Blacks and the Military in American History: A New Perspective* (New York: Praeger).

54. Troutman, 1987, 146.

55. Edward G. Longacre, 2003, *A Regiment of Slaves: The Fourth United States Colored Infantry, 1863–1866* (Mechanicsburg, PA: Stackpole Books), 15.

56. U.S. War Department, 1880–1901. *The War of the Rebellion: A Compilation of the Official Records of the Union and Confederate Armies* (Washington, DC: U.S. Government Printing Office; http://cdl.library .cornell.edu/moa/browse.monographs/waro .html); Morris MacGregor and Bernard C. Nalty, 1977, *Blacks in the United States Armed Forces: Basic Documents*, vol. 2 (Wilmington, DE: Scholarly Resources), 96; John W. Blassingame, 1967, "The Recruitment of Colored Troops in Kentucky, Maryland, and Missouri: 1863–1865," *The Historian* 29(4): 533–45.

57. Gatthaar, 1990, 14–16.

58. Ibid.

59. David C. Rankin, 2004, *Diary of a Christian Soldier: Rufus Kinsley and the Civil War* (Cambridge: Cambridge University Press), 106.

60. Jerome Mushkat (Ed.), 2002, *A Citizen-Soldier's Civil War: The*

Letters of Brevet Major General Alving C. Voris (DeKalb, IL: Northern Illinois University Press), 232.

61. Lewis, 1982, 107.

62. Quoted by Joseph Edward Stevens, 1999, *1863: The Rebirth of a Nation* (New York: Bantam Books), 112.

63. Works Progress Administration, 2002.

64. Longacre, 2003, 14–16.

65. Glatthaar, 1990, 68.

66. Troutman, 1987, 169.

67. Ibid., 179.

68. Glatthaar, 1990, 69–70.

69. Ibid., 75.

70. Susie King Taylor, 1902, *Reminiscences of My Life in Camp with the 33d United States Colored Troops Late 1st S. C. Volunteers* (Boston: Author; http://docsouth.unc.edu/neh/taylorsu/taylor su.html), 9–35.

71. Jacob Metzer, 1981, "The Records of the U.S. Colored Troops as Historical Source: An Exploratory Examination," *Historical Methods* 14: 123–32.

72. Rankin, 2004, 24.

73. Works Progress Administration, 2002.

74. See, for example, Berlin et al., 1998.

75. Hargrove, 1988, 214–15.

76. Glatthaar, 1990.

77. U.S. National Archives, n.d., Regimental Letter Book of the 10th USCT, National Archives Record Group 94 (Washington, DC).

78. Glatthaar, 1990, 76.

79. Longacre, 2003, 14.

80. Glatthaar, 1990, 72.

81. Kent, 1976,. 214–15.

82. Quoted in McPherson, 1997, 48.

83. John Gerber, 1955, "Mark Twain's 'Private Campaign,'" *Civil War History* 1: 37–60.

84. Grant, 1996, 144–45.

85. Quoted in Henry L. Williams, 2005, *The Lincoln Story Book*, the Project Gutenberg EBook (http://www.gutenberg.org/dirs/etext05/8linc10h.htm).

86. Hess, 1997, 18–19, 137.

87. Bauer, 1977, 56–57.

88. Hess, 1997, 6.

89. Quoted in Quaife, 1959, 196–97.

90. Quoted in Donald, 1975,84–85.

91. Bauer, 1977.

92. Harris and Niflot, 1998, 8.

93. Michael Sikora, 1998, "Das 18. Jahrhundert: Die Zeit der Deserteure," in *Armeen und ihreDeserteure: Vernachlässigte Kapitel einer Militärgeschichte der Neuzeit* (Göttingen, Germany: Vandenhoeck & Ruprecht).

94. McPherson, 1997, 81–82.

Chapter 4
Heroes and Cowards

1. Victor Davis Hanson, 2001, *Carnage and Culture: Landmark Battles in the Rise of Western Power* (New York: Doubleday); John Keegan, 1993, *A History of Warfare* (New York: Alfred A. Knopf).

2. Thucydides, 1950, *The History of the Peloponnesian War*, translated by Richard Crawley (New York: E. P. Dutton), 335.

3. Ibid.

4. Linderman, 1987, 16.

5. A. J. Motley, quoted by Robert L. O'Connell, 1980, *Of Arms and Men: A History of War, Weapons, and Aggression* (New York: Oxford University Press), 118.

6. Quoted in Keegan, 1993, 20.

7. Ibid.

8. Quoted in Michael Glover, 1979, *The Napoleonic Wars: An Illustrated History, 1792–1815* (London: Batsford), 216.

9. Quoted in Linderman, 1987, 74.

10. Bauer, 1977, 247.

11. Antony Beevor, 1998, *Stalingrad* (New York: Viking Press).

12. Dieter Knippschild, 1998, "Deserteure im Zweiten Weltkrieg: Der Stand der Debatte," in Ulrich Bröckling and Michael Sikora (Eds.), *Armeen und ihre Deserteure: Vernachlässigte Kapitel einer Militärgeschichte der Neuzeit* (Göttingen, Germany: Vandenhoeck & Ruprecht).

13. Quoted in Linderman, 1987, 59.

14. Alan I. Forrest, 1990, *The Soldiers of the French Revolution* (Durham, NC: Duke University Press), 160.

15. McPherson, 1997, 113.

16. Quoted in Harris and Niflot, 1998, 81.

17. Richard M. Trimble (Ed.), 2000, *Brothers 'Til Death: The Civil War Letters of William, Thomas, and Maggie Jones, 1861– 1865, Irish Soldiers in the 48th New York Volunteer Regiment* (Macon, GA: Mercer University Press), 42.

18. McPherson, 1997, 118.

19. Thomas Wentworth Higginson, 2004, *Army Life in a Black Regiment* (http://manybooks.net/titles/higginsoetext04 armyl10.html; first published 1869), 98.

20. Ibid., 100.

21. Stouffer et al., 1949, 169.

22. John Dollard, 1943, *Fear in Battle* (New Haven, CT: Institute of Human Relations, Yale University), 555.

23. McPherson, 1997, 86; Stouffer et al., 1949, 109.

24. Quoted in Stouffer et al., 1949, 136.

25. Linderman, 1987, 265.

26. Quoted in Jonathan Shay, 2002, *Odysseus in America: Combat Trauma and the Trials of Homecoming* (New York: Scribner), 208.

27. Ibid., 210.

28. Quoted in Hess, 1997, 117.

29. Louis Menand, 2001, *The Metaphysical Club* (New York: Farrar, Straus, and Giroux), 43.

30. Quaife, 1959, 163.

31. Edward A. Shils and Morris Janowitz, 1948, "Cohesion and Disintegration in the Wehrmacht in World War II, *Public Opinion Quarterly* 12(2): 280–315.

32. John Keegan, 1976, *The Face of Battle* (Harmondsworth, Middlesex, U.K.: Penguin Books), 276.

33. Quoted in McPherson, 1997, 157.

34. Ibid., 160.

35. Ibid., 161.

36. Peter S. Bearman, 1991, "Desertion as Localism: Army Unit Solidarity and Group Norms in the U.S. Civil War," *Social Forces* 80: 321–42.

37. McPherson, 1997, 137.

38. Mark De Wolfe Howe (Ed.), 1969, *Touched With Fire: Civil War Letters and Diary of Oliver Wendell Holmes, Jr., 1861– 1864* (New York: Da Capo Press), 18.

39. Kent, 1976, 311.

40. Stouffer et al., 1949, 36–37.

41. Quoted in Victor Davis Hanson, 1999, *The Soul of Battle: From Ancient Times to the Present Day, How Three Great Liberators Vanquished Tyranny* (New York: Anchor Books), 168.

42. Ibid., 231.

43. Ibid., 227.

44. Ibid., 230.

45. Thomas Wentworth Higginson (Ed.), 1866, *Harvard Memorial Biographies*, vol. 1 (Cambridge, MA: Sever and Francis; digital edition 2005 by Google), 301.

46. Ibid., 321.

47. Quoted in Carol Bundy, 2005, *The Nature of Sacrifice: A Biography of Charles Russell Lowell, Jr., 1835–1864* (New York: Farrar, Straus, and Giroux), 431.

48. Ibid., 432.

49. Quaife, 1959, 163.

50. Harris and Niflot, 129.

51. Lewis, 1982,26.

52. Higginson, 2004, 160.

53. Ibid., 160.

54. Ibid., 101.

55. Quoted in Glatthaar, 1990, 109.

56. William Darryl Henderson, 1985, *Cohesion: The Human Element in Combat* (Washington, DC: National Defense University Press); Reuven Gal, 1986, *A Portrait of the Israeli Soldier* (Westport, CT: Greenwood Press).

57. Quaife, 1959, 239.

58. Quoted in McPherson, 2007, 147.

59. Ibid., 147.

60. Ibid., 140.

61. Quoted in Berlin et al., 1998, 131–32.

62. Robert W. Fogel, 1989, *Without Consent or Contract: The Rise and Fall of American Slavery* (New York: W. W. Norton), 384.

63. Shils and Janowitz, 1948.

64. McPherson, 1997, 77–89.

65. Ibid., 9.

66. Fogel, 1989, 369–87.

67. McPherson, 1997, 176.

68. Keegan, 1976, 276.

69. McPherson, 1997, 155–62.

70. Stouffer et al., 1949, 108–110.

71. We estimate a hazard model. For white soldiers, time until desertion depends on company occupational, birthplace, and age diversity, the fraction of the company dying within the last 6 months, the fraction of Union victories within the last 6 months, the percent of the county of enlistment voting for Lincoln, year of enlistment, volunteer status, the population of the city of enlistment, whether the soldier was literate, whether he was married, age at enlistment, total household personal property wealth in 1860, country of birth, occupation, height at enlistment, and the region of the country the regiment was from. For black soldiers time until desertion depends on company birthplace and age diversity, the fraction of a company that was free, whether the company contained a fellow soldier from the same plantation, whether there was an abolitionist officer in the regiment, slave status, year of enlistment, occupation at enlistment, whether a bounty was paid and whether one was due, whether the soldier was light-skinned, whether the soldier was born in a Confederate state, age, whether the Civil War was ongoing, whether the regiment was a fighting regiment, and the fraction of Union victories within the last 6 months. For estimation details and the statistical results see Costa and Kahn (2003a, 2006).

72. Lewis, 1982, 67.

73. Ibid., 43.

74. Ibid., 82.

75. Ibid., 43.

76. Linderman, 1987, 23.

77. Ella Lonn, 1928, *Desertion During the Civil War* (New York: Century Co.), 22, 41.

78. Ibid., 148.

79. U.S. War Department, 1884, Series 1, Vol, 10, Part 1, 267.

80. Newton Robert Scott, 2008 (http://www.civilwarletters .com).

81. Hess, 1997, 89.

82. Glatthaar, 1990, 200.

83. Quoted in McPherson, 1997, 5.

84. Russell Duncan, 1999, *Where Death and Glory Meet: Colonel Robert Gould Shaw and the 54th Massachusetts Infantry* (Atlanta, GA: University

of Georgia Press); Luis F. Emilio, 1894, *The History of the 54th Regiment of Massachusetts Volunteer Infantry, 1863–1865* (Boston: Boston Book Co.).

85. Quoted in Hanson, 2001, 5.

86. Ibid., 231.

87. Stouffer et al., 1949, 108–110.

Chapter 5
POW Camp Survivors

1. Lawrence Malkin, 2001, "Prisoners of War," in Robert Cowley and Geoffrey Parker (Eds.), *Reader's Companion to Military History* (Boston: Houghton Mifflin), 368–69.

2. Quoted in Henry J. Webb, 1948, "Prisoners of War in the Middle Ages," *Military Affairs* 12(1): 46–49.

3. Ibid.

4. Ibid.

5. Malkin, 2001.

6. Ibid.

7. James Ford Rhodes, 1904, *History of the United States of America: From the Compromise of 1850 to the McKinley-Bryan Campaign of 1896*, vol. 5, *1864–1866* (New York: Macmillan), 507–8.

8. In our random sample of white infantry companies, roughly 38 percent of the 553 men held at Andersonville died there. In the National Park Service's Andersonville database, 40 percent of the men listed died there. During the trial of Captain Wirz, the surviving commanding officer at Andersonville, one statement put the number of prisoners at more than 30,000 and the number of deaths at more than 13,000. Another put the number of prisoners at about 45,000. These statements yield a mortality rate of 29 to 43 percent. See U.S. War Department, 1880–1901, Series II, Vol. VIII, 615, 781.

9. Leo Eitinger, 1964, *Concentration Camp Survivors in Norway and Israel* (Oslo: Universitetsforlaget).

10. Paul Schmolling, 1984, "Human Reactions to the Nazi Concentration Camps: A Summing Up" *Journal of Human Stress* 10(3): 108–20.

11. Primo Levi, 1961, *Survival in Auschwitz: The Nazi Assault on Humanity*, translated by Stuart Woolf (New York: Collier).

12. Anne Applebaum, 2003, *Gulag: A History* (New York: Doubleday), 380.

13. David R. Jones, 1980, "What the Repatriated Prisoners of War Wrote about Themselves," *Aviatation, Space, and Environmental Medicine* 51(6): 615–17.

14. Brian MacArthur, 2005, *Surviving the Sword: Prisoners of the Japanese in the Far East, 1942–45* (New York: Random House), 269.

15. Ibid., 62–137.

16. Andrew D. Carson, 1997, *My Time in Hell: Memoir of an American Soldier Imprisoned by the Japanese in World War II* (Jefferson, NC: McFarland), 149.

17. MacArthur, 2005, 155.

18. John McElroy, 1879, *Andersonville: A Story of Rebel Military Prisons, Fifteen Months a Guest of the So-Called Southern Confederacy. A Private Soldier's Experience in Richmond, Andersonville, Savannah, Millen, Blackshear, and Florence* (Toledo, OH: D. R. Locke), 170.

19. Robert H. Kellogg, 1865 *Life and Death in Rebel Prisons* (Hartford, CT: L. Stebbins), 67.

20. Jim Janke (Ed.), n.d., "Memoirs of Thomas Newton, Pvt. Co. I, 6th Wisconsin" (http://homepages.dsu.edu/jankej/ civilwar/newton .htm).

21. Leon Basile (Ed.), 1981, *The Civil War Diary of Amos E. Stearns, a Prisoner at Andersonville* (Rutherford, NJ: Farleigh Dickinson University Press and London: Associated University Presses).

22. McElroy, 1879, 110.

23. Sneden, 2000, 268.

24. John Ransom, 1963, *John Ransom's Andersonville Diary* (New York: Berkley Books), 93.

25. See, for example, Lisa F. Berkman, 1995, "The Role of Social Relations in Health Promotion," *Psychosomatic Medicine* 57(3): 245–54.

26. Steve W. Cole, Louise C. Hawkley, Jesusa M. Arevalo, Caroline Y. Sung, Robert M. Rose, and John T. Cacioppo, 2007, *Genome Biology* 8(9): R189.1-R189.13 (http://genomebiology.com/2007/8/9/R189).

27. Lucius W. Barber, 1894, *Army Memoirs of Lucius W. Barber, Company "D," 15th Illinois Volunteer Infantry, May 24, 1861, to Sept. 30, 1865.* Chicago: J.M.W. Jones Stationery and Printing Co., p. 169.

28. Washington Davis, 1888, *Camp-Fire Chats of the Civil War; Being the Incident, Adventure and Wayside Exploit of the Bivouac and Battlefield,*

as Related by the Veteran Soldiers Themselves (Cincinnati, OH: Cincinnati Publishing Co.), 112.

29. Carson, 1997, 36.

30. Quoted in Ovid L. Futch, 1972, "Prison Life at Andersonville," in William B. Hesseltine (Ed.), 1930, *Civil War Prisons* (Kent, OH: Kent State University Press), 9–31.

31. Rhodes, 1904, 507.

32. Estimated from the figures in U.S. Department of Veterans Affairs (2004) and from http://www.cwc.lsu.edu/cwc/ other/stats/warcost .htm.

33. U.S. War Department, 1880–1901, Series II, Vol. IV, 777.

34. See U.S. War Department, 1880–1901, Series II, Vol. VII, 607.

35. Estimated from the Fogel sample of white veterans.

36. See http://www.sonofthesouth.net/leefoundation/the- civil-war .htm.

37. Ransom, 1963, 142.

38. Basile, 1981, 116.

39. Lonnie R. Speer, 1997, *Portals to Hell: Military Prisons of the Civil War* (Mechanicsburg, PA: Stackpole Books), 332.

40. Testimony from the trial of Captain Wirtz, reprinted in Ransom, 1963.

41. William Marvel, 1994, *Andersonville: The Last Depot* (Chapel Hill: University of North Carolina Press), 79, 170.

42. Speer, 1997, 276.

43. William Best Hesseltine, 1930, *Civil War Prisons: A Study in War Psychology* (Columbus: Ohio State University Press); Speer, 1997, *Portals to Hell*.

44. Hesseltine, 1930, 156.

45. Kellogg, 1865, 58–59.

46. Warren Lee Goss, 1866, *The Soldier's Story of His Captivity at Andersonville, Belle Isle, and Other Rebel Prisons* (Boston: Lee & Shepard; reproduced 2001 by Digital Scanning, Scituate, MA), 75.

47. Ibid., 77.

48. Marvel, 1994, 79.

49. McElroy, 1879, 538.

50. Ibid., 225–26.

51. Speer, 1997, 58.

52. McElroy, 1879, 225.

53. Speer, 1997, 263.

54. Sneden, 2000, 229.

55. Marvel, 1994, 75; McElroy, 1879, 208.

56. Marvel, 1994, 75–79.

57. Marvel, 1994, 78–80.

58. McElroy, 1879, 102.

59. Goss, 1866, 104.

60. Lawson H. Carley, n.d., http://www.scriptoriumnovum .com/c /p/carley.html.

61. 1879, 211–12.

62. Ibid., 67.

63. Ibid., 167.

64. Sneden, 2000, 222.

65. Alberto Alesina and Eliana La Ferrara, 2000, "Participation in Heterogeneous Communities," *Quarterly Journal of Economics* 115(3): 847–904; George A. Akerlof and Rachel E. Kranton, 2005, "Identity and the Economics of Organizations," *Journal of Economic Perspectives* 19(1): 9–32.

66. McElroy, 1879, 222.

67. Marvel, 1994, 111.

68. Robert C. Ellickson, 1991, *Order without Law: How Neighbors Settle Disputes* (Cambridge, MA: Harvard University Press); Avinash Dixit, 2004, *Lawlessness and Economics: Alternative Modes of Governance* (Princeton, NJ: Princeton University Press).

69. Alberto Alesina, Reza Baqir, and William Easterly, 1999, "Public Goods and Ethnic Division," *Quarterly Journal of Economics* 114(4): 1243–84.

70. Edward P. Lazear, 1999a, "Culture and Language," *Journal of Political Economy* Suppl. 107(S6): 95–126; idem, 1999b, "Globalization and the Market for Team-Mates," *Economic Journal* 109(454): 15–40.

71. McElroy, 1879, 235.

72. Ibid., 341.

73. Ibid., 209

74. For an admittedly pro-Southern view, see Hesseltine, 1930.

75. McElroy, 1879, 339.

76. We estimate a hazard model in which time until death depends on the number of friends, the total number of men in the camp, the fraction of the company dying before capture, the POW's occupation

at enlistment, his place of birth, his rank, his age at captivity, his height at enlistment, his household personal property wealth in 1860, his marital status in 1860, his literacy, whether he was wounded 10 days before capture, whether he enlisted in a city of 50,000 or more, the year and the month, and the POW camp. A detailed description of the analytical methods and the statistical results is given in Costa and Kahn (2007b).

77. We recognize that if only those who could walk could be transferred, the characteristics of friends who were transferred in may differ from those of friends who were already there. Our instrumental variables strategy assumes that a POW's unobserved health is uncorrelated with transfer status.

78. A searchable version of the database is available on-line as part of the Soldiers and Sailors system (http://www.itd.nps .gov/cwss).

79. U.S. War Department, 1880–1901, Series II, Vol. VIII, 789.

80. We estimate a probit model in which we examine how the probability of survival depended on the number of men in the regiment at Andersonville, the number of men in the company, the number of men with the same last name in the company, the fraction of men with the same last name in the regiment, the number of men from the same hometown in the camp, the POW's rank and ethnicity and his year of capture, and the state of the regiment. We also estimate separate models for the Irish, Germans, and French, in which we examine how the probability of survival depended on the number of men in the company, the number of men of the same ethnicity in the company, the POW's rank, whether he was from a small town, and his year of capture.

81. Sneden, 2000, 149.

82. Basile, 1981, 48.

83. J. P. Ray (Ed.), 1981, *The Diary of a Dead Man, 1862–1864* (New York: Eastern Acorn Press), 196.

84. Jackman and Hadley, 1891, 217, 227.

85. Ibid.,228.

86. Quoted in Lesley J. Gordon, 2002, "'Surely They Remember Me': The 16th Connecticut in War, Captivity, and Public Memory," in Paul A. Cimbala and Randall M. Miller (Eds.), *Union Army Soldiers and the Northern Home Front* (New York: Fordham University), 327–60.

87. Goss, 1866, 22.

88. McElroy, 1879, 52–60.

89. Ibid., 65–134.

90. Janke, 2008.

91. Carley, n.d.

92. McElroy, 1879, 110.

93. Carson, 1997, 20, 24.

94. Davis, 1888, 125.

95. Goss, 1866, 76–77.

96. Ibid., 76.

97. Davis, 1888, 110–11.

98. McElroy, 1879, 261.

99. Except for a few officers of the colored troops, those with a rank higher than sergeant still wore sergeants' stripes, either because their commissions had arrived at regimental headquarters after they were captured or because they had not yet been mustered in (Marvel 1994: 112).

100. Higginson, 2004, 91.

101. Gavan Daws, 1994, *Prisoners of the Japanese: POWs of World War II in the Pacific* (New York: William Morrow), 139.

102. McElroy, 1879, 170.

103. Levi, 1961, 79.

104. Ibid., 81.

105. Sneden, 2000, 235.

106. McElroy, 1879, 222

107. Marvel, 1994, 96–144.

108. Ibid., 144.

109. Sneden, 2000, 190.

110. Basile, 1981, 114.

111. Quoted in Linderman, 1987, 260.

112. Levi, 1961, 159.

113. Sneden, 2000, 229.

114. McElroy, 1879, p. 646.

Chapter 6
The Homecoming of Heroes and Cowards

1. Frances Clarke, 2002, "'Honorable Scars': Northern Amputees and the Meaning of Civil War Injuries," in Paul A. Cimbala and Ran-

dall M. Miller (Eds.), *Union Army Soldiers and the Northern Home Front* (New York: Fordham University), 361–94.

2. Jackman and Hadley, 1891, 395–96.

3. Quoted in Blight, 2001, 149.

4. Ibid., 86.

5. Ibid., 198–201.

6. Ray,1981, 391.

7. Jackman and Hadley, 1891, 395.

8. David E. Long, 1994, *The Jewel of Liberty: Abraham Lincoln's Re-Election and the End of Slavery* (Mechanicsburg, PA: Stackpole Books), 283.

9. James M. McPherson, 1988, *Battle Cry of Freedom: The Civil War Era* (New York: Oxford University Press), 595.

10. John C. Waugh, 1997, *Re-Electing Lincoln: The Battle for the 1864 Presidency* (New York: Crown), 211.

11. McPherson, 1988, 595.

12. Lonn, 1928, 161, 204.

13. From a letter to Secretary of War Edwin M. Stanton after the trial, signed by thirteen officers of Conzet's regiment and in the *Registers of the Records of the Proceedings of the U.S. Army General Court-Martial, 1809–1890.* See http://www.archives .gov/publications/prologue/1998 /winter/union-court-martials .html.

14. Dora L. Costa and Matthew E. Kahn, 2007a, "Deserters, Social Norms, and Migration," *Journal of Law and Economics* 50: 323–53.

15. Robert W. Fogel, 1992, "Problems in Modeling Complex Dynamic Interactions: The Political Realignment of the 1850s," *Economics and Politics* 4(3): 215–54.

16. Costa and Kahn, 2007a.

17. Ibid.

18. Fogel, 1992.

19. Frank L. Klement, 1999, *Lincoln's Critics: The Copperheads of the North* (Shippensburg, PA: White Mane Books), 43–52.

20. Waugh, 1997, 210.

21. Ellickson, 1991,8.

22. Ira S. Dodd, 1898, *The Song of the Rappahannock* (New York: Dodd, Mead), 206.

23. Ibid., 205–6.

24. Quoted in Linderman, 1987, 92.

25. In the 1875 case of *Goetcheus v. Matthewson* (61 NY 420) the

Court of Appeals of New York decided a case in which the plaintiff sued election officials who had denied him the right to vote in the 1868 election because he refused to answer questions about being a deserter. The defendant-officials claimed they were charged by the state constitution with determining the eligibility of voters and the 1865 federal law authorized them to question the plaintiff about desertion. The court held that the 1865 act of Congress denied the rights of citizens only to those convicted of desertion by a competent court and that election officials were not authorized to determine this fact independently.

26. Lonn, 1928, 202–7; U.S. War Department, 1880–1901, Series III, Vol. 5, 1900, 110.

27. Jon Elster, 1998, "Emotions and Economic Theory," *Journal of Economic Literature* 36: 47–74.

28. Eugene Kandel and Edward P. Lazear, 1992, "Peer Pressure and Partnerships," *Journal of Political Economy* 100(4): 801– 17; Ernst Fehr and Klaus M. Schmidt, 1999, "A Theory of Fairness, Competition, and Cooperation," *Quarterly Journal of Economics* 114(3): 817–68; David K. Levine, 1998, "Modeling Altruism and Spitefulness in Experiments," *Review of Economic Dynamics* 1: 593–622; Matthew Rabin, 1993, "Incorporating Fairness into Game Theory and Economics," *American Economic Review* 83(5): 1281–302.

29. Lonn, 1928, 179.

30. Robert I. Alotta, 1978, *Stop the Evil: A Civil War History of Desertion and Murder* (San Rafael, CA: Presidio Press); Arnold M. Shankman, 1980, *The Pennsylvania Antiwar Movement, 1861– 1865* (Cranbury, NJ: Associated University Presses).

31. Lonn, 1928, 198–208.

32. U.S. War Department 1880–1901, Series III, V: 110–11.

33. We use probit models to estimate how the probability of a state move and the probability of a move of more than 350 km depends on deserter status, the vote for McClellan in 1864 in county of enlistment, the interaction between deserter status, and the vote for McClellan, age at enlistment, place of birth, occupation at enlistment, volunteer status, whether the soldier received a bounty, whether the soldier was owed a bounty, personal property wealth in 1860, whether the soldier was literate, whether the soldier was married in 1860, population in the city of enlistment, and state of enlistment. For details see Costa and Kahn (2007a).

34. We estimate a probit model of the probability of being found that depends on the variables listed in note 33 as well as whether the soldier had an uncommon name and county of enlistment characteristics such as the share of the county labor force in manufacturing and the share of the foreign-born population. A detailed discussion of potential sample biases, estimation strategies, and statistical results is available in Costa and Kahn (2007a).

35. Alexis de Tocqueville, 2000, *Democracy in America*, translated by Harvey C. Mansfield and Delba Winthrop (Chicago: University of Chicago Press), 268–69.

36. Ferrie, 2005.

37. Estimated from the Integrated Public Use census sample.

38. Of course, we need to assume that neither war horror nor company social capital directly affects the migration decision.

39. Costa and Kahn, 2007a.

40. Estimates are from a conditional logit model in which each soldier decides to which state or territory to move on the basis of its characteristics, conditional on his being a state mover. Each observation is a person's potential state choice. The soldier's choice depends on the state's percentage of the vote for McClellan, distance from state of enlistment, whether the state had a law disenfranchising deserters, and interactions with deserter status. See Costa and Kahn (2007a) for details.

41. Steckel (1983) documents that migration in the United States had traditionally been along the same latitude because farmers could grow familiar crops in similar climate zones.

42. McPherson,1997,145.

43. Shankman, 1980.

44. Elster, 1998.

45. Alexandra Barahona de Brito, Carmen González-Enríquez, and Paloma Aguilar (Eds.), 2001, *The Politics of Memory: Transitional Justice in Democratizing Societies* (Oxford: Oxford University Press); Robert O. Paxton, 1998, foreword, in *Vichy: An Ever-Present Past*, by Éric Conan and Henry Rousso (Hanover, NH: Dartmouth University Press), ix–xiii.

46. George R. Goethals and Richard F. Reckman, 1973, "The Perception of Consistency in Attitudes" *Journal of Experimental Social Psychology* 9(3): 491–501; Michael Ross and Michael Conway. 1986, "Remembering One's Own Past: The Construction of Personal Histories," in R. M. Sorrentino and E. T. Higgins (Eds.), *Handbook of*

Motivation and Cognition: Foundations of Social Behavior (New York: Guilford Press), 122–44.

47. Pieter Lagrou, 2000, *The Legacy of Occupation: Patriotic Memory and National Recovery in Western Europe, 1945–65* (Cambridge: Cambridge University Press).

48. Gordon Wright, 1962, "Reflections on the French Resistance (1940–1944)," *Political Science Quarterly* 77(3): 336–49.

49. Barbara Miller, 1999, *Narratives of Guilt and Compliance in Unified Germany: Stasi Informers and Their Impact on Society.* (London: Routledge), 109–10.

50. Quoted in Blight, 2001, 298.

51. Lonn, 1928, v.

Chapter 7
Slaves Become Freemen

1. Joshua D. Angrist and Alan B. Krueger, 1994, "Why Do World War II Veterans Earn More Than Nonveterans?" *Journal of Labor Economics* 12(1): 74–97; Joshua D. Angrist, 1990, "Lifetime Earnings and the Vietnam Era Draft Lottery: Evidence from Social Security Administrative Records," *American Economic Review* 80(3): 313–36.

2. Daron Acemoglu, David H. Autor, and David Lyle, 2004, "Women, War, and Wages: The Effect of Female Labor Supply on the Wage Structure at Midcentury," *Journal of Political Economy* 112(3): 497–551.

3. Mushkat, 2002, 66.

4. Glatthaar, 1990, 243.

5. Quoted in Nell Irvin Painter, 1992, *Exodusters: Black Migration to Kansas after Reconstruction* (New York: W.W. Norton), 74.

6. Works Progress Administration, 2000.

7. Thomas Holt, 1979, *Black Over White: Negro Political Leadership in South Carolina during Reconstruction* (Urbana: University of Illinois Press), 76.

8. Ibid., 50.

9. Taylor, 1902, 54.

10. Calculated from the random sample of USCT and from the 1900 and 1910 Integrated Public Use census samples.

11. Works Progress Administration, 2000.

12. Ibid.

13. Quoted in Glatthaar, 1990, 79.

14. We estimate three separate probit models of the probability of migration across states, regions, and city sizes. We also estimate two separate probit models for the probability of literacy and a name change. In our probit models the outcomes depend on company and age diversity, the fraction of the company that was free, whether the company had an abolitionist officer, the fraction of the company enlisting in a large city (when examining moves across different size cities), whether the regiment traveled to a new region (when examining state and regional moves), whether the regiment traveled to a city (when examining moves across different size cities), year of enlistment, occupation at enlistment, birth cohort, whether the soldier was light-skinned, whether the soldier was born in a Confederate state, the number of days served, whether the regiment was a fighting regiment, whether the individual was promoted, the fraction of the company that was promoted, the fraction of the company that died in service, whether the recruit was injured during the war, and, in examining migration probabilities, literacy. We also estimate conditional logit models of the probability of move to a particular state, assum- ing that the soldier has moved, where each observation is his choice of potential states. This probability depends on whether the regiment was there, the fraction of men in the company from that state, the fraction of the state population that was black, distance from the enlistment state, and interactions with writing ability. A detailed description of the data, analytical methods, and statistical results is available in Costa and Kahn (2006).

15. Painter, 1992, 76.

16. Taylor, 1902, 59.

17. Works Progress Administration, 2000.

18. Glatthaar, 1990, 252.

19. Berlin et al., 1998, 173.

20. Quoted in Painter, 1992, 74.

21. Taylor, 1902, 73.

22. Quoted in Painter, 1992, 85–86.

23. Ibid., 133.

24. Steven Hahn, 2003, *A Nation Under Our Feet: Black Political Struggles in the Rural South from Slavery to the Great Migration* (Cambridge, MA: Harvard University Press), 219, 280.

25. Painter, 1992, 78.

26. Works Progress Administration, 2000.

27. Lee J. Alston and Joseph P. Ferrie, 1999, *Southern Paternalism and the American Welfare State: Economics, Politics, and Institutions in the South, 1865–1965* (Cambridge: Cambridge University Press), 133–34.

28. Paul D. Escott, 1985, *Many Excellent People: Power and Privilege in North Carolina, 1850–1900* (Raleigh: University of North Carolina Press), 185.

29. Quoted in Painter, 1992, 154.

30. Ibid., 183.

31. Hahn, 2003, 283.

32. Quoted in Holt, 1979, 122.

33. Quoted in Eric Foner, 2005, *Forever Free: The Story of Emancipation and Reconstruction* (New York: Alfred A. Knopf), 196.

34. Holt, 1979, 63, 188.

35. Foner, 2005, 195–98.

36. Chulhee Lee, 2005, "Health, Information, and Migration: Geographic Mobility of Union Army Veterans, 1860–1880," National Bureau of Economic Research Working Paper No. 11027 (Cambridge, MA: National Bureau of Economic Research).

37. Works Progress Administration, 2000.

38. Ibid.

39. William J. Collins and Robert A. Margo, 2006, "Historical Perspectives on Racial Differences in Schooling in the United States," in Eric Hanushek and Finis Welch (Eds.), *Handbook of the Economics of Education*, vol. 1 (New York: North-Holland).

40. Quoted in Edwin S. Redkey (Ed.), 1992, *A Grand Army of Black Men: Letters from African-American Soldiers in the Union Army, 1861–1865* (Cambridge: Cambridge University Press), 68.

41. Ibid.

42. Keith P. Wilson, 2002, *Campfires of Freedom: The Camp Life of Black Soldiers During the Civil War* (Kent, OH: Kent State University Press), 87.

43. Ibid., 84.

44. Ibid., 87.

45. Ibid., 88.

46. Holt, 1979, 82.

47. Wilson, 2002, 87.

48. James M. McPherson, 1965, *The Negro's Civil War: How Amer-*

ican Blacks Felt and Acted During the War for the Union. (New York: Vintage Civil War Library), 115–35.

49. Quoted in Holt, 1979, 82.

50. Taylor, 1902, 21.

51. Higginson, 2004, 19.

52. Wilson, 2002, 103.

53. Ibid., 103.

54. Ibid., 106.

55. Ibid., 101–2.

56. Ibid., 99.

57. Ibid., 106.

58. Glatthaar, 1990, 227.

59. Some companies served fewer days than the regular three-year term because they formed late and were disbanded when the war ended.

60. Donald Robert Shaffer, 2004, *After the Glory: The Struggles of Black Civil War Veterans* (Lawrence: University Press of Kansas), 100–1.

61. Works Progress Administration, 2000.

62. Ibid.

63. George Arnold, 1887, quoted in Blight, 2001, 198.

64. Quoted in Longacre, 2003, 177.

65. Quoted in Blight, 2001, 198.

66. Works Progress Administration, 2000.

67. Ibid.

68. Bruce Sacerdote, 2005, "Slavery and the Intergenerational Transmission of Human Capital," *Review of Economics and Statistics* 87(2): 217–34.

Chapter 8
Learning from the Past

1. McPherson, 1997.

2. Ted Genoways and Hugh H. Genoways (Eds.), 2001, *A Perfect Picture of Hell: Eyewitness Accounts by Civil War Prisoners from the 12th Iowa* (Iowa City: University of Iowa Press), 39.

3. For a review, see Linton C. Freeman, 2004, *The Development of Social Network Analysis: A Study in the Sociology of Science* (Vancouver: Empirical Press).

4. Marc Sageman, 2004, *Understanding Terror Networks* (Philadelphia: University of Pennsylvania Press), 114.

5. Donatella della Porta, 1988, "Recruitment Processes in Clandestine Political Organizations: Italian Left-Wing Terrorism," *International Social Movement Research* 1: 155–59.

6. Sageman, 2004, 133.

7. Scott Atran, 2003, "Genesis of Suicide Terrorism," *Science* 299: 1534–39.

8. Andrea Elliott, 2007, "Where Boys Grow Up to Be Jihadis," *New York Times Magazine*, Nov. 26, 2008, 70.

9. Bruce Sacerdote, 2001, "Peer Effects with Random Assignment: Results for Dartmouth Roommates," *Quarterly Journal of Economics* 116(2): 681–704.

10. David Marmaros and Bruce Sacerdote, 2002, "Peer and Social Networks in Job Search," *European Economic Review* 46(4–5): 870–79.

11. Michael Kremer and Dan M. Levy, 2003, "Peer Effects and Alcohol Use Among College Students," NBER Working Paper No. 9876 (Cambridge, MA: National Bureau of Economic Research).

12. Bruce Sacerdote, 2007, "How Large are the Effects from Changes in Family Environment? A Study of Korean-American Adoptees," *Quarterly Journal of Economics* 122(1): 119–57.

13. Alexandre Mas and Enrico Moretti, in press, "Peers at Work," *American Economic Review*.

14. Kaivan Munshi, 2003, "Networks in the Modern Economy: Mexican Migrants in the U.S. Labor Market," *Quarterly Journal of Economics* 118(2): 549–99.

15. Esther Duflo and Emmanuel Saez, 2003, "The Role of Information and Social Interactions in Retirement Plan Decisions: Evidence from a Randomized Experiment," *Quarterly Journal of Economics* (118): 815–42.

16. Marianne Bertrand, Erzo Luttmer, and Sendhil Mullainathan, 2000, "Network Effects and Welfare Cultures," *Quarterly Journal of Economics* 115(3): 1019–55.

17. Kullervo Rainio, 1966, "A Study of Sociometric Group Structure: An Application of a Stochastic Theory of Social Interaction," in J. Berger, M. Zelditch, and B. Anderson (Eds.), *Sociological Theories in Progress*, vol. 1 (Boston: Houghton Mifflin); Nancy B. Tuma and Maureen T. Hallinan, 1979, "The Effects of Sex, Race and Achievement on Schoolchildren's Friendships," *Social Forces* 57: 1265–85.

18. Marmaros and Sacerdote, 2002.

19. Henderson, 1985, 26.

20. Quoted in Kate Murphy, 2004, "After Enron, a Sunless Year in a Tiny Cell" *New York Times*, Sunday Business, News and Analysis, June 20, 5.

21. Robert J. MacCoun, 1993. "What Is Known about Unit Cohesion and Military Performance," In *Sexual Orientation and U.S. Military Personnel Policy: Options and Assessment* (Santa Monica, CA: RAND), 283–331 (http://www.rand.org/pubs/monograph_reports/MR323/mr323.pref.pdf).

22. Alberto Alesina and Eliana La Ferrara, 2002, "Who Trusts Others?" *Journal of Public Economics* 85(2): 207–34.

23. Jacob L. Vigdor, 2004, "Community Composition and Collective Action: Analyzing Initial Mail Response to the 2000 Census," *Review of Economics and Statistics* 86(1): 303–12.

24. Erzo F. P. Luttmer, 2001, "Group Loyalty and the Taste for Redistribution," *Journal of Political Economy* 109(3): 500–28.

25. James M. Poterba, 1997, "Demographic Structure and the Political Economy of Public Education," *Journal of Policy Analysis and Management* 16(1): 48–66; Amy Rehder Harris, William N. Evans, and Robert M. Schwab, 2001, "Education Spending in an Aging America," *Journal of Public Economics* 83(3): 449–72.

26. Claudia Goldin and Lawrence F. Katz, 1999, "Human Capital and Social Capital: The Rise of Secondary Schooling in American, 1910 to 1940," *Journal of Interdisciplinary History* 29: 683–723.

27. Alesina et al., 1999.

28. Alesina and La Ferrara, 2002; Edward L. Glaser, David I. Laibson, Jose A. Scheinkman, and Christine L. Soutter, 2000, "Measuring Trust," *Quarterly Journal of Economics* 115(3): 715–1090.

29. Edward Miguel and Mary Kay Gugerty, 2005, "Ethnic Diversity, Social Sanctions, and Public Goods in Kenya," *Journal of Public Economics* 89(11–12): 2325–68.

30. Eliana La Ferrara, 2002, "Inequality and Group Participation: Theory and Evidence from Rural Tanzania," *Journal of Public Economics* 85(2): 235–73; Peter H. Lindert, 1996, "What Limits Social Spending?" *Explorations in Economic History* 33(1): 1–34.

31. Dean S. Karlan, 2007, "Social Connections and Group Banking," *Economic Journal* 117(February): F52-F84.

32. Mia Tuan, 1998, *Forever Foreigners or Honorary Whites? The Asian Ethnic Experience Today* (New Brunswick, NJ: Rutgers University Press).

33. C. N. Lee, n.d., "By the Numbers: Dating, Marriage, and Race in Asian America" (http://www.imdiversity.com/Villages/Asian/family _lifestyle_traditions/le_interracial_dating.asp).

34. Joel Perlman and Mary C. Waters, 2004, "Intermarriage Then and Now: Race, Generation, and the Changing Meaning of Marriage," in Nancy Foner and George M. Fredrickson (Eds.), *Not Just Black and White: Historical and Contemporary Perspectives on Immigration, Race, and Ethnicity in the United States* (New York: Russell Sage Foundation), 262–77.

35. Will Herberg, 1955, *Protestant, Catholic, Jew: An Essay in American Religious Sociology* (Garden City, NY: Doubleday).

36. Alan M. Dershowitz, 1997, *The Vanishing American Jew: In Search of Jewish Identity for the Next Century* (Boston: Little, Brown).

37. John Pencavel, 1998, "Assortative Mating by Schooling and the Work Behavior of Wives and Husbands," *American Economic Review* 88(2): 326–29.

38. Dora L. Costa and Matthew E. Kahn, 2003b, "Civic Engagement and Community Heterogeneity: An Economist's Perspective," *Perspectives on Politics* 1(1); idem, 2003c, "Understanding the American Decline in Social Capital, 1952–1998," *Kyklos* 56(1): 17–46.

39. Costa and Kahn, 2007b, 2007c.

40. Alesina and La Ferrara, 2000.

41. Putnam, 2007.

42. Costa and Kahn, 2007b, 2007c.

43. David Anderson, 2006, "What's a Little Money Between Friends? A Lot When One Friend Just Bought a Million-Dollar Apartment and the Other Is Subsisting on Frozen Dinners," *New York Magazine*, Nov. 6.

44. Sarah H. Dolgonos and Daniela J. Lamas, 2000, "Many Protested Randomization, but Minority Groups were Among the Most Vocal," *Harvard Crimson*, June 8.

45. Johanne Boisjoly, Greg J. Duncan, Michael Kremer, Dan M. Levy, and Jacque Eccles, 2006, "Empathy or Antipathy? The Impact of Diversity," *American Economic Review* 96(5): 1890–905.

46. Marmaros and Sacerdote, 2006.

47. http://web.worldbank.org.

48. La Ferrara, 2003.

49. Quoted in Joyce Cohen, 1998, "If You're Thinking of Living in

Howard Beach, Queens; An Urban Enclave with Prow to the Sea," *New York Times*, Oct. 25.

Appendix
Records and Collection Methods

1. Regimental Books stored at the National Archives, Washington, D.C. (record group 94.2.2).

2. Fogel, 1993, 5–43.

3. Dora L. Costa, 1998, *The Evolution of Retirement: An American Economic History, 1880–1990* (Chicago: University of Chicago Press), 160.

4. Ibid., 197–212.

5. For full details, see Costa and Kahn, 2007a.

BIBLIOGRAPHY

Acemoglu, Daron, David H. Autor, and David Lyle. 2004. "Women, War, and Wages: The Effect of Female Labor Supply on the Wage Structure at Midcentury." *Journal of Political Economy* 112(3): 497–551.

Adams, Capt. John G. B. 1899. *Reminiscences of the Nineteenth Massachusetts Regiment.* Boston: Wright, Potter Printing Co. http://sunsite.utk.edu/civil-war/Mass19.html.

Aizer, Anna, and Janet Currie. 2004. "Networks or Neighborhoods? Correlations in the Use of Publicly-Funded Maternity Care in California." *Journal of Public Economics* 88(12): 2573–85.

Akerlof, George A., and Rachel E. Kranton. 2005. "Identity and the Economics of Organizations." *Journal of Economic Perspectives* 19(1): 9–32.

———. 2000. "Economics and Identity." *Quarterly Journal of Economics* 115(3): 715–53.

Alesina, Alberto, Reza Baqir, and William Easterly. 1999. "Public Goods and Ethnic Division." *Quarterly Journal of Economics* 114(4): 1243–84.

Alesina, Alberto, and Eliana La Ferrara. 2002. "Who Trusts Others?" *Journal of Public Economics* 85(2): 207–34.

———. 2000. "Participation in Heterogeneous Communities" *Quarterly Journal of Economics* 115(3): 847–904.

Alesina, Alberto, Enrico Spolaore, and Romain Wacziarg. 2000. "Economic Integration and Political Disintegration." *American Economic Review* 90(4): 1276–96.

Alotta, Robert I. 1978. *Stop the Evil: A Civil War History of Desertion and Murder.* San Rafael, CA: Presidio Press.

Alston, Lee J., and Joseph P. Ferrie. 1999. *Southern Paternalism and the American Welfare State: Economics, Politics, and Institutions in the South, 1865–1965.* Cambridge: Cambridge University Press.

Amsden, David. 2006. "What's a Little Money Between Friends? A Lot When One Friend Just Bought a Million-Dollar Apartment and the Other Is Subsisting on Frozen Dinners." *New York Magazine*, October 29. http://nymag .com/guides/money/2006/23486.

Angrist, Joshua D. 2004. "American Education Research Changes Tack." *Oxford Review of Economic Policy* 20(2): 198–212.

———. 1990. "Lifetime Earnings and the Vietnam Era Draft Lottery: Evidence from Social Security Administrative Records." *American Economic Review* 80(3): 313–36.

Angrist, Joshua D., and Alan B. Krueger. 1994. "Why Do World War II Veterans Earn More Than Nonveterans?" *Journal of Labor Economics* 12(1): 74–97.

Applebaum, Anne. 2003. *Gulag: A History*. New York: Doubleday.

Atran, Scott. 2003. "Genesis of Suicide Terrorism." *Science* 299 (March 7): 1534–39.

Barahona de Brito, Alexandra, Carmen González-Enríquez, and Paloma Aguilar (Eds.). 2001. *The Politics of Memory: Transitional Justice in Democratizing Societies*. Oxford: Oxford University Press.

Barber, Lucius W. 1894. *Army Memoirs of Lucius W. Barber, Company "D," 15th Illinois Volunteer Infantry, May 24, 1861, to Sept. 30, 1865*. Chicago: J.M.W. Jones Stationery and Printing Co.

Basile, Leon (Ed.). 1981. *The Civil War Diary of Amos E. Stearns, a Prisoner at Andersonville*. Rutherford, NJ: Fairleigh Dickinson University Press; London: Associated University Presses.

Bauer, K. Jack (Ed.). 1977. *Soldiering: The Civil War Diary of Rice C. Bull, 123rd New York Volunteer Infantry*. San Rafael, CA: Presidio Press.

Bayer, Patrick, Stephen L. Ross, and Giorgio Topa. 2005. "Place of Work and Place of Residence: Informal Hiring Networks and Labor Market Outcomes." NBER Working Paper No. 11019. Cambridge, MA: National Bureau of Economic Research.

Bearman, Peter S. 1991. "Desertion as Localism: Army Unit Solidarity and Group Norms in the U.S. Civil War." *Social Forces* 80: 321–42.

Beevor, Antony. 1998. *Stalingrad*. New York: Viking.

Berkman, Lisa F. 1995. "The Role of Social Relations in Health Promotion." *Psychosomatic Medicine* 57(3): 245–54.

Berlin, Ira, Joseph P. Reidy, and Leslie S. Rowland (Eds.). 1998. *Freedom's Soldiers: The Black Military Experience in the Civil War*. Cambridge: Cambridge University Press.

Bernstein, Iver. 1990. *The New York City Draft Riots: Their Significance for American Society and Politics in the Age of the Civil War*. New York: Oxford University Press.

Bertrand, Marianne, Erzo Luttmer, and Sendhil Mullainathan. 2000. "Network Effects and Welfare Cultures." *Quarterly Journal of Economics* 115(3): 1019–55.

Blassingame, John W. 1967. "The Recruitment of Colored Troops in Kentucky, Maryland, and Missouri: 1863–1865." *The Historian* 29(4): 533–45.

Blight, David W. 2001. *Race and Reunion: The Civil War in American Memory*. Cambridge, MA: Harvard University Press.

Boisjoly, Johanne, Greg J. Duncan, Michael Kremer, Dan M. Levy, and Jacque Eccles. 2006. "Empathy or Antipathy? The Impact of Diversity." *American Economic Review* 96(5): 1890–1905.

Bowen, William G., and Derek Bok. 1998. *The Shape of the River: Long-Term Consequences of Race in College and University Admissions*. Princeton, NJ: Princeton University Press.

Brooke, John L. 1989. *The Heart of the Commonwealth: Society and Political Culture in Worcester County, Massachusetts, 1713–1861*. Cambridge: Cambridge University Press.

Bundy, Carol. 2005. *The Nature of Sacrifice: A Biography of Charles Russell Lowell, Jr., 1835–1864*. New York: Farrar, Straus, and Giroux.

Burrage, Henry S. 1884. *History of the Thirty-Sixth Regiment Massachusetts Volunteers, 1862–1865*. Boston: Press of Rockwell and Churchill.

Carley, Lawson H. n.d. http://www.scriptoriumnovum.com/c/p/carley /htm.

Carson, Andrew D. 1997. *My Time in Hell: Memoir of an American Soldier Imprisoned by the Japanese in World War II*. Jefferson, NC: McFarland.

Chamberlain, Joshua Lawrence. 1993. *The Passing of the Armies*. New York: Bantam Books. First published 1915.

Charnwood, Godfrey Rathbone Benson, Lord. 1917. *Abraham Lincoln*. Garden City, NY: Henry Holt.

Clarke, Frances. 2002. "'Honorable Scars': Northern Amputees and the Meaning of Civil War Injuries." In Paul A. Cimbala and Randall M. Miller (Eds.), *Union Army Soldiers and the Northern Home Front*. New York: Fordham University, 361–94.

Cohen, Joyce. 1998. "If You're Thinking of Living in Howard Beach, Queens: An Urban Enclave with Prow to the Sea." *New York Times*, October 25.

Cole, Steve W., Louise C. Hawkley, Jesusa M. Arevalo, Caroline Y.

Sung, Robert M. Rose, and John T. Cacioppo. 2007. *Genome Biology* 8(9): R189.1–R189.13. http://genomebiology .com/2007/8/9/R189.

Collins, William J., and Robert A. Margo. 2006. "Historical Perspectives on Racial Differences in Schooling in the United States." In Eric Hanushek and Finis Welch (Eds.), *Handbook of the Economics of Education*. Vol. 1. New York: North-Holland.

Costa, Dora L. 1998. *The Evolution of Retirement: An American Economic History, 1880–1990*. Chicago: University of Chicago Press.

Costa, Dora L., and Matthew E. Kahn. 2007a. "Deserters, Social Norms, and Migration." *Journal of Law and Economics* 50: 323–53.

———. 2007b. "Surviving Andersonville: The Benefits of Social Networks in POW Camps." *American Economic Review* 97(4): 1467–87.

———. 2006. "Forging a New Identity: The Costs and Benefits of Diversity in Civil War Combat Units for Black Slaves and Freemen." *Journal of Economic History* 66(4): 936–62.

———. 2004. "Changes in the Value of Life: 1940–1980." *Journal of Risk and Uncertainty* 29(2): 159–80.

———. 2003a. "Cowards and Heroes: Group Loyalty in the American Civil War." *Quarterly Journal of Economics* 118(2): 519–48.

———. 2003b. "Civic Engagement and Community Heterogeneity: An Economist's Perspective." *Perspectives on Politics* 1(1).

———. 2003c. "Understanding the American Decline in Social Capital, 1952–1998." *Kyklos* 56(1): 17–46.

Davis, Washington. 1888. *Camp-Fire Chats of the Civil War; Being the Incident, Adventure and Wayside Exploit of the Bivouac and Battlefield, as Related by the Veteran Soldiers Themselves*. Cincinnati, OH: Cincinnati Publishing Co.

Daws, Gavan. 1994. *Prisoners of the Japanese: POWs of World War II in the Pacific*. New York: William Morrow.

de Jong, Greta. 2002. *A Different Day: African American Struggles for Justice in Rural Louisiana, 1900–1970*. Chapel Hill: University of North Carolina Press.

della Porta, Donatella. 1988. "Recruitment Processes in Clandestine Political Organizations: Italian Left-Wing Terrorism." *International Social Movement Research* 1: 155–59.

Dershowitz, Alan M. 1997. *The Vanishing American Jew: In Search of Jewish Identity for the Next Century*. Boston: Little, Brown.

Dixit, Avinash. 2004. *Lawlessness and Economics: Alternative Modes of Governance*. Princeton, NJ: Princeton University Press.

Dodd, Ira S. 1898. *The Song of the Rappahannock*. New York: Dodd, Mead.

Dolgonos, Sarah H., and Daniela J. Lamas. 2000. "Many Protested Randomization, But Minority Groups Were Among the Most Vocal." *Harvard Crimson*, June 8. http://www.the crimson.com/archives/aspx.

Dollard, John. 1943. *Fear in Battle*. New Haven, CT: Institute of Human Relations, Yale University.

Donald, David Herbert (Ed.). 1975. *Gone for a Soldier: The Civil War Memoirs of Private Alfred Bellard*. Boston: Little, Brown.

DuBois, W.E.B. 1967. *The Philadelphia Negro: A Social Study*. New York: Schocken Books. First published 1899.

Duflo, Esther, and Rema Hanna. 2005. "Monitoring Works: Getting Teachers to Come to School." NBER Working Paper No. 11880. Cambridge, MA: National Bureau of Economic Research.

Duflo, Esther, and Emmanuel Saez. 2003. "The Role of Information and Social Interactions in Retirement Plan Decisions: Evidence from a Randomized Experiment." *Quarterly Journal of Economics* (118): 815–42.

Duncan, Russell. 1999. *Where Death and Glory Meet: Colonel Robert Gould Shaw and the 54th Massachusetts Infantry*. Atlanta: University of Georgia Press.

Easterly, William, and Ross Levine. 1997. "Africa's Growth Tragedy: Policies and Ethnic Divisions." *Quarterly Journal of Economics* 112(4): 1203–50.

Eitinger, Leo. 1964. *Concentration Camp Survivors in Norway and Israel*. Oslo: Universitetsforlaget.

Ellickson, Robert C. 1991. *Order without Law: How Neighbors Settle Disputes*. Cambridge, MA: Harvard University Press.

Elliott, Andrea. 2007. "Where Boys Grow Up to Be Jihadis." *New York Times Magazine*, November 26, p. 70.

Elster, Jon. 1998. "Emotions and Economic Theory." *Journal of Economic Literature* 36: 47–74.

Emilio, Luis F. 1894. *The History of the 54th Regiment of Massachusetts Volunteer Infantry, 1863–1865*. Boston: Boston Book Co.

Escott, Paul D. 1985. *Many Excellent People: Power and Privilege in North Carolina, 1850–1900*. Raleigh: University of North Carolina Press.

Fatout, Paul (Ed.). 1961. *Letters of a Civil War Surgeon*. Purdue University Studies, Humanities Series. Lafayette, IN: Purdue Research Foundation.

Fehr, Ernst, and Klaus M. Schmidt. 1999. "A Theory of Fairness, Competition, and Cooperation." *Quarterly Journal of Economics* 114(3): 817–68.

Ferrie, Joseph P. 2005. "The End of American Exceptionalism? Mobility in the U.S. Since 1850." *Journal of Economic Perspectives* 19(3): 199–215.

Fogel, Robert William. 1993. "New Sources and New Techniques for the Study of Secular Trends in Nutritional Status, Health, Mortality, and the Process of Aging." *Historical Methods* 26(1): 5–43.

———. 1992. "Problems in Modeling Complex Dynamic Interactions: The Political Realignment of the 1850s." *Economics and Politics* 4(3): 215–54.

———. 1989. *Without Consent or Contract: The Rise and Fall of American Slavery.* New York: W. W. Norton.

Foner, Eric. 2005. *Forever Free: The Story of Emancipation and Reconstruction.* New York: Alfred A. Knopf.

Foner, Jack D. 1974. *Blacks and the Military in American History: A New Perspective.* New York: Praeger.

Fonvielle, Chris E., Jr. 1997. *The Wilmington Campaign: Last Rays of Departing Hope.* Mechanicsburg, PA: Stackpole Books.

Forrest, Alan I. 1990. *The Soldiers of the French Revolution.* Durham, NC: Duke University Press.

Freeman, Linton C. 2004. *The Development of Social Network Analysis: A Study in the Sociology of Science.* Vancouver, BC: Empirical Press.

Futch, Ovid L. 1972. "Prison Life at Andersonville." In William B. Hesseltine (Ed.), *Civil War Prisons.* Kent, OH: Kent State University Press, 9–31.

Gal, Reuven. 1986. *A Portrait of the Israeli Soldier.* Westport, CT: Greenwood Press.

Genoways, Ted, and Hugh H. Genoways (Eds.). 2001. *A Perfect Picture of Hell: Eyewitness Accounts by Civil War Prisoners from the 12th Iowa.* Iowa City: University of Iowa Press.

Gerber, John. 1955. "Mark Twain's 'Private Campaign.'" *Civil War History* 1: 37–60.

Glaeser, Edward L., David I. Laibson, Jose A. Scheinkman, and Christine L. Soutter. 2000. "Measuring Trust." *Quarterly Journal of Economics* 115(3): 715–1090.

Glatthaar, Joseph T. 1990. *Forged in Battle: The Civil War Alliance of Black Soldiers and White Officers.* New York: Free Press.

Glauber, Bob. 2004. "Ex-NFL Player Dies in Combat." http://www.SpokesmanReview.com. April 24.

Glover, Michael. 1979. *The Napoleonic Wars: An Illustrated History, 1792–1815*. London: Batsford.

Goethals, George R., and Richard F. Reckman. 1973. "The Perception of Consistency in Attitudes." *Journal of Experimental Social Psychology* 9(3): 491–501.

Goldin, Claudia, and Lawrence F. Katz. 1999. "Human Capital and Social Capital: The Rise of Secondary Schooling in American, 1910 to 1940." *Journal of Interdisciplinary History* 29: 683–723.

Gordon, Lesley J. 2002. "'Surely They Remember Me': The 16th Connecticut in War, Captivity, and Public Memory." In Paul A. Cimbala and Randall M. Miller (Eds.), *Union Army Soldiers and the Northern Home Front*. New York: Fordham University, 327–60.

Goss, Warren Lee. 1866. *The Soldier's Story of His Captivity at Andersonville, Belle Isle, and Other Rebel Prisons*. Boston: Lee & Shepard. Reproduced 2001 by Digital Scanning, Scituate, MA.

Gould, Benjamin Apthorp. 1869. *Investigations in the Military and Anthropological Statistics of American Soldiers*. New York: Hurd and Houghton, for the United States Sanitary Commission.

Grant, Ulysses S. 1996. *Personal Memoirs of U.S. Grant*. Lincoln: University of Nebraska Press.

Grinker, Roy Richard, and John Paul Spiegel. 1945. *Men Under Stress*. Philadelphia: Blakiston.

Guiso, Luigi, Paola Sapienza, and Luigi Zingales. 2004. "The Role of Social Capital in Financial Development." *American Economic Review* 94(3): 526–56.

Hahn, Steven. 2003. *A Nation Under Our Feet: Black Political Struggles in the Rural South from Slavery to the Great Migration*. Cambridge, MA: Harvard University Press.

Haney, C., W. C. Banks, and P. G. Zimbardo. 1973. "Study of Prisoners and Guards in a Simulated Prison." *Naval Research Reviews* 9: 1–17.

Hanson, Victor Davis. 2001. *Carnage and Culture: Landmark Battles in the Rise of Western Power*. New York: Doubleday.

———. 1999. *The Soul of Battle: From Ancient Times to the Present Day, How Three Great Liberators Vanquished Tyranny*. New York: Anchor Books.

Hargrove, Hondon B. 1988. *Black Union Soldiers in the Civil War*. Jefferson, NC: McFarland.

Harris, Amy Rehder, William N. Evans, Robert M. Schwab. 2001. "Education Spending in an Aging America." *Journal of Public Economics* 83(3): 449–72.

Harris, Robert F., and John Niflot (Eds.). 1998. *Dear Sister: The Civil War Letters of the Brothers Gould*. Westport, CT: Praeger.

Harrison, Glenn W., and John A. List. 2004. "Field Experiments." *Journal of Economic Literature* 42(4): 1009–55.

Hattaway, Herman M. 1997. "The Civil War Armies: Creation, Mobilization, and Development." In Stig Föster and Jörg Nagler (Eds.), *On the Road to Total War: The American Civil War and the German Wars of Unification, 1861–1871*. Cambridge: German Historical Institute and Cambridge University Press.

Healy, David. 1997. *The Anti-Depressant Era*. Cambridge, MA: Harvard University Press.

Heckman, James J. 1992. "Randomization and Social Policy Evaluation." In Charles Manski and Irwin Garfinkel (Eds.), *Evaluating Welfare and Training Programs*. Cambridge, MA: Harvard University Press, 201–30.

Henderson, W. Darryl. 1985. *Cohesion: The Human Element in Combat*. Washington, DC: National Defense University Press.

Herberg, Will. 1955. *Protestant, Catholic, Jew: An Essay in American Religious Sociology*. Garden City, NY: Doubleday.

Hershberg, Theodore (Ed.). 1981. *Philadelphia: Work, Space, Family, and Group Experience in the Nineteenth Century*. New York: Oxford University Press.

Hess, Earl J. 1997. *The Union Soldier in Battle: Enduring the Ordeal of Combat*. Lawrence: University Press of Kansas.

Hesseltine, William Best. 1935. "The Propaganda Literature of Confederate Prisons." *The Journal of Southern History* 1(1): 56–66.

———. 1930. *Civil War Prisons: A Study in War Psychology*. Columbus: Ohio State University Press.

Higginson, Thomas Wentworth. 2004. *Army Life in a Black Regiment*. http://manybooks.net/titles/higginsoetext04armyl10.html. First published 1869.

——— (Ed.). 1866. *Harvard Memorial Biographies*. Vol. 1. Cambridge, MA: Sever and Francis. Digital edition 2005 by Google.

Holt, Thomas. 1979. *Black Over White: Negro Political Leadership in South Carolina during Reconstruction*. Urbana: University of Illinois Press.

Holzer, Harry J. 1987. "Informal Job Search and Black Youth Unemployment." *American Economic Review* 77(3): 446–52.

Horowitz, Tony. 1998. *Confederates in the Attic*. New York: Pantheon Books.

Howe, Mark De Wolfe (Ed.). 1969. *Touched With Fire: Civil War Letters and Diary of Oliver Wendell Holmes, Jr.* New York: Da Capo Press.

Ioannides, Yannis M., and Linda Datcher Loury. 2004. "Job Information Networks, Neighborhood Effects, and Inequality." *Journal of Economic Literature* 42(4): 1056–93.

Jackman, Capt. Lyman, and Amos Hadley. 1891. *History of the Sixth New Hampshire Regiment in the War for the Union.* Concord, NH: Republican Press Association.

Jacobs, Jane. 1969. *The Economy of Cities.* New York: Vintage Books.

Janke, Jim (Ed.). n.d. "Memoirs of Thomas Newton, Pvt., Co. I, 6th Wisconsin." http://homepages.dsv.edu/jankej/civilwar/ Newton.htm.

Jones, David R. 1980. "What the Repatriated Prisoners of War Wrote about Themselves." *Aviation, Space, and Environmental Medicine* 51(6): 615–17.

Kandel, Eugene, and Edward P. Lazear. 1992. "Peer Pressure and Partnerships." *Journal of Political Economy* 100(4): 801–17.

Karlan, Dean S. 2007. "Social Connections and Group Banking." *Economic Journal* 117(February): F52–F84.

———. 2005. "Using Experimental Economics to Measure Social Capital and Predict Financial Decisions." *American Economic Review* 95(5): 1688–99.

Keegan, John. 1993. *A History of Warfare.* New York: Alfred A. Knopf.

———. 1976. *The Face of Battle.* Harmondsworth, Middlesex, U.K.: Penguin Books.

Kellogg, Robert H. 1865. *Life and Death in Rebel Prisons.* Hartford, CT: L. Stebbins.

Kemp, Thomas R. 1990. "Community and War: The Civil War Experience of Two New Hampshire Towns." In Maris A. Vinovskis (Ed.), *Toward a Social History of the American Civil War.* Cambridge: Cambridge University Press, 1–30.

Kent, Arthur A. (Ed.). 1976. *Three Years with Company K: Sergt. Austin C. Stearns Company K 13th Mass. Infantry (Deceased).* Cranbury, NJ: Associated University Presses.

Kershaw, Alex. 2003. *The Bedford Boys: One American Town's Ultimate D-Day Sacrifice.* London: DaCapo Press.

Klement, Frank L. 1999. *Lincoln's Critics: The Copperheads of the North.* Shippensburg, PA: White Mane Books.

Knack, Stephen, and Philip Keefer. 1997. "Does Social Capital Have an Economic Pay-Off? A Cross-Country Investigation." *Quarterly Journal of Economics* 112(4): 1251–88.

Knippschild, Dieter. 1998. "Deserteure im Zweiten Weltkrieg: Der Stand der Debatte." In Ulrich Bröckling and Michael Sikora (Eds.), *Armeen und ihre Deserteure: Vernachlässigte Kapitel einer Militärgeschichte der Neuzeit.* Göttingen, Germany: Vandenhoeck & Ruprecht.

Kramer, Michael S., and Stanley Shapiro. 1984. "Scientific Challenges in the Application of Randomized Trials." *JAMA* 252: 2739–45.

Kremer, Michael, and Dan M. Levy. 2003. "Peer Effects and Alcohol Use Among College Students." NBER Working Paper No. 9876. Cambridge, MA: National Bureau of Economic Research.

La Ferrara, Eliana. 2003. "Kin Groups and Reciprocity: A Model of Credit Transactions in Ghana." *American Economic Review* 93(5): 1730–51.

———. 2002. "Inequality and Group Participation: Theory and Evidence from Rural Tanzania." *Journal of Public Economics* 85(2): 235–73.

Lagrou, Pieter. 2000. *The Legacy of Occupation: Patriotic Memory and National Recovery in Western Europe, 1945–65.* Cambridge: Cambridge University Press.

Lazear, Edward P. 1999a. "Culture and Language." *Journal of Political Economy* Suppl. 107(S6): 95–126.

———. 1999b. "Globalization and the Market for Team-Mates." *Economic Journal* 109(454): 15–40.

Lee, Chulhee. 2005. "Health, Information, and Migration: Geographic Mobility of Union Army Veterans, 1860–1880." NBER Working Paper No. 11027. Cambridge, MA: National Bureau of Economic Research.

Lee, C. N. n.d. "By the Numbers: Dating, Marriage, and Race in Asian America." http://www.imdiversity.com/Villages/Asian/ family_lifestyle_traditions/le_interracial_dating.asp.

Levi, Primo. 1961. *Survival in Auschwitz: The Nazi Assault on Humanity.* Translated by Stuart Woolf. New York: Collier.

Levine, David K. 1998. "Modeling Altruism and Spitefulness in Experiments." *Review of Economic Dynamics* 1: 593–622.

Lewis, A. S. (Ed.). 1982. *My Dear Parents: An Englishman's Letters Home from the American Civil War.* London: Victor Gollancz.

Linderman, Gerald F. 1987. *Embattled Courage: The Experience of Combat in the American Civil War*. New York: Free Press.

Lindert, Peter H. 1996. "What Limits Social Spending?" *Explorations in Economic History* 33(1): 1–34.

Livingstone, William. 1900. *Livingstone's History of the Republican Party*. Detroit, MI: Wm. Livingstone.

Long, David E. 1994. *The Jewel of Liberty: Abraham Lincoln's Re-Election and the End of Slavery*. Mechanicsburg, PA: Stackpole Books.

Longacre, Edward G. 2003. *A Regiment of Slaves: The 4th United States Colored Infantry, 1863–1866*. Mechanicsburg, PA: Stackpole Books.

———. 1999. *Joshua Chamberlain: The Soldier and the Man*. Conshohoken, PA: Combined Publishing.

Lonn, Ella. 1928. *Desertion During the Civil War*. New York: Century Co.

Luttmer, Erzo F. P. 2001. "Group Loyalty and the Taste for Redistribution." *Journal of Political Economy* 109(3): 500–28.

MacArthur, Brian. 2005. *Surviving the Sword: Prisoners of the Japanese in the Far East, 1942–45*. New York: Random House.

MacCoun, Robert J. 1993. "What Is Known about Unit Cohesion and Military Performance." In *Sexual Orientation and U.S. Military Personnel Policy: Options and Assessment*. Santa Monica, CA: RAND, 283–331. http://www.rand.org/pubs/ monograph_reports/MR323/ mr323.pref .pdf.

MacGregor, Morris, and Bernard C. Nalty. 1977. *Blacks in the United States Armed Forces: Basic Documents*. Vol. 2. Wilmington, DE: Scholarly Resources.

Malkin, Lawrence. 2001. "Prisoners of War." In Robert Cowley and Geoffrey Parker (Eds.), *Reader's Companion to Military History*. Boston: Houghton Mifflin, 368–69.

Marmaros, David, and Bruce Sacerdote. 2006. "How Do Friendships Form?" *Quarterly Journal of Economics* 121(1): 79–119.

———. 2002. "Peer and Social Networks in Job Search." *European Economic Review* 46(4–5): 870–79.

Marrs, Elijah P. 1969. *Life and History of the Rev. Elijah P. Marrs, First Pastor of Beargrass Baptist Church, and Author*. Miami, FL: Mnemosyne Publishing Co. First published 1885 by the Bradley and Gilbert Company, Louisville, KY.

Marvel, William. 1994. *Andersonville: The Last Depot*. Chapel Hill: University of North Carolina Press.

Mas, Alexandre, and Enrico Moretti. In press. "Peers at Work." *American Economic Review.*

McDonald, Patrick. n.d. "Opportunities Lost, The Battle of Cold Harbor." http://www.civilwarhome.com/coldharbor summary.htm.

McElroy. John. 1879. *Andersonville: A Story of Rebel Military Prisons, Fifteen Months a Guest of the So-Called Southern Confederacy: A Private Soldier's Experience in Richmond, Andersonville, Savannah, Millen, Blackshear, and Florence.* Toledo, OH: D. R. Locke.

McPherson, James M. 2007. *This Mighty Scourge: Perspectives on the Civil War.* Oxford: Oxford University Press.

———. 1997. *For Cause and Comrades: Why Men Fought in the Civil War.* New York: Oxford University Press.

———. 1988. *Battle Cry of Freedom: The Civil War Era.* New York: Oxford University Press.

———. 1965. *The Negro's Civil War: How American Blacks Felt and Acted During the War for the Union.* New York: Vintage Civil War Library.

Menand, Louis. 2001. *The Metaphysical Club.* New York: Farrar, Straus, and Giroux.

Metzer, Jacob. 1981. "The Records of the U.S. Colored Troops as Historical Source: An Exploratory Examination." *Historical Methods* 14: 123–32.

Miguel, Edward, and Mary Kay Gugerty. 2005. "Ethnic Diversity, Social Sanctions, and Public Goods in Kenya." *Journal of Public Economics* 89(11–12): 2325–68.

Milgram, Stanley. 1963. "Behavioral Studies of Obedience." *Journal of Abnormal and Social Psychology* 67: 371–78.

Miller, Barbara. 1999. *Narratives of Guilt and Compliance in Unified Germany: Stasi Informers and their Impact on Society.* London: Routledge.

Mitchell, Reid. 1990. "The Northern Soldier and His Community." In Maris A. Vinovskis (Ed.), *Toward a Social History of the American Civil War.* Cambridge: Cambridge University Press, 1-30.

Moffitt, Robert A. 2004. "The Role of Randomized Field Trials in Social Science Research: A Perspective from Evaluations of Reforms of Social Welfare Programs." *American Behavioral Scientist* 47(5): 506–40.

Moretti, Enrico. 1999. "Social Migrations and Networks: Italy 1889–1913." *International Migration Review* 33(3): 640–57.

Moses, Jefferson. 1911. *The Memoirs, Diary, and Life of Private Jefferson*

Moses, Company G, 93rd Illinois Volunteers. http://www .ioweb.com /civilwar.

Munshi, Kaivan. 2003. "Networks in the Modern Economy: Mexican Migrants in the U.S. Labor Market." *Quarterly Journal of Economics* 118(2): 549–99.

Murphy, Kate. 2004. "After Enron, a Sunless Year in a Tiny Cell." *New York Times*, SundayBusiness; News and Analysis, June 20, 5.

Mushkat, Jerome (Ed.). 2002. *A Citizen-Soldier's Civil War: The Letters of Brevet Major General Alving C. Voris.* DeKalb: Northern Illinois University Press.

National Park Service. 2007. "Other Slaves at Monocacy." Updated July 10. http://www.nps.gov/mono/historyculture/ei_ others.htm.

O'Connell, Robert L. 1980. *Of Arms and Men: A History of War, Weapons, and Aggression.* New York: Oxford University Press.

Painter, Nell Irvin. 1992. *Exodusters: Black Migration to Kansas after Reconstruction.* New York: W.W. Norton.

Palaca, Joseph. 1989. "AIDS Drug Trials Enter New Age." *Science Magazine*, Oct. 6, 19–21.

Paxton, Robert O. 1998. Foreword. In *Vichy: An Ever-Present Past*, by Éric Conan and Henry Rousso. Hanover, NH: Dartmouth University Press, ix–xiii.

Pencavel, John. 1998. "Assortative Mating by Schooling and the Work Behavior of Wives and Husbands." *American Economic Review* 88(2): 326–29.

Perlman, Joel, and Mary C. Waters. 2004. "Intermarriage Then and Now: Race, Generation, and the Changing Meaning of Marriage." In Nancy Foner and George M. Fredrickson (Eds.), *Not Just Black and White: Historical and Contemporary Perspectives on Immigration, Race, and Ethnicity in the United States.* New York: Russell Sage Foundation, 262–77.

Peskin, Allan. 1999. *Garfield: A Biography.* Kent, OH: Kent State University Press.

Pfeffer, Jeffrey. 1997. *New Directions for Organization Theory.* New York: Oxford University Press.

Poterba, James M. 1997. "Demographic Structure and the Political Economy of Public Education." *Journal of Policy Analysis and Management* 16(1): 48–66.

Putnam, Robert. 2007. "*E Pluribus Unum*: Diversity and Community

in the Twenty-first Century. The 2006 Johan Skytte Prize Lecture."
Scandinavian Political Studies 30(2): 137–74.

———. 2000. *Bowling Alone: The Collapse and Revival of American Community*. New York: Simon and Schuster.

Quaife, Milo M. (Ed.). 1959. *From the Cannon's Mouth: The Civil War Letters of General Alpheus S. Williams*. Detroit: Wayne State University Press and the Detroit Historical Society.

Rabin, Matthew. 1993. "Incorporating Fairness into Game Theory and Economics." *American Economic Review* 83(5): 1281-302.

Rainio, Kullervo. 1966. "A Study of Sociometric Group Structure: An Application of a Stochastic Theory of Social Interaction." In J. Berger, M. Zelditch, and B. Anderson (Eds.), *Sociological Theories in Progress*. Vol. 1. Boston: Houghton Mifflin, 102–23.

Rankin, David C. 2004. *Diary of a Christian Soldier: Rufus Kinsley and the Civil War*. Cambridge: Cambridge University Press.

Ransom, John. 1963. *John Ransom's Andersonville Diary*. New York: Berkley Books.

Ray, J. P. (Ed.) 1981. *The Diary of a Dead Man, 1862–1864*. New York: Eastern Acorn Press.

——— (Ed). 1992. *A Grand Army of Black Men: Letters from African-American Soldiers in the Union Army, 1861–1865*. Cambridge: Cambridge University Press.

Rhea, Gordon C. 2002. *Cold Harbor: Grant and Lee, May 26-June 3 1864*. Baton Rouge: Louisiana State University Press.

Rhodes, James Ford. 1904. *History of the United States of America: From the Compromise of 1850 to the McKinley-Bryan Campaign of 1896*. Vol. 5, *1864–1866*. New York: Macmillan.

Rosenzweig, Roy. 1983. *Eight Hours for What We Will: Workers and Leisure in an Industrial City, 1870–1920*. New York: Cambridge University Press.

Ross, Michael, and Michael Conway. 1986. "Remembering One's Own Past: The Construction of Personal Histories." In R. M. Sorrentino and E. T. Higgins (Eds.), *Handbook of Motivation and Cognition: Foundations of Social Behavior*. New York: Guilford Press, 122–44.

Roth, Margaret Brobst (Ed.). 1960. *Well, Mary: Civil War Letters of a Wisconsin Volunteer*. Madison: University of Wisconsin Press.

Sacerdote, Bruce. 2007. "How Large Are the Effects from Changes in Family Environment? A Study of Korean American Adoptees." *Quarterly Journal of Economics* 122(1): 119–57.

————. 2005. "Slavery and the Intergenerational Transmission of Capital." *Review of Economics and Statistics.* 87(2): 217–34.

————. 2001. "Peer Effects with Random Assignment: Results for Dartmouth Roommates." *Quarterly Journal of Economics* 116(2): 681–704.

Sageman, Marc. 2004. *Understanding Terror Networks.* Philadelphia: University of Pennsylvania Press.

Schmolling, Paul. 1984. "Human Reactions to the Nazi Concentration Camps: A Summing Up." *Journal of Human Stress* 10(3): 108–20.

Scott, Newton Robert. http://www.civilwarletters.com. Prepared August 17, 1994; revised March 1, 2008.

Shaffer, Donald Robert. 2004. *After the Glory: The Struggles of Black Civil War Veterans.* Lawrence: University Press of Kansas.

Shankman, Arnold M. 1980. *The Pennsylvania Antiwar Movement, 1861–1865.* Cranbury, NJ: Associated University Presses.

Shay, Jonathan. 2002. *Odysseus in America: Combat Trauma and the Trials of Homecoming.* New York: Scribner.

Sherif, Muzafer, O. J. Harvey, B. Jack White, William R. Hood, and Carolyn W. Sherif. 1961. *Intergroup Conflict and Cooperation: The Robbers Cave Experiment.* Norman: University of Oklahoma Book Exchange. http://psychclassics.yorku.ca/Sherif.

Sherman, William T. 1876. *Memoirs of General William T. Sherman.* New York: D. Appleton.

Shils, Edward A., and Morris Janowitz. 1948. "Cohesion and Disintegration in the Wehrmacht in World War II." *Public Opinion Quarterly* 12(2): 280–315.

Sikora, Michael. 1998. "Das 18. Jahrhundert: Die Zeit der Deserteure." In *Armeen und ihre Deserteure: Vernachlässigte Kapitel einer Militärgeschichte der Neuzeit.* Göttingen, Germany: Vandenhoeck & Ruprecht.

Smith, Dan. 2003. "Seasoning Disease Environment, and Conditions of Exposure: New York Union Army Regiments and Soldiers." In Dora L. Costa (Ed.), *Health and Labor Force Participation over the Life Cycle: Evidence from the Past.* Chicago: University of Chicago Press for the National Bureau of Economic Research.

Smith, Vernon L., Gerry L. Suchanek, and Arlington W. Williams. 1988. "Bubbles, Crashes, and Endogenous Expectations in Experimental Spot Asset Markets." *Econometrica* 56(5): 1119–51.

Sneden, Robert Knox. 2000. *Eye of the Storm.* Edited by Charles E. Bryan and Nelson D. Lankford. New York: Free Press.

Spann, Edward K. 1996. "Union Green: The Irish Community and the Civil War." In Ronald H. Bayor and Timothy J. Meagher (Eds.), *The New York Irish*. Baltimore: Johns Hopkins University Press, 193–209.

Speer, Lonnie R. 1997. *Portals to Hell: Military Prisons of the Civil War*. Mechanicsburg, PA: Stackpole Books.

Steckel, Richard H. 1983. "The Economic Foundations of East-West Migration during the 19th Century." *Explorations in Economic History* 20(1): 14–36.

Stevens, Joseph Edward. 1999. *1863: The Rebirth of a Nation*. New York: Bantam Books.

Stouffer, Samuel A., Arthur A. Lumsdaine, Marion Harper Lumsdaine, Robin M. Williams, Jr., M. Brewster Smith, Irving L. Janis, Shirley A. Star, and Leonard S. Cottrell, Jr. 1949. *The American Soldier: Combat and Its Aftermath*. Vol. II. Princeton, NJ: Princeton University Press.

Taylor, Susie King. 1902. *Reminiscences of My Life in Camp with the 33d United States Colored Troops Late 1st S. C. Volunteers*. Boston: Author. http://docsouth.unc.edu/neh/taylorsu/taylorsu.html.

Thompson, Morton. 1949. *The Cry and the Covenant*. New York: Garden City Books.

Thucydides. 1950. *The History of the Peloponnesian War*. Translated by Richard Crawley. New York: E. P. Dutton.

Tocqueville, Alexis de. 2000. *Democracy in America*. Translated by Harvey C. Mansfield and Delba Winthrop. Chicago: University of Chicago Press.

Trimble, Richard M. (Ed.) 2000. *Bothers 'Til Death: The Civil War Letters of William, Thomas, and Maggie Jones, 1861–1865, Irish Soldiers in the 48th New York Volunteer Regiment*. Macon, GA: Mercer University Press.

Troutman, Richard L. (Ed.). 1987. *The Heavens Are Weeping: The Diaries of George Richard Browder, 1852–1886*. Grand Rapids, MI: Zondervan Publishing House.

Truxall, Aida Cragg (Ed.). 1962. *"Respects to All": Letters of Two Pennsylvania Boys in the War of the Rebellion*. Pittsburgh: University of Pittsburgh Press.

Tuan, Mia. 1998. *Forever Foreigners or Honorary Whites? The Asian Ethnic Experience Today*. New Brunswick, NJ: Rutgers University Press.

Tuma, Nancy B., and Maureen T. Hallinan. 1979. "The Effects of Sex, Race and Achievement on Schoolchildren's Friendships." *Social Forces* 57: 1265–85.

U.S. Bureau of Labor Statistics. 2004a. "Census of Fatal Occupational Injuries." Table A-5. Fatal Occupational Injuries by Occupation and Event or Exposure, All United States, 2004. http://www.bls.gov/iif /oshwc/cfoi/cftb0200.pdf.

———. 2004b. "May 2004 National Occupational Employment and Wage Estimates." http://www.bls.gov/oes.

U.S. Department of Veterans Affairs. 2006. "Fact Sheet: America's Wars." http://www1.va.gov/opa/fact/amwars.asp.

U.S. National Archives. n.d. Regimental Letter Book of the 10th USCT. Record Group 94. Washington, DC.

U.S. Provost Marshall General. 1866. *Final Report*, United States House of Representatives, Executive Document No. 1, 39th Congress, 1st Session, Series Numbers 1251, 1252, 1866.

U.S.War Department. 1880–1901. *The War of the Rebellion: A Compilation of the Official Records of the Union and Confederate Armies*. Washington, DC: U.S. Government Printing Office. http://cdl.library .cornell.edu/moa/browse.monographs/waro .html.

Vinovskis, Maris. 1990. "Have Social Historians Lost the Civil War? Some Preliminary Demographic Speculations." In Maris A. Vinovskis (Ed.), *Toward a Social History of the American Civil War.* Cambridge: Cambridge University Press, 1–30.

Vigdor, Jacob L. 2004. "Community Composition and Collective Action: Analyzing Initial Mail Response to the 2000 Census." *Review of Economics and Statistics* 86(1): 303–12.

Voltz, John. 2/10/1865. University Libraries of Virginia Tech. http:// spec.libvt.edu/voltz.

Waugh, John C. 1997. *Re-Electing Lincoln: The Battle for the 1864 Presidency*. New York: Crown Publishers.

Webb, Henry J. 1948. "Prisoners of War in the Middle Ages." *Military Affairs* 12(1): 46–49.

Westwood, Howard C. 1992. *Black Troops, White Commanders, and Freedmen During the Civil War*. Carbondale: Southern Illinois University Press.

Wheeler, Richard (Ed.). 1976. *Voices of the Civil War*. New York: Thomas Y. Crowell Co.

Wiley, Bell Irvin. 1952. *The Life of Billy Yank*. Indianapolis, Indiana: Bobbs-Merrill.

Williams, Henry L. 2005. *The Lincoln Story Book*. The Project Gutenberg EBook. http://www.gutenberg.org/dirs/etext05/ 8linc10h.htm.

Wilson, Keith P. 2002. *Campfires of Freedom: The Camp Life of Black Soldiers During the Civil War*. Kent, OH: Kent State University Press.

Wimmer, Larry. 2003. "Reflections on the Early Indicators Project: A Partial History." In Dora L. Costa (Ed.), *Health and Labor Force Participation over the Life Cycle: Evidence from the Past*. Chicago: University of Chicago Press for the National Bureau of Economic Research, 1–10.

Woodworth, Steven E. 1998. *Six Armies in Tennessee: The Chickamauga and Chattanooga Campaigns*. Lincoln: University of Nebraska Press.

Works Progress Administration. Federal Writers Project. *Slave Narratives* (database online). Provo, UT: Ancestry.com, 2000. Original data from Works Project Administration. Federal Writers Project. *Slave Narratives: A Folk History of Slavery in the United States from Interviews with Former Slaves*. Washington, DC: n.p.

Wright, Gordon. 1962. "Reflections on the French Resistance (1940–1944)." *Political Science Quarterly* 77(3): 336–49.

INDEX

Brown, John, 241
Brown's Ferry, 16–17
Bruce, Blanche K., 200
Buckland, 107
Buckley, Charles, 205
Bull, Rice, 58, 74–75, 78, 89
Bureau of Colored Troops, 63, 72
Burma-Thailand railway, 122
Buttler, Henry, 67–68

Camp William Penn, 112
Canada, 48, 172
cannons, 76
Carley, Lawson, 134, 146
Carson, Andrew, 122, 124, 148
Castle Thunder, 18
Catholics, 28, 94, 166–67, 222
Cayuga County, 15–16, 177–78
census records, 9, 34, 179, 191, 230–31
Chamberlain, Joshua, 1, 57, 59, 61
Charleston, 20, 128
Chattanooga, 16
Chickahominy River, 11
Chickasaw Bluffs, 97
Childs, Rhoda Ann, 198
Chinese Americans, 222
civic engagement. *See* community
Civil War: army building and, 46–79; community support for, 162–69 (*see also* community); data sources for, 30–36, 227–42; death rates of, 3; delayed draft in, 46–47;

deserters and, 2–3 (*see also* deserters); discipline and, 47, 72–83, 93; economic disadvantages from, 187–88; family losses and, 160; fascination with, 26–27; Fogel database for, 34–36; impact of, 2–3; internal divisions caused by, 27–28; as liberty against despotism, 84–85; as life-altering experience, 187–89; moral high ground and, 117–18; motivation for fighting, 83–116; national myth of, 186; North/South division of, 27–28; opposition to, 164, 166, 183–84; participation rates in, 36, 69; POWs and, 121 (*see also* prisoners of war [POWs]); reasons for, xx, 26–45; Reconstruction and, 200–201, 211; soldier's life and, 74–79; as War of Northern Aggression, 27; web sites for, 27
Clausewitz, 82–83
Coffee, Silas J., 112–14
Coffin, Charles, 58
Cohin, Pierre, 84
Cold Harbor, 11–13, 119, 215
Coleman, 217
colleges, 36, 57–58, 224–25
Colt, Samuel, 205
combat exercises, 220
Communist Party, 185–86
Community, xvii; altruism and, 3–5; anthropological studies of, 217; betrayal and, 6; cohe-